THE LEGACY OF D. H. LAWRENCE

THE LEGACY OF D. H. LAWRENCE

New Essays

Edited by
Jeffrey Meyers
Professor of English
University of Colorado

St. Martin's Press   New York

Editorial matter, Introduction and Chapter Four © Jeffrey Meyers 1987; Chapter One © John Bayley 1987; Chapter Two © James Gindin 1987; Chapter Three © William M. Chace 1987; Chapter Five © Roberts W. French 1987; Chapter Six © Eugene Goodheart 1987; Chapter Seven © Kingsley Widmer 1987.

All rights reserved. For information, write:
Scholarly & Reference Division,
St. Martin's Press, Inc., 175 Fifth Avenue, New York, NY 10010

First published in the United States of America in 1987

Printed in Hong Kong

ISBN 0-312-47804-6

Library of Congress Cataloging-in-Publication Data
The Legacy of D. H. Lawrence.
Bibliography: p.
Includes index.
1. Lawrence, D. H. (David Herbert), 1885–1930—Influence.
2. English literature—20th century—History and criticism.
3. American literature—20th century—History
and criticism.   I. Meyers, Jeffrey.
PR6023.A93Z655   1987   823'.912   86-6591
ISBN 0-312-47804-6

For Francis King

Contents

	Acknowledgments	ix
	Notes on the Contributors	x
	Introduction *Jeffrey Meyers*	1
1	LAWRENCE AND THE MODERN ENGLISH NOVEL *John Bayley*	14
2	LAWRENCE AND THE CONTEMPORARY ENGLISH NOVEL *James Gindin*	30
3	LAWRENCE AND ENGLISH POETRY *William M. Chace*	54
4	LAWRENCE AND TRAVEL WRITERS *Jeffrey Meyers*	81
5	LAWRENCE AND AMERICAN POETRY *Roberts W. French*	109
6	LAWRENCE AND AMERICAN FICTION *Eugene Goodheart*	135
7	LAWRENCE'S CULTURAL IMPACT *Kingsley Widmer*	156
	Notes	175
	Index	200

Acknowledgments

The editor is grateful for the generous letters from and interviews with many of the writers considered in this book: Robert Bly, Melvyn Bragg, Robert Creeley, Lawrence Durrell, Allen Ginsberg, Graham Greene, Seamus Heaney, Ted Hughes, the late Christopher Isherwood, Galway Kinnell, Doris Lessing, Norman Mailer, the late Bernard Malamud, Karl Shapiro, Alan Sillitoe, Gary Snyder, Sir Stephen Spender, David Storey and Keith Waterhouse.

Notes on the Contributors

John Bayley is Warton Professor of English Literature and Fellow of St. Catherine's College, Oxford University. He is the author of *The Romantic Survival* (1956), *The Character of Love* (1960), *Tolstoy and the Novel* (1966), *Pushkin* (1971), *The Uses of Division* (1976), *An Essay on Hardy* (1978), *Shakespeare and Tragedy* (1981) and *Selected Essays* (1984).

William M. Chace is Professor of English and Vice Provost for Academic Planning and Development at Stanford University. Author of *The Political Identities of Ezra Pound and T. S. Eliot* (1973), *Lionel Trilling: Criticism and Politics* (1980), editor of *James Joyce: A Collection of Critical Essays* (1974) and *An Introduction to Literature* (1985), he has also written essays on a wide variety of modern authors.

Roberts W. French is Professor of English at the University of Massachusetts. He has published essays in *College English*, *The Nation*, *Massachusetts Review*, *Milton Quarterly* and *Walt Whitman Review*. His chapter on Lawrence and Whitman appeared in *D. H. Lawrence and Tradition*, edited by Jeffrey Meyers (1985).

James Gindin, Professor of English at the University of Michigan, has won Fulbright, National Endowment for the Humanities and Guggenheim fellowships. He is the author of *Postwar British Fiction* (1962), *Harvest of a Quiet Eye: The Novel of Compassion* (1971), *The English Climate: An Excursion into a Biography of John Galsworthy* (1979) and *John Galsworthy's Life and Art* (1986).

Eugene Goodheart is the Edytha Macy Gross Professor of Humanities at Brandeis University. He is the author of *The Utopian Vision of D. H. Lawrence* (1963), *The Cult of the Ego: The Self in Modern Literature* (1968), *Culture and the Radical Conscience* (1973),

The Failure of Criticism (1978) and *The Skeptic Disposition in Contemporary Criticism* (1984).

Jeffrey Meyers is Professor of English at the University of Colorado and Fellow of the Royal Society of Literature. He is the author or editor of 22 books, including biographies of Katherine Mansfield (1978), Wyndham Lewis (1980) and Ernest Hemingway (1985), *Wyndham Lewis: A Revaluation* (1980) and *Hemingway: The Critical Heritage* (1982), several books on T. E. Lawrence and George Orwell, *Fiction and the Colonial Experience* (1973), *Painting and the Novel* (1975), *A Fever at the Core* (1976), *Married to Genius* (1977), *Homosexuality and Literature* (1977), *Disease and the Novel* (1985), *The Craft of Literary Biography* (1985), *D. H. Lawrence and the Experience of Italy* (1982) and *D. H. Lawrence and Tradition* (1985).

Kingsley Widmer is Professor of English at San Diego State University. Among his several hundred publications are eight books of literary and cultural criticism: *The Art of Perversity: D. H. Lawrence's Shorter Fictions* (1962), *Henry Miller* (1963), *The Literary Rebel* (1965), *The Ways of Nihilism: Herman Melville's Short Novels* (1970), *The End of Culture: Essays on Sensibility in Contemporary Society* (1973), *Paul Goodman* (1980), *Edges of Extremity: Problems of Literary Modernism* (1980) and *Nathanael West* (1982).

> Poet and sculptor, do the work,
> Nor let the modish painter shirk
> What his great forefathers did.
>
> Yeats, "Under Ben Bulben"

> Every masterpiece is the cry of a precursor, and rallies beyond time, in the black frost of eternity, its companions yet to come.
>
> Lucien Daudet

Introduction

JEFFREY MEYERS

The Legacy of D. H. Lawrence is a sequel and complement to *D. H. Lawrence and Tradition*, a collection of seven original essays that I edited for the Athlone Press and the University of Massachusetts Press in 1985. *Lawrence and Tradition* shows how Lawrence interprets, revalues, absorbs and transforms the work of Blake, Carlyle, Ruskin, George Eliot, Hardy, Whitman and Nietzsche. The contributors all assume that Lawrence's use of the style, forms and ideas of his predecessors is positive, that his fiction, poetry and criticism derive their resonance, meaning and value—and much of their inspiration—from his vital connection to significant authors of the nineteenth century.

The Legacy of Lawrence looks forward rather than backward. For Lawrence not only followed and developed a tradition, but also inspired one. After his death, the *Manchester Guardian* stated: "Mr. Lawrence was a writer who has exercised a more potent influence, perhaps, over his generation than any of his contemporaries."[1] But his impact extended well beyond his own generation. He became the most influential writer of the twentieth century and is, after Shakespeare, "the most widely studied author in the English language."[2]

Lawrence's influence was personal as well as literary. All the friends of Lawrence whom I have met—Dorothy Brett, Rebecca West, David Garnett, A. S. Frere, Juliette Huxley, Enid Hilton, Montague Weekley, Richard Murry, Barbara Weekley Barr, Julian Morrell Vinogradoff and John Carswell—were immediately and forcefully struck, as Aldous Huxley was, by "a being, somehow, of another order, more sensitive, more highly conscious, more capable of feeling than even the most gifted of common men."[3]

The Legacy of D. H. Lawrence traces the literary and cultural influence of Lawrence's ideas and his art on the English and American novelists, poets and travel writers who responded to his sympathetic temperament and discovered in his work forms of expression that could be transformed and developed, recreated and reaffirmed. This work illuminates Lawrence as well as the writers he influenced, and reveals how his art has survived through association and transmission. Lawrence did not, like Pound, make a conscious and deliberate attempt "to set up the equivalent of a Berlitz or extra-mural course in poetics."[4] But he did pass on to significant successors his subject matter, structure, style, themes and tone. His literary genius enlarged their perceptions, refined their sensibilities and inspired their emulation. The authoritative contributions and concerted effort in this book are well suited to this immense and important subject, for no single scholar has the breadth of knowledge to draw together all the complex connections between Lawrence and the modern authors who came under his dynamic and stimulating influence.

There is overwhelming evidence to contradict Anthony Burgess' assertion: "No potential writer would ever take Lawrence as a model."[5] W. H. Auden's ideas on education, popular culture, politics, psychology and religion—even the uninhibited, lyrical and dogmatic reviews he wrote for *Scrutiny* in the 1930s—were influenced by Lawrence, whom he considered a great genius. In his Foreword to *The Orators* (1932), Auden acknowledged: "Over the whole work looms the shadow of that dangerous figure, D. H. Lawrence the Ideologue, author of *Fantasia of the Unconscious* and those sinister novels *Kangaroo* and *The Plumed Serpent*." Auden alludes to the treatise on homosexuality that Lawrence mysteriously destroyed in 1917 ("O Goat with the Compasses, hear us"). And in the first ode he links his own fate with Lawrence's, suggests he has survived to transmit the Master's beliefs and refers to: "The hour in the night when Lawrence died and I came/Round from the morphia." Auden reaffirmed his admiration a quarter of a century later and said: "Lawrence has been and remains one of my literary heroes, one of the few modern writers whom I constantly reread."[6]

Stephen Spender has said that from his undergraduate days until the present he has had tremendous admiration for Lawrence: a sacred writer and a visionary genius. Spender believes that Tolstoy, Blake, Carlyle, Ruskin and Lawrence communicate an extraordinary prophetic energy that has a physical effect and makes you feel more alive.[7] Spender rejects repression and expresses pure Lawrencean doctrine in his famous poem, "I Think Continually of Those Who Were Truly Great":

What is precious is never to forget
The essential delight of the blood drawn from ageless springs
Breaking through rocks in worlds before our earth.
Never to deny its pleasure in the morning simple light
Nor its grave evening demand for love.

For Christopher Isherwood, Lawrence was perhaps the greatest writer in modern times as well as the least dreary, stuffy and formal. He was truly a poet in every respect; a model not only for Isherwood's travel books, but for all his writings. Isherwood admired Lawrence's spontaneous and illuminating description of people, his ability to catch the actual intuitive moment in an extraordinary way, and hoped to capture and cultivate his flashes of insight.[8]

Lawrence's powerful sense of the mysterious, Dionysian forces in nature, his desire "to realise the tremendous *non-human* quality of life,"[9] had a powerful effect on the poems of Dylan Thomas and (reinforced by Thomas) on the poetry of Ted Hughes. Both Lawrence and Thomas shared a Nonconformist background and were thoroughly versed in the Bible. Both expressed the same intense rage, pantheistic vitalism, veneration of the life force and vision of sex as a spiritual good that would make man healthy and whole. Thomas' reference to "Bird beast and flower" in the second line of "A Refusal to Mourn" is an act of homage to Lawrence. And, as Karl Shapiro notes, "like D. H. Lawrence he is always hurling himself back into childhood and the childhood of the world."[10] Keith Sagar writes that Hughes "is very Lawrentian in his opposition to rationalism, humanism, and certain aspects of science; in his insistence on the sacredness, miraculousness of Nature; in his belief in the need for an ego-death and a resurrection in individuals; and in his belief in the ability of two people to reconstitute each other in marriage."[11]

Seamus Heaney has provided a fascinating account of the

influence of Lawrence's energy, fluidity and sexual imagery on his work: "One of the first poems that made an incision into unexpected parts of me was Lawrence's short 'Discord in Childhood,' " which he read in a practical criticism class. *Sons and Lovers* "was a genuine experience and wakened me in my late teens in a way I was not used to being awakened by a book."

But it was the Lawrence which I discovered extra-murally, as it were, that came home with most verifying force. I never thought of him as one of my guardian voices, however. You know how young poets invent their own lineage and opt for a story of how they began to write under the influence of so and so—in that scenario, Hopkins and Hughes were part of my English caste and Patrick Kavanagh among the Irish. And it is indeed true that these were the freeing influences. Obvious to myself at the time. But it would probably be true to say that Lawrence's example was a corroborating one. His solidarity with the underground silent part of the psyche and of the society. His chthonic energy. His sexualizing of ground and growths. All of that was entirely sympathetic to me and I felt naturally at home with his way of responding. When I was teaching *The Rainbow* in the late sixties, I was always affected by a number of the scenes there as if they were dream memories of my own—Anna being carried out into the stable, Will and Anna stooking the corn. I still love the forthrightness and impatience and sudden unmediated quality of much of his poetry. I also think the essay on the poetry of the living present is one of the best statements by a practising poet about the essential differences between kinds of lyric and keep asking myself if it is possible for anybody except Lawrence to opt so unreservedly for living present. Shakespeare the playwright, perhaps. Fluid, molten, quivering, all that—very persuasive as a version of how the lyric poet would like things to be but unless that lyric poet is a genius, not altogether a credible record of how things usually are.[12]

Lawrence inspired the English novelists as well as the poets. Aldous Huxley was a close friend of Lawrence during his final years and wrote a brilliant introduction to his edition of Lawrence's *Letters* in 1932. Though temperamentally and artistically remote from Huxley, Lawrence influenced Huxley's radical change from rationalism to mysticism. Lawrence's dynamic vitalism had a positive effect on the rather desiccated Huxley, who expressed Lawrence's sense of social responsibility in the essays in *Do What You Will* (1929).

Lawrence appears in Huxley's fiction as frequently as Middleton Murry appeared in Lawrence's. He portrayed Lawrence as Kingham in "Two or Three Graces" (1926), as Rampion in *Point Counter Point* (1928), as Miles Fanning in "After the Fireworks" (1929), as John Savage in *Brave New World* (1932) and as Henry Maartens in *The Genius and the Goddess* (1955). In *Eyeless in Gaza* (1936), the sleepless Anthony reads *The Man Who Died*.

Lawrence's influence on George Orwell was also significant. Like Lawrence, who states, "I write because I want folk—English folk—to alter, and have more sense,"[13] Orwell was a rebel and a prophet intensely dissatisfied with the decaying spirit of England and the sharp decline of European civilization. Disenchantment with the modern age led Orwell to idealize the recent past of his childhood as Lawrence idealized the distant past of his race. Lawrence turned inward and treated the disease and the cure in an extremely personal way: he wanted to make a new world by radically changing the feelings of men and women. Orwell tried to find social solutions to the crisis of civilization felt within the individual: he attempted to make himself and others aware of their responsibility and their capacity to deal with political problems. Orwell writes of Lawrence:

> What he is demanding is a movement away from our mechanised civilisation, which is not going to happen, and which he knows is not going to happen. Therefore his exasperation with the present turns once more into an idealisation of the past. . . . The ultimate subject-matter of nearly all Lawrence's books is the failure of contemporary men, especially in the English-speaking countries, to live their lives intensely enough.[14]

Lawrence's impress is apparent in several of Orwell's works in the 1930s. Orwell's comment on the repressive and sterile milieu of the rectory in "Daughters of the Vicar" (1911), "Probably Lawrence had watched . . . the underfed, downtrodden, organ-playing daughter of a clergyman wearing out her youth, and had a sudden vision of her escaping into the warmer world of the working class,"[15] reveals that the story inspired the conception and theme of *A Clergyman's Daughter* (1935). In *Women in Love* (1920) and Orwell's *The Road to Wigan Pier* (1937), the emotional sterility of the mine owners is contrasted to the inextinguishable warmth and vitality of the oppressed working people, and reflected in the deathly ugliness of the landscape.[16]

A man named Mellors gives George Bowling the racing tip that provides his escape money in *Coming Up For Air* (1939); and, like Lawrence's Mellors, Bowling rises to the officer class during the war and becomes, temporarily, a gentleman. Lawrence's story "The Thorn in the Flesh" is mentioned in the novel and Bowling enjoys reading *Sons and Lovers*. More significantly, the mood of *Coming Up For Air*, and indeed of many of Orwell's works in the thirties, is close to the dark prophecies of Lawrence's letters and to the opening sentences of *Lady Chatterley's Lover*: "Ours is essentially a tragic age, so we refuse to take it tragically. The cataclysm has happened, we are among the ruins."

Alan Sillitoe identified with Lawrence's landscape and writes: "After I was fourteen and bought a bicycle I took that road [to Matlock] . . . puffing up out of Nottingham through Apsley and Cinderhill. There is a colliery at this latter place, depicted as Tinder Mill in *Sons and Lovers*."[17] The postwar working-class novelists—Sillitoe, John Wain, Keith Waterhouse, David Storey as well as Melvyn Bragg and Doris Lessing—were influenced by Lawrence's love–hate attitude toward the beauty and ugliness of the industrial Midlands, which he called "the country of my heart."[18] These writers also followed Lawrence in his use of dialect and demotic speech, his intimate portrayal of the life of colliers and factory workers, his rage at the suffocating class snobbery in England and in the transcendence of class (and sometimes race) in *Chatterley*-influenced novels like Lessing's *The Grass is Singing* (1950) and Sillitoe's *The Death of William Posters* (1965).

Sillitoe, Storey and Bragg have recently described their intense response to Lawrence. Sillitoe writes of his reaction to the sense of place in the Midlands novels:

I read *The Rainbow* when I was 22 and thought it marvellous—
as it is. Then I went on to read *everything* else. ... I was
avidly interested in all of it, more the Nottinghamshire
works than others. ... Lawrence did open my eyes to
Nottinghamshire. Maybe my work shows more traces of
Lawrence's influence than I imagine: though I can't see it,
maybe an outsider can.[19]

David Storey places Lawrence in the Romantic tradition and
explains what he learned from the potent perception of *Sons and
Lovers*:

I first read him when I started writing myself. The indissoluble
link is one of background, but not so much one of
temperament. I've always seen Lawrence as a romantic. ...
I find *Sons and Lovers* his "best" novel, and discern affectation
and pretension, to a degree, dominating much of his fiction
which came after. ... In *Sons and Lovers* the potency of the
material—its ability, and even need, still to affect him—gave
an urgency and thereby a directness to his writing. ... An
instance of this is the effectiveness of the father (Morel)
where hatred acted on Lawrence as a restraint, invoking an
objectivity in the presentation of his character to such a
degree that the scene [in chapter 6] where he is called out of
the colliery and leans against the truck and weeps must be
one of the most moving in the book. ...
In this sense I took a "perception" from Lawrence, but not
a "realisation"—using him, thereby, in a constructive way, I
hope, in the process, however, of creating something
different.[20]

Melvyn Bragg notes the force on his own fiction of Lawrence's
descriptive power, social themes and prophetic insight:

I didn't start writing fiction until I was 20/21. By that time I
had a good knowledge of D. H. Lawrence's chief works and
felt—as I did with a few other writers—that he had already,
in a sense, "written my story/fiction." ... I hope that
Lawrence's particularity of description, especially of intense
cohabitation and the real/symbolic abutment of Industry and
Nature, has percolated into my work. ... Lawrence has

undoubtedly been what could perhaps be called a guardian—someone Up There whose drive and genius grew out of a social/geographical/economic/intellectual soil so similar to my own that, at times, I felt he had said all there was to be said about what I myself had experienced or imagined.

The older I get the more I respect his boldness and—despite much accompanying "bad writing"—his determination to use fiction for inspirational views and indeed, finally, even laws of life.[21]

Lawrence, who spent several years in New Mexico and wrote the seminal *Studies in Classic American Literature*, also had a potent impact on the lives as well as the works of American writers. As he told Amy Lowell: "In direction I am more than half American. I always write really towards America: my listener is there."[22] The "direct utterance from the instant, whole man" in Lawrence's poetry has influenced both William Carlos Williams and Karl Shapiro.[23] The latter has recently emphasized the "American" aspect of Lawrence:

I think every modern American poet is in Lawrence's debt. His use, his perfection of the "spoken" verse, the clarity of his own voice in the birds, beasts and flowers poems and in the love poems is something that has colored all our poetry. Lawrence was very American, the Brits still take him with a grain of salt, one of the few moderns who really understood Whitman and learned from him. Lawrence marches on. Young readers and writers are still shocked into recognition by him. He is still a chanticleer, the escaped cock himself. He gave Auden the shivers; that was the England in Auden. I think Lawrence taught everybody the best free verse and the brightest imagery in the clearest of voices, even when he screeched. He is still a big model, a permanence.[24]

Theodore Roethke's "loose and open rhythms, the closely-observed details of natural growth, the frank confession, the sense of desecration . . . evoke the spirit of D. H. Lawrence, to whose works Roethke was deeply devoted in the early 1930's."[25] Roethke's "The Bat," "The Pike" and "Snake" are clearly indebted to and enriched by *Birds, Beasts and Flowers*. Shortly before his death, Roethke acknowledged his profound debt to Lawrence's primordial immediacy:

> In terms of immediate influence, I read a lot of Lawrence's prose, almost all of it, and I wrote a paper on him once. But, I mean, *The White Peacock* and *Sons and Lovers* dented me the most. . . . I think Lawrence's poetry is more important than the prose. . . . Lawrence talks about the immediate moment. That's what the poem, in a sense, should capture. I think Lawrence is, of course, often self-indulgent, but in the great runs we can feel into primordial kinds of life. I mean, that sense of identity.[26]

Roethke placed Lawrence with the "blood-thinkers or intuitives," with the "special writers for whom [he had] a real enthusiasm."[27] Like Lawrence, Roethke was intensely conscious of the human body, which he vividly and evocatively placed in its proper environment. He learned to use Lawrence's flowing rhythms, which were closely related to the pulse of blood and of nature, and declared: "We must permit the poetry to extend consciousness as far, as deeply, as particularly as it can."[28]

Robert Bly has also acknowledged Lawrence's powerful impact on his work:

> I was grateful to Lawrence for carrying that subtlety of seeing into our own culture, and giving it a place and habitation so near to all living poets. To grant consciousness to non-human creatures—how difficult for people raised in Christian symbology! Without intending to we suddenly throw a rock at a motionless thirsty snake, and so we "lose our chance" with "one of the lords of the universe." Lawrence's "Snake" and "Fish" belong with [Francis] Ponge's "Horse" and "Trees Lose Parts of Themselves Inside a Circle of Fog" as masterpieces of subtle seeing; and those masterly generous acts of attention that we call D. H. Lawrence's poems lie underneath all my "Morning Glory" and seeing poems.[29]

Galway Kinnell testified to Lawrence's continuing influence on the poetical generation after Roethke when he stated: "Lawrence is among the great germinal poets of modern times.

I love his love poems and animal poems; I like less the didactic and social ones. . . . His best love poems move us so far into mystery. They turn into acts of cosmic adoration. In some of them love of one person passes into worship of sexuality itself."[30]

Allen Ginsberg feels that Lawrence supplemented and reinforced the Williams lineage from Whitman. Lawrence criticizes Whitman and rejects the body, but enters into a non-genital "heart relation" with other men. He is a model for specific detail, minute particulars, vivid facts, colorful images, spurts of perception; for awareness, abundance, profusion, dramatic movement, touches of sharp description, use of subjective facts about his own life. Ginsberg admires his rhythm and experiments with open form, his bold pioneering, his making new rules, especially in the animal and flower poems, in "Bat" and in "Ship of Death." Lawrence seemed wide open and abandoned, but he was also disciplined. He had strong content and was a major innovator.[31] Ginsberg, who shared Gary Snyder's sense of a mystical, Lawrencean revelation, described how his friend "suddenly realized 'everything is alive'—the entire universe is alive. Every sentient being is alive, like myself."[32]

Lawrence had a strong effect on American novelists who adopted his primitivism, emphasis on instinct and interest in the adjustment of consciousness. Wyndham Lewis, who attacked Lawrence's primitivism in *Paleface* (1929), quoted Hemingway's observation: "Lawrence you know was Anderson's God in the old days—and you can trace his effect all through A's stuff."[33] Though Hemingway satirized Anderson's sentimental *Dark Laughter* (1925) in *The Torrents of Spring* (1926), he too came under Lawrence's influence.

Hemingway's coy device of calling his wife and traveling companion P. O. M. (Poor Old Mama) in *Green Hills of Africa* was probably taken from Lawrence, who refers to his wife as Q. B. (Queen Bee) in *Sea and Sardinia*. "The Short Happy Life of Francis Macomber" and several other stories express a Lawrencean hostility to castrating women and portray the struggle for domination in marriage. Like Lawrence, Hemingway exalted the primitive element in man in his Spanish and Cuban fiction; and he learned from Lawrence how to express what he felt about a country, how to bring alive a landscape and convey the "spirit of place." Just as Lawrence believed in the therapeutic effect of shedding "one's sicknesses in books," so Hemingway maintained: "If he wrote it he could get rid of it. He had gotten rid of many things by writing them."[34]

William Jay Smith noted that Tennessee Williams also fell under the sway of the deity, that his "great god was D. H. Lawrence" who influenced the mystic confluence of sex, nature and power in Williams' early prose and poetry.[35] Williams dedicated *Battle of Angels* (1940) to the memory of Lawrence, did a dramatic adaptation of Lawrence's story "You Touched Me" (1945) and wrote a poignant play about Lawrence's death, *I Rise in Flame, Cried the Phoenix* (1941). Williams' biographer remarks that *Kingdom of the Earth* (1968) shows an obvious homage to *The Virgin and the Gipsy* in its "connection between repressed sexuality, an imminent flood and the nature of proprietorship."[36]

Norman Mailer, whose anal-orgasmic "The Time of Her Time" (1958) was clearly inspired by Lawrence, has suggested his immediate and lasting intellectual and emotional debt to the Master:

> Lawrence's main influence for me was *Lady Chatterley's Lover*. I had the privilege of reading it back in 1941 in the unexpurgated edition. That was in the Treasure Room of Widener Library. ... It changed my sex life, or rather, accelerated it into a direction it had been proceeding on nicely by itself. I accepted Lawrence's thesis about untrammeled and illimitable rights and liberties and pleasure of sexual love and the union between the two. I don't think anyone ever before, whether in literature or personal life, had stated it so forcefully for me, that one could not have sex without love, or love without sex, period. Now, as I know from the other side of 40-plus years, that is an extraordinary thesis, and can be half-right, or all-wrong, as well as absolutely so. For this reason, Lawrence's hypothesis has lived with me as my own, with all the excitement of an ongoing hypothesis that you can never quite confirm or deny (hypotheses are so much more life-giving than obsessions!). At any rate, such is my essential debt to Lawrence. His other works I admire, and I think he was a great writer, but *Lady Chatterley* changed my life.[37]

As early as 1912 Lawrence prophetically wrote: "I think the new generation is rather different from the old. I think they will read me more gratefully."[38] Lawrence was in direct touch with the sources of vitality and could clearly see the sickness of society. He was hostile to competitive, material, industrial, technological society, and to the power structures and self-destructive tendencies of the modern state. He wanted to eliminate all the hypocrisy and cant in religion and sex, to create an entirely new and life-enhancing system of values. His frank erotic manifestoes emphasized blood consciousness, instinct and passion; they saw sex as an instrument for social regeneration and tried to create a new dialectic in the relations of men and women. He searched for spiritual values outside Christianity, was attracted to the traditional life of Latins and Indians, and longed for an elite community of fellow spirits.[39]

Lawrence's social impact—especially after the trial of *Lady Chatterley's Lover* in 1960 and the first English edition of the novel (1961) which sold 3,225,000 copies in the first eight months[40]—influenced the abolition of state censorship, freedom of language, sexual permissiveness, public homosexuality, nudity and the salvation of touch: "I think we come into knowledge (unconscious) of the most vital parts of the cosmos through touching things."[41] Philip Larkin wryly observed in "Annus Mirabilis":

> Sexual intercourse began
> In nineteen sixty-three
> (Which was rather late for me)—
> Between the end of the *Chatterley* ban
> And the Beatles' first LP.[42]

And the would-be seducer at a tropical fishing pool in William Boyd's witty novel, *A Good Man in Africa*, invokes the dark gods of *The Plumed Serpent*: "Christ, he thought to himself, D. H. Lawrence couldn't have arranged or directed that episode any more skilfully—the violence, the blood, the male aggression, the admiring female—the very air throbbed with felt life. Furthermore, Morgan suddenly thought, if DHL was anywhere near right she should be a pushover now."[43]

It is ironic that Lawrence became the prophet of the sexual revolution in the 1960s and patron saint of the new youth culture, with its hot tubs and massage parlors, for these movements have distorted his gospel and carried his ideas to repugnant extremes. The "philosophy" of Hugh Hefner, for example, is a direct though debased derivative: " 'Playboyism' ... says that 'we must not be afraid or ashamed of sex, sex is not necessarily limited to marriage, sex is oxygen, mental health. Enough of virginity, hypocrisy, censorship, restrictions. Pleasure is to be preferred to sorrow.' "[44] As Huxley noted as early as 1932: "Lawrence's doctrine is constantly invoked by people, of whom Lawrence himself would passionately have disapproved, in defence of a behaviour, which he would have found deplorable or even revolting."[45]

CHAPTER ONE

Lawrence and the Modern English Novel

JOHN BAYLEY

In an age of faith the novel hardly exists. The form, as we know it, comes most into its own when life is seen to offer nothing but life itself. The one who sees it the most graphically is the novelist, and it is his task and opportunity to offer the realisation of life in art which will—at least implicitly—fulfil his reader's sense of what life can be.

The classic Russian novel vividly demonstrates this. Turning, as it were, to the novel for a sense of what life can be, the Russians use the phrase *zhivaya zhizn*—"living life." Most of our experience, that is to say, is of mere existence, but there are moments when we are conscious of the thing itself, of *joie de vivre* (the French equivalent) as a positive blessing; and it is these moments which the novelist builds into his art, turning them into a whole language and pattern of being. Something as simple and yet as radical as this is really the impulse that underlies what we call Modernism in twentieth-century art, and particularly the art of the novel. It is behind what Joyce called the Epiphany; what Proust made the purpose and theme of his long novel to recapture; what Virginia Woolf strove in her novels to give the reader as a continuous and conscious awareness.

Consciousness is indeed the hallmark of this new technique. "Well, life itself is life," as D. H. Lawrence remarks in one of his letters, and the tautology expresses what matters to him and what matters to the novel: the continuous consciousness of life. By critics of the great modern novelists the use of the word as a kind of talisman or rallying-cry can be overdone. Lawrence's chief partisan, F. R. Leavis, tells us so often that what matters in a novelist is "the sense of where life flows" that he becomes repetitive and tedious. Gogol and Tolstoy and Dostoyevsky had that sense all right, but they did not make a fuss about it. All three in their various ways, and as artists, understood deep down that life was what mattered, but all three, as men, agonised over what seemed to them the much more important questions of faith and belief. Both Gogol and Tolstoy abandoned the novel out of a sense of guilt and misery, convinced that salvation lay elsewhere. In the perspective of history their anguished state of mind is an interesting example of the transition in art between an age of faith and an age which believes only in life itself. Chaucer's *Troilus and Criseyde*, we might note in passing, is sometimes spoken of as the first psychological novel, but Chaucer no more had the sense of "life itself" than had the classic writers who were his models, back to Virgil and Homer. His novel in poetry ends with a palinode in which the hero is removed after death to the ninth sphere of heaven, from where he is conscious of the utter triviality and unimportance of the human world, while his author exhorts us to turn from worldly loves and joys to the contemplation of heavenly ones. Yet in his story of the two lovers Chaucer shows as acute a sense of sexual relations, of living, human desires and preoccupations, as do Tolstoy and D. H. Lawrence.

Lawrence is of course one of the great Modernists, and of him it might be said, as James Joyce said of Hemingway, that "he has reduced the veil between literature and life, which is what every writer strives to do." Every Modernist writer, that is, every modern novelist. Joyce's admiring comment was made specifically about Hemingway's story "A Clean, Well-Lighted Place," a story in which the café described in the title might be said to stand as an image for life itself, all that there is, a place to hold on to in a world of *nada*. To reduce the veil between literature and life—indeed virtually to equate the two—is indeed the goal of the major modern novelist, the goal equally of Hemingway, of Joyce and of Lawrence.

It follows that the novelist's commitment to life is identified with his commitment to art—"one life one writing," as Robert Lowell put it in a poem. Lawrence, Hemingway, Joyce, they lived as they wrote in the deepest, most intimate sense; not only making their writing out of the way they had to live, but living totally in the way their writing demanded. Lawrence intuited that a purely secular kind of fiction, which expressed and demanded the whole being of its author, was in some sense an American discovery, and one that his study of American literature shows that he greatly admired. Literature was at last concerning itself with the physical basis of life, striving to come as close to the body as it was possible to do. To quote Joyce on Hemingway again: "He would never have written it if his body had not allowed him to live it." The same thing, ironically enough, is true of Lawrence. His physical frailty gave him that vivid apprehension of being which lived in what he wrote.

It is ironical, too, that this break-through of Modernism, implicit in its new styles, should now be seen by structuralist critics as just another form of "literariness," a linguistic code of the fictional to be read in the same way as any other. Lawrence would scarcely be pleased. Of course the new criticism is right on its own terms and from its own point of view. Yet so too is the common reader, in his impression that this writing has indeed narrowed the gap between literature and life, if only because it is so intent on what constitutes the sensation of living. It is significant that no writer or reader of novels, in an earlier period, would have seen the point of Joyce's observation. It would have seemed as meaningless as trying to narrow the gap between body and soul. And if readers of novels, or more likely students as readers of novels, are successfully conditioned by today's critical attitudes, it will come to seem meaningless again: we shall all take for granted that the codes of literary language and the processes of living can never approach one another.

But the modern spirit, with which Lawrence is inevitably associated, took for granted the notion of wholeness—one life, one writing—with no dichotomy between body and soul any more than between life and literature. And what distinguished Lawrence and his peers most sharply from other and earlier novelists was the absence of the kinds of dichotomy earlier writers took for granted. The importance of these becomes clearer if we think of Lawrence in his time, and in relation to novelists like Henry James and Ford Madox Ford. Ford was among the first to see what Lawrence, as expressed in the Lawrencean style, would be at, and he admired that style deeply. His own novel, *The Good Soldier*, is not only contemporary with *Women in Love* but is attempting to do the same kind of thing: to give the feel of life in its time. It does not signify that Ford's "literariness" seems quite inadequate to its task, while Lawrence's triumphantly fulfils it. What matters, again, is the intention; and Ford's intention was to foreground the feel of a doomed society: to make the reader intellectually aware of it, even though his style has no ability to give the feel of it.

The Good Soldier has become a Modernist text by reason of its literary devices—the equivocal narrator, the indirect presentation of evidence. Lawrence's devices are more purely his own, and besides they do not feel like devices. But it is worth noting that Lawrence's conception of character—an aspect of his developing technique he took very seriously—is also implicit in Ford, just as it is in the later Henry James. To be sure, Lawrence's claims for what he was doing are more consciously combative and committed. He wanted to convey not how men and women behave as individuals but what the man *is*, what the woman *is*, and he wanted to do this as a part of his gospel and philosophy of life. But in practice both Ford and James do very much the same thing, not for ideological reasons but as part of the groundwork of their art. James' characters are submerged in the whole rich stylistic pattern of his later novels, in their "density of felt life"; while Ford hardly expects the reader to believe in his characters as individuals but rather as elements in a social atmosphere, pointers to and portents of a way of life gone rotten behind the façade.

The general tendency, therefore, in aiming at "life itself" where the novel is concerned, and with whatever degree of consciousness on the novelist's part, is to remove individual and component features, to break down the normal dichotomies, to present a seamless whole, an appearance—at least—that life and literature have become one. There is little difference here between Henry James' noble plea that the art of the novelist "makes life," and Joyce's or Lawrence's assumption that life itself is what matters. In both cases the novel has ceased to perform its traditional role as an artificial entertainment, has become instead a serious matter, *the* serious matter, no more "capable of the absolute"—for Lawrence—than ordinary daily experience, yet helping the reader to live by the way it merges so closely with that experience.

It is clear that Lawrence was influenced by the Russians, by Tolstoy in particular, and particularly in the matter of "life itself." The goal of the novelist is to teach his readers how to live. Lawrence's friendship—incidentally one of his steadiest and least stormy—with the Russian-Jewish translator S. S. Koteliansky went with the general atmosphere and aspirations of the literary world he entered through his relationship—initially almost that of understanding father and brilliant son—with Edward Garnett, whose wife was the translator of Dostoyevsky. Lawrence entered into this contemporary worship of the great Russians in his own way, using them and then rejecting them, more especially rejecting Dostoyevsky. But he never rejected the general message of the Russian novel, which was that life is everything, that the novel is a vessel of life, the act of writing most concerned with it, and that the forms and traditions of the genre count for nothing beside this fact. Tolstoy had himself observed that no outstanding Russian "novel" of the nineteenth century conformed to the received and conventional idea of the genre, but that each was in its own way *sui generis*, and we can be sure that Lawrence himself would have endorsed this judgment where the modern novel was concerned, just as his own fictional work confirms it.

All the more remarkable, then, that Lawrence's own influence on the English novels that came after him should be relatively slight. His own direct influence, that is. Obviously the novel after him was never quite the same again: he entered the bloodstream of fiction in English in the way that Henry Crawford, in Jane Austen's *Mansfield Park*, describes Shakespeare as being "in the blood" of all English writers and readers. But if we think of the immediate and lasting effect that Richardson had on the English and French novel of sensibility, and all the equivocations of the inner life; or the ways in which Dickens influenced not only the English but the European, the Russian and the American novel, then we must admit that Lawrence is not, after all, so very important in the development of the English novel since his time. His impact on continental literature has always been marginal; except as a curiosity the French have hardly bothered with him, taking on trust what T. S. Eliot pronounced in a lecture at the Sorbonne, that "*il écrit extrêmement mal*," and preferring such elegant stylists as Charles Morgan. Moreover they considered, with some justification, that his message about sex held nothing for them, and that the subject had already been fully explored in the French novel.

The problem, of course, is just what Tolstoy said it was. Since Lawrence's novels are unique, and like nothing else, they could produce few children. You can imitate the form of the novels of Sir Walter Scott but not that of *Women in Love*. And so to the extent that Lawrence exercised any direct influence it tended to be bad, just as—in its own different way—the influence of *War and Peace* has produced a whole crop of inferior works of Russian fiction, approximating to it in subject and scale, but trying to reproduce in terms of genre a work that is essentially outside such considerations. And it is a singular fact, which goes some way towards explaining why its influence on the international scene has been so much less than during the previous hundred years, that the novel in England during the twentieth century has become more and more individualistic, with an individualism which in its case has tended towards the provincial.

The novels of the Powys brothers, for instance, and particularly those of John Cowper Powys, might loosely be associated with those of Lawrence in terms of mode and message, of a common *Zeitgeist*. But they are in fact different in temperament and imagination, exhibiting in different ways that particular sort of quirky individuality which has resigned from the mysteriously authoritative status of the generally accepted canonical novel. Their admirers think that *Wolf Solent* and *Weymouth Sands*, by John Cowper Powys, are among the greatest novels of the century, but Powys never has and never will acquire the canonical status of Joyce, Faulkner or Lawrence. His style is as unauthoritative as his philosophy, his sense of human freedom—sexual freedom above all—too eccentric and unserious to impose itself in the way that the personalities of a Lawrence, or a Henry Miller, have done.

Lawrence's direct influence tended to be bad, too, because he inculcated a pretension to authority which less inspired writers could not sustain. The great novel has its own ways of securing our submission which the merely talented and opinionated writer, in the mould of H. G. Wells or Aldous Huxley, can only imitate factitiously. Huxley's convictions and prescriptions, morally civilised and humane as most of them are, stand apart from his novels like a suit of clothes. Huxley's friendship with and admiration for Lawrence led to his willed acceptance of much of the Lawrencean message, including that of the "living death" (as opposed to "living life") in which the modern world exists, and which must be overcome by new manifestations of the human spirit. But he strikes one as a sceptic and rationalist who is trying to be a mystic, and the Lawrencean mysticism is of a non-transferable kind. Novelists like Lawrence Durrell and James Hanley, who obviously came under Lawrence's spell, cannot be said to have profited from it except in a rather similar way and in terms of attitudes and ideas. The way they actually write shows conscious signs of trying to escape from Lawrence, into corresponding kinds of richness and vividness cultivated on their own.

The one aspect of narrative genre in which Lawrence's influence has been really pervasive, and significantly fruitful, has been in the development of the story form, whether nouvelle or short story proper. Here it is a peculiar forcefulness which is the dominant effect passed on, and which is as evident in English writers like V. S. Pritchett and Elizabeth Bowen as it is in America, where it makes a natural combination with the inheritance of Hemingway. The Lawrencean legacy here is one of a powerfully satiric undertone, of a sharp psychological diagnosis establishing itself in a characteristic atmosphere, the atmosphere, say, of "The Captain's Doll," or of "Jimmy and the Desperate Woman." We can see today what a very marked affiliation there is, too, between the stories of Kipling and those of Lawrence, as if Lawrence had instinctively, and perhaps unconsciously, adopted the pungent local product after his brief encounter with Chekhov, whom he handed over, as it were, to the sensibilities of Katherine Mansfield.

But the surprising thing about the novel of the thirties, at least in England, is the way in which it ignored and turned away from Lawrence, perhaps in necessary self-defence; turning away, too, from any assumption of the novel as vessel of life, the medium that teaches one how to live. The counter-revolution in the English novel, if one can call it that, laid a much greater emphasis on form, on the creation of a completely coherent and individual fictional world. It may be here, indeed, that the element of provinciality begins to make its appearance in the English novel, the quality of *snugness*, of the novelist operating in an enclosed world of his own. It could even be fancied, in this connection, that P. G. Wodehouse (much admired by, among others, Evelyn Waugh) was a more potent if unacknowledged influence than was Lawrence himself. Certainly many of the best novelists of the period—Ivy Compton-Burnett, Anthony Powell, Patrick Hamilton, Graham Greene and Evelyn Waugh too—strike one at this distance as having a special quality of Englishness about them, in a snug but limiting sense; and it is this insulated and encapsulated form which is quite alien to anything Lawrence ever wrote.

Although so many of Graham Greene's novels (and *England Made Me* is a very Lawrencean title) are set in foreign parts, they are enclosed inside a form and a formula—a small hell from which the Catholic faith offers a glimpse of salvation—which is the novelist's response to the diminished and depressing England of his home and upbringing. Lawrence's disillusion with his native country never takes this form, and never seems to seek to create—as these other novelists do—a special form of private Englishness to offset the general sense of letdown by England itself. In contrast to his successors, Lawrence is in no constricting sense an "English" novelist. And to contrast *The Plumed Serpent* and *Mornings in Mexico* with *The Power and the Glory* and *The Lawless Roads* is to see that Lawrence is a wholly international writer who is not bringing to his subject—in this case Mexico—his own special way of writing a novel, and his own localised English viewpoint. Nor could Lawrence ever have seen the novel, as these later novelists involuntarily do, as in some sense a *protection* against life.

It is true that Lawrence could use traditional fiction, in its conventional and formal sense, as a vehicle to convey some of his more dogmatic assertions and fantasies. When he simply wrote about how he was living or had lived—as in the family and holiday scenes of *Sons and Lovers*, the social tableaux of *Women in Love*, the Australian suburban sequences in *Kangaroo*—he was at one with his writing, and his writing itself does all the necessary work on us for him. This indeed is life, in the new sense in which the novel is its vessel. But, even in *Kangaroo*, the relationship plotted up between Kangaroo himself and the Lawrencean hero is like something "out of a novel," because it has to convey straight one of the thematic patterns of Lawrence's ideology—the possibilities of *Blutbrüderschaft*. "The Woman Who Rode Away" shows even more clearly how Lawrence can use cliché scenes from fiction to convey his ideas. The Woman stands in a very obvious relation to the popular novel genre of the twenties and thirties in which girls are carried off by sheikhs or savage tribes, and find a new and more fulfilling way of life away from the deadness of their accustomed society. On the other hand, in "The Princess" and in *St Mawr*, although the heroines themselves are typecast as girls of the period, Lawrence's intelligence reverses any expected contrast between wilderness and corrupt society, or noble savage and etiolated man about town. "Living life" is not a facile affair of the difference between one way of life and another.

One complex difficulty here, which affects the whole nature of influence, is that what seems wholly "natural" in Lawrence becomes "fictional" when it is imitated, perhaps unconsciously, by another writer. A comic instance of this is that even so unLawrencean a novelist as Evelyn Waugh can lapse involuntarily into a Lawrencean style of utterance when wishing to describe a lyrical sex relation. Charles Ryder, in *Brideshead Revisited*, describes how he began a passionate affair with the heroine on board an ocean liner, and was first "made free of her narrow loins." The word "loins," common in Lawrence's vocabulary and native to his way of writing, sounds absurdly mannered when used in a different style of fiction. But, interestingly, Lawrence himself always had trouble, ever since his first novel, *The White Peacock*, with the relations between the fictional and the "living" sides of his work. Of all his novels only *Sons and Lovers* is wholly free from the standard ploys and devices of fiction, which become increasingly conspicuous in the later ones, in such episodes as the gunfight sequence in *The Plumed Serpent*, imported from its original in the thriller or cowboy tale. In *Lady Chatterley's Lover* he uses the hoary fictional device, beloved by Hardy, of the grand lady in love with a man from a humble class. Of course there is a conscious element of irony here, with Lawrence deliberately injecting new life into a fictional situation, but this only accentuates the lack of harmony between the two. Tolstoy, the other great proclaimer of "living life," is always careful to make a seamless whole, so that we cannot tell where life ends and fiction begins.

Certainly Lawrence misconceived some of the consequences of his way of doing things. It is effective that the title of *Lady Chatterley's Lover* suggests a solid perspective of fiction, reaching back to the Victorian sensationalist novel, like Mary Braddon's

Lady Audley's Secret (1862). Lawrence is out to create a new kind of sensation. But this new demonstration of "life," as represented by the lovers and their relation, as opposed to the deathly routines and reflexes of the post-war upper classes, is compromised by the ironies, intended and unintended, of its literary setting. Even the famous four-letter words have the air of coming out of books rather than out of life: however much they reverse the pattern they still exhibit self-consciously the literary tradition of a lovers' language. It is an interesting case of life and literature colliding, because Lawrence has sought to give to literature the supreme authenticity of words used in the crudest living context, and in the context of the book they take on a bizarrely bookish sound. Joyce used them in *Ulysses* much more successfully because he placed them in the context of men's talk—soldiers' talk—in which they are naturally at home. Four-letter words are not tender, and never have been, and in seeking to make them appear so Lawrence shows very clearly how his imagination of "life" clashed with the ordinary facts about it. His sexual imagination fantasised about men, never about women—there are no physical descriptions of women in his work in any way comparable in vividness to those of the men—and he tried to graft his fantasy of a man's world—complete with four-letter words and lyrical images of men like Mellors washing, their breeches slipping off their slender loins—on to a willed presentation of tenderness and love in a heterosexual situation.

Lady Chatterley's Lover thus remains an extraordinary hybrid, in which satire and fantasy, literature and "living life," come together with the maximum incongruity, held together only by the magic of Lawrence's personality and style. It explains why the influence of Lawrence on other writers, insofar as it was a matter of imitation, tended to be bad; and why English novelists with a real talent of their own did their best to insulate themselves from contact with this disconcerting genius who brought life and the novel so incongruously together. They had no inclination to strive to reduce the veil between literature and life, and indeed would have regarded the notion of doing so as all but meaningless. Henry Green, Evelyn Waugh and Anthony Powell were creating worlds of their own in fiction, and their watchword—if they had one—would not have been Joyce's comment but Henry James' passionate assertion, which H. G. Wells professed not to be able to understand, that it is the *novel* which "makes life, makes interest."

It is James and Proust, not Lawrence, who are most behind the modern English novel. Virginia Woolf too, and Rosamond Lehmann and Elizabeth Taylor, silently repudiate Lawrence in an argument which goes back to Flaubert and beyond, demonstrating in their novels not the supremacy of life but what James called "the force and beauty" of the fictional process. Lawrence was still alive and writing when E. M. Forster tried—however quietly and placatingly—to aestheticise him in *Aspects of the Novel*, to claim him for form rather than for life. To modern criticism the argument appears unreal, for to recent critics what is under discussion cannot be "life," but only different aspects of "literariness." And yet the debate between life and literature had fire in its time, and gave a theoretical basis to what later novelists instinctively felt about Lawrence.

In the later Lawrence scenario "living life" and "living death" confront one another in an opposition that is in fact built into the novel's form, rather as Vronsky–Anna and Kitty–Levin are opposed in *Anna Karenina*, and it is this kind of opposition which turns out in the end to be the most influential that Lawrence produced. Its chief result is what might be termed the inherently superior hero, the Rupert Birkin of *Women in Love*, or the gamekeeper Mellors in *Lady Chatterley's Lover*. This superiority is the logical consequence of novel and hero as vessel of life. He who is closest to life is king, and the novelist must logically be identified with his hero, since in writing the novel he is demonstrating his own closeness to life. So significant a development for the novel is the Lawrencean superior hero that he crops up continually in later fiction, as I shall show in a moment, even in the work of novelists who have no other connection with Lawrence or his message.

Paul Morel of *Sons and Lovers* is not yet a superior hero, but in some ways a very conventional figure from the fiction of a slightly earlier period, who is learning his way about life like the hero of a *Bildungsroman*. Lawrence concentrates on understanding and displaying his relations with his mother and the girls, themselves powerfully perceived and presented individuals. Morel's nature, with its ordinary charm, talents and weaknesses, is also well defined, in a way unsuited to the hero as vessel of life, to what the man *is*, or should be. Gilbert Noon, in the brilliant unpublished and unfinished novel which Lawrence wrote in the first days of his marriage, is presented in rather the same way, but with a degree of Wellsian brio and facetiousness which makes him more attractive. Very significantly, too, Noon is cuckolded by his German mistress, just as Lawrence so frequently was by Frieda. That aspect of ordinary human experience was not proper for the later hero, who was to be the vessel of life.

It is logical that the novelist who is telling us that life itself is the thing should himself be the supreme being in whom life resides. What is in a sense harder to understand, though it proves Lawrence's genius, is why readers should have been ready to accept this. There is a difference between our acceptance of the truth—his own particular truth—in a novelist's world, and the assent we are required to give to the absolute superiority of Lawrence's vision of life. We do assent, in some degree, or the magic would not work upon us, but this involves the characteristic dual response which the reader experiences not only with Lawrence but with a great writer like Hemingway. The effect at first reading is dazzling and hypnotic; no vision of life seems so vivid and so authentic. But later on the reader adopts a more critical attitude, both to the novelist and to his way of seeing things. Such a dual response is not uncommon where highly original novelists of the modernist epoch are concerned. But, whereas in the case of Virginia Woolf, say, the novelist seems almost the passive vehicle for her own vision, in the case of Lawrence or Hemingway the novelist is himself by implication the greatest when it comes to living, the implicit hero at the business. Even James Joyce, for all his image of the artist as aloof and withdrawn, is identified with his creation, in fact portrays in Leopold Bloom the hero in whom the true mode of living unexpectedly resides.

But Lawrence was in the most obvious sense the prime mover in the mystique of living. Related forms of superiority, commonly met with in the modern and Modernist novel, are encountered even in such unexpected writers as Evelyn Waugh and Graham Greene. Although the Church occupies in their novels the same absolute position that life itself does in Lawrence, the remarkably pervasive influence of his modes of superiority has spread to their characters and situations, and to the status implicitly claimed by the authors as well. The superiority of their heroes—Tony Last in *A Handful of Dust*, Guy Crouchback in the *Officers and Gentlemen* sequence, Scobie in *The Heart of the Matter*—seems due less to their symbolic status, as representatives of old and absolute values and beliefs, than to an identity with their creators in the kind of distinction and style which they most admire in life. Superiority, in whose establishment Lawrence was perhaps the greatest influence, has itself also become an established literary convention, and today we take it for granted even in the conventions of the thriller and the detective story. Sherlock Holmes was a marvellous detective, but no one would suppose that his "life style" was being held up to us, as is for instance that of Ian Fleming's James Bond, as an exemplar of how to do it.

It is probably true that novelists have always ministered to their reader's hankering for superiority, but in more indirect ways, which did not set out to offer an exemplar of the ideal "living" man. For Jane Austen it was an affair of manners and of morals, an implicit standard which it was assumed the reader would recognise and endorse, and from which most of the author's creations were falling away in ways that were droll, touching, always entertaining. The "communal novel" as it might be called, in contrast to the "living novel" of which Lawrence is a chief exponent, not only survives today but has made something of a comeback. Barbara Pym, like Jane Austen, is concerned not with life as life but with the traditional concept of a society of which the members are engaged in helping each other through the business as best they can. The novelist is one of them: her task to comfort and amuse, since we are all in it together. But life for Lawrence is in the end an absolute affair: the only thing, and the most important thing, and for that reason something which cannot be shared or communalised.

Nothing in this context is more significant than Lawrence's criticism of the relation of Vronsky and Anna Karenina in Tolstoy's novel. Both in prose criticism and in doggerel verse he reiterates his conviction that Tolstoy has betrayed his lovers, and that "a pair of rebels like Anna and Vronsky" could have taught Russia, and the world generally, how to live. The fallacy of which Lawrence in his saner moments was perfectly well aware, is that "living" in the Lawrencean sense is a solitary process: you cannot teach other people how to do it, even through the novel; and, though he and Frieda might successfully go off together and indulge in what Frieda, in her embarrassing parody of the Lawrencean style, called "the splendour of living," this was not what Tolstoy had in mind, nor was it a possibility for the lovers that he presents in *Anna Karenina*. The love of Anna and Vronsky withers, becomes sterile, finally flickers out, because they *need* conventional human society and the normal human relationships that go with marriage, children, an occupation. As Tolstoy observed in his diary, whichever way he planned the story it always came out the same in the end. He could not go against what he perceived to be the passive instincts of ordinary people, the inability of "love," in the sense that Vronsky and Anna have chosen and willed it, to survive the human and social pressures to which the individual must accede if he is to find happiness.

That process, in however multiple a variety, is the message of the traditional novel. *Anna Karenina* is a grand climactic example of that novel. Hence Lawrence's need to rewrite it, to remould it nearer to his own heart's desire, his own personal credo. But we may wonder today, and with hindsight, whether the real achievement of Lawrence as a writer is not a wholly personal one, and exemplary only in the sense that it is so personal and so solitary. The living magic of his writing, particularly when we are young, is enough in itself. The sex message no longer seems so real or relevant; the social combativeness makes little sense any more. What remains is precisely Lawrence's gift for life, as a thing in itself. And though he alleges that "the novel, and the novel alone, can help you," it remains a fact that the traditional novel—and it still survives—is concerned not with life in his sense, but with society.

He himself was too fundamentally sensible not to realise this. With hindsight again we can see how some of his best work contradicts itself in subtle ways, producing a more traditional moral than Lawrence himself would have consciously permitted. Take his nouvelle "The Fox." The young soldier in it gets his way, marries his girl, destroys the "unhealthy" feminine set-up which tried to keep him out. It is on the face of it a triumph of disruption, paralleling the way Lawrence himself had destroyed the "unreal" marriage of the Weekleys, and borne Frieda off to a solitude *à deux*. "Life" has overcome "death." But this is not the true story, as Lawrence knows quite well, because his soldier and girl are not himself and Frieda, but a well-realised, quite commonplace young couple. The soldier thinks that by getting his way, getting his will, he must have found happiness, "the blue flower." But he has not. He is left restless and unsatisfied, and when he speaks to his woman it is "with pain in his face." As the epigraph to his verse novel, *Eugene Onegin*, Pushkin quoted the cultured Swiss banker Jacques Necker, who had remarked that "morality is in the nature of things." It is the nature of things, in this sense, that the novel knows how to bring out. So does "The Fox." The story, like many good stories of the period, knows that human beings continually seek to realise a dream of their own, usually at the expense of others; and that such a dream, even if realised or partly realised, cannot in the nature of things bring happiness.

Lawrence himself indulged in such dreams, dreams of Rananim, the ideal community bossed by himself, the ideal society, like that of the Indians to whom the woman rode away. And it is ironic, as I have already observed, that when he takes such things seriously he writes in the bad style of a conventional novel, as if for him what was not "living," but an artificial exercise of the will and the imagination, could only present itself in the style of an "unreal" novel. It is relevant to compare "The Fox," with its close and surprising linkage to old truths the good novel has long known how to tell, with Joyce's story "The Dead," or Elizabeth Bowen's story "Mysterious Kor." In both the symbolic resources of Modernism are used to deploy a deep moral of an old kind, one not necessarily fully present to the consciousness of the story's creator. Joyce's feeling in the tale is indeed for life itself, the felt life so marvellously conveyed in the party, its unfinished animation, its restorative banality. All this awakens the old human dream, the dream of something lost and perfect in the past, and Gabriel's sympathy with his wife enables him to enter this dream, and soothe himself too on the verge of sleep with its treacherous perfection. Such dreams belong to death, not life; and the subtle ambivalence of the tale puts the two together so that we can choose ourselves which is which.

In "Mysterious Kor" the shabby, exhausted provisional nature of wartime London life contrasts with the cold and perfect country of a girl's dream. Her friend, a girl of different instincts, knows nothing of it, and hardly knows herself how much she is committed to ordinary living. Both stories, I suspect, would have been well understood by Lawrence, though perhaps at a level of his creative mind which was free from his surface beliefs and preoccupations. At that level Lawrence knew very well indeed how to distinguish between the necessities of living—even if living were an end in itself—and what is to humans the equally necessary world of delusion, dream and unreality. "Life itself is life," but it includes everything that humans, and the novelists who write of them, have to experience in it. However much it is his own, Lawrence's best work has essentially the same qualities, and the same perceptions, as those found in the best of other modern, and Modernist, fiction; and it would be surprising if this were not so. His fiction is weakest where it relies on traditional fiction's methods and messages, or revives its own version of them. Lawrence's sententiousness now appears in much the same light as that of Thackeray or Dickens or Meredith; but his vision, and the words in which it found immediate utterance, remain fresh and new.

CHAPTER TWO

Lawrence and the Contemporary English Novel

JAMES GINDIN

Literary influence permeates the culture at different levels of recognition and consciousness. At one end of a hypothetical continuum, echoes of a strong literary presence are quick, referential tags, like brand-name recognition; at the other, they penetrate more deeply, seeming to become a central part of the consciousness and perspective through which subsequent fictional experience is seen and presented. With the fiction of D. H. Lawrence, the process assimilating the distinctive literary voice into the general culture has been going on since the 1950s, along with a growing critical understanding of Lawrence's art. Earlier, when Lawrence was likely to be hailed uncritically as prophet or excoriated as demon, roles magnified by his iconoclasm, his singular voice, and the many controversies he both provoked and engendered, his work seemed entirely new and strange, not part of a discernible literary tradition. Critics polarized, regarded him as issuing the call for salvation or fulminating clouds of pernicious nonsense, often playing him in tandem against Joyce, one or the other the reigning genius, the scourge or the end of modern fiction. But time and judgment have humanized Lawrence and connected him with a literary past. While regarding his distinctive and important work as closer to the prophet than to the demon, they have established a continuity that encourages the assimilation of Lawrence into subsequent fiction. That some of the assimilation is only referential and superficial testifies to its wide currency; that some of it is much deeper, more intrinsic, indicates its continuing vitality.

The assimilation of Lawrence has been easiest, most audible, in so far as he is understood as the voice of a particular region and class. The placement of the Nottinghamshire miner's son is the most convenient starting point for tracing Lawrencean echoes in subsequent fiction, although not necessarily the one leading to the most far-reaching or accurate assimilation. Other local and class voices from past fiction, some of which like Thomas Hardy's and Arnold Bennett's ante-dated Lawrence's, can sometimes be heard more resoundingly in recent fiction. Although Lawrence illustrates a significant version of the clash between a local voice and a cosmopolitan, middle-class, London-centered one, other and different local voices may be, in particular instances, more relevant sources. In the general widening and dissemination of the literary culture through more of the society over the past century, contemporary representations of cultural clash need owe little to Lawrence.

One basically non-Lawrencean contemporary voice, placed initially in the tradition of the provincial, is that of Keith Waterhouse. Even the use of Yorkshire dialect in Waterhouse's well-known *Billy Liar*, for example, exaggerated in the elaborate and self-invented speech of old Councillor Duxbury, is as much a "lie" as are Billy's stories in relation to his provincial experience. Waterhouse does not use Lawrence's sense of dialect to reveal local character and social class. Rather, in Waterhouse's world, the local speech, like the local society, is simply a comically rendered barrier to the growing imagination of the contemporary young man. Lawrence does function in Waterhouse's world, but it is only the brand-name Lawrence, the figure widely diffused in the general culture. In *Billy Liar*, when Billy, meditating on the conflict between his own lies and those in the world around him, retires to the basement lavatory at the funeral home where he works, a loutish contemporary is sure he is spending all this time reading *Lady Chatterley's Lover*—a quick social reference that signals 1959, the year in which *Billy Liar* was published. The use of Lawrence is similar in one of Waterhouse's later novels, *Maggie Muggins, or Spring in Earl's Court* (1981). The novel chronicles the adventures and survival of Maggie, a denizen of pubs and bed-sitters in London, living a rackety life in rebellion from her middle-class provincial Doncaster family. At one point, she recalls an earlier lover in Leeds (her half-way house on the way to London): he was a red-bearded former art-student who sold old books from a barrow, his "morose expression . . . all very soulful and D. H. Lawrenceish," a "sulkpot." Waterhouse's world is certainly not as superficial as these references suggest, for his comically treated themes, like Billy's inability to leave and finally test the life he imagines in London, reflect the constant problems and incapacities of his characters to live, individually or culturally, with the finer worlds they can imagine. Sometimes, the clashes between actual settings and worlds imagined explode into violent madness, as in *Jubb* (1963) or in the heart attack that ends the differences between imagination and reality for the principal character in *Thinks* (1984). (Waterhouse presents the entire novel through what the character thinks, never what he says directly.) The heart attack is the product of his "magnificent Hallelujah chorus of sustained and bellowing rage." Waterhouse's world, although redolent with social and cultural references, is finally one of individual pathology. Lawrence's world is one of relationships, individual, social and cultural; his "Hallelujah chorus," positively and negatively, usually both simultaneously, is never a single heart attack, but an organic connection that is sexual, social and racial.

Another contemporary novelist who deals with depictions and themes of the provincial for whom Lawrence seems chiefly referential is John Wain. Wain's treatment of provincial life varies, developing from the provincial as unpretentious, unaffected by cosmopolitan competition and self-inflation, in *The Contenders* (1958), to the provincial as an authentic discovery by the rootless outsider in *A Winter in the Hills* (1970) and *The Pardoner's Tale* (1978). In all these novels, the provincial is a locus of value, but it is a value outside of class and historical time, not the richly complex combinations of class and geography represented in Lawrence's early novels. Wain describes relatively little of his provincial settings in specific terms. He begins *The Contenders* in the provincial town that "mustn't be named," although a number of the details suggest the Potteries and some of the treatments of industrial geography and characters seen through their dress, poses and surroundings are more reminiscent of Arnold Bennett than of Lawrence. Wain's provincial narrator claims that "Spring in North Staffordshire is much the same as spring anywhere else, so I won't bother to describe it." Thematically, the provinces are said to produce an "originality" consumed in the competitive mass of London, but little specific sense of that local "originality" is conveyed in the novel. The novel works defensively, negatively, on the value of the *un*pretentious or the satirical rejection of the confusing presences of contemporary life. *A Winter in the Hills* describes the Welsh village, with fondness and imagination, from the point of view of the sensitive off-season tourist. Little interior sense of the clashes or classes of the village is conveyed, rather a statement of its authenticity in contrast to the rest of the modern world. Almost the only social theme that Lawrence and Wain share is an extreme aversion to the "bully," a word both writers frequently use for anyone who would impose himself or his political ideas on others. Both want to protect the identity of the individual in an age of massive, compelling social systems. Yet, even on this point, Wain's aversion to bullying seems closer to that of Bennett, George Orwell or the resistance of many of his generation to the equivalently virulent forms of totalitarianism represented by Communism and Fascism, than it is to Lawrence's idea of the violation of another's being, which is personal and social simultaneously.

Even when relationships form the subject matter of Wain's fiction, his treatment and points of view demonstrate no connection with those of Lawrence. Wain's *A Travelling Woman* (1959) is centrally concerned with sexual relationships, but these focus on deceptions, plots and contrivances, most of which take place in London, a texture of ratiocinative duplicity remote from any Lawrencean treatment of sex. Affairs are plots, and plot, the arrangement of unexpected happenings, is central to all Wain's fiction. *A Travelling Woman* exhausts all its contrivances and combinations, satirizing them as immoral, in a novel whose concluding note is the morality of stasis, of solace, of the description of the philosopher's garden in terms of "let the soil rest." Sexuality is contrived, ratiocinative, aggressive and immoral; the moral life is finally asexual.

Sexuality is seen as more deeply attractive in some of Wain's later fiction. In *The Pardoner's Tale*, a novelist, in both his life and his fiction (separate stories, separate plots that are connected imaginatively and thematically), falls in love with a woman who represents uninhibited sexuality, religion and music simultaneously. Through her, he begins to escape a lifetime of inhibition and privacy, to devote himself to what he cannot entirely understand. But she unexpectedly jilts him after her big concert in London, and he, passive in life as his protagonist is passive in fiction, is unexpectedly saved by the return of the duller and more knowable woman who had jilted him at the beginning of the novel. Wain's sexual plots are often circles, his protagonists, caught in the middle, became spectators of what happens to them. And Lawrence, if present at all in representing the possibility of a desirable sexual relationship, is shunted aside, or perhaps deliberately reversed, in favor of a safe retreat. A rare specific reference in Wain's work dismisses Lawrence entirely. The seventeen-year-old protagonist in *Young Shoulders* (1982), who wants to create the ideal of a "World Free Zone," the complete obverse of anything provincial, is attracted by both the sexual woman he meets in a Lisbon cabaret and the image of his dead sister. He wonders if there is a female-ness or woman-ness "like that Lawrence book they pushed down our throats in sixth form English." But he easily abandons the speculation when he discovers that he can create the "World Free Zone" in his imagination.

More intrinsic use of Lawrence is apparent in the fiction of Melvyn Bragg. Bragg has, in essays, indicated his interest in Lawrence, just as Wain has written searchingly and well about Bennett. Bragg has also stated that his "fictional self" is the character Douglas Tallentire in *A Place in England* (1970), the second novel of a pair—the first is *The Hired Man* (1969)—which traces three generations of a family beginning with a Cumberland agricultural laborer. When Douglas is at Oxford, trying to become a writer, he wonders if he might become the first English writer "really" from the working classes, the first undiluted specimen of the breed with "no school-teacher-mother-literary-uncle in the background." He considers and rejects various earlier possibilities: "If only Lawrence's mother had not been so classy." At least as far as the novel goes, this statement of the purity and specialness of class representation seems to stand unmodified, a simpler version of class experience than Lawrence ever sanctioned. Elements in the pair of novels echo Lawrence's *The Rainbow*: the representative of the first generation as a miner, then, after a pit accident, the shift to agricultural work; the meticulous descriptions of farms and class resentments against owners or bosses; the sense of physical love connected with class in *The Hired Man*; the combination of love and a suppressed, almost strangulated, domestic hostility in the couple representing the second generation; the confusions in the second generation, when, after the Second World War, the representative leaves declining farmwork to sell insurance, then to manage a pub.

Yet, in other, perhaps more crucial, respects, Bragg does not echo Lawrence. Bragg's prose is precise, meticulous, graphic, not suggestive or metaphysical at all. His treatment of class and social issues is also very different, for Bragg's voice emphasizes class solidarity and justifies resentment against owners or landlords, especially during the decade-long slump of the 1930s. The triumphant scenes in Bragg are most often those of the colorful local carnival, the assemblage of class and locality, frequently in celebration of a public event like a coronation. Especially after the Second World War, as he describes the Welfare State, changes in education and the problems in running a pub, Bragg is visibly writing a chronicle of the social history of England from the point of view of the Cumberland working classes—Noël Coward's *Cavalcade*, extended in time and detail.

When dealing centrally with women, Bragg seems closer to internalizing Lawrence, as in *The Silken Net* (1974). A young woman, orphaned at fifteen (her father was an English artist killed in the First World War, her mother a French aristocrat), lives in Cumberland with her bachelor uncle and spinster aunt. After a brief flirtation with an elegant Richmond cousin does not work out, she spends nine years in the isolated Cumberland town, dry years of what the author indicates are unconscious frustration, reminiscent of those of Alvina Houghton in Lawrence's *The Lost Girl*. Sexually awakened by a local "roughneck," Bragg's protagonist debates between the appeal of the body and that of words or literature, as represented by her suddenly returned elegant cousin. Like Louisa in "Daughters of the Vicar," she marries the man who represents body, against the opposition of her family. All the strains of the relationship, expressed socially (he wants to manage a pub, Bragg's frequent symbol for community), sexually and in attitudes toward their children over the next twenty years, convey a Lawrencean complexity, a balance of love and hostility that holds for a long time and eventually fails.

When dealing with domestic arguments and partial reconciliations, Bragg writes with a resonance not often apparent in his fiction. In one scene, when her son is temporarily home from Oxford, the woman tries to describe to him her need for independence and freedom within the context of her marriage by quoting and explaining Lawrence's poem that begins "Not I, not I, but the wind that blows through me . . . .." At these particular points, Bragg's use of Lawrence is more than referential, it is the conscious echo of a more fully developed and influential version of experience. Other of Bragg's later novels, as he moves his focus away from Cumberland, seem to have no connection with Lawrence. *Love and Glory* (1983), for example, set in New York and London, describes shifting loves, pains and infidelities among television producers, actresses and psychiatrists. In a rush of plot and aimlessness, no one really relates to anyone. The characters originally from Cumberland are distinguished from others only by conveying an impression of intensity, by a response to amorphous experience that seems more painful or deeply felt than that of others. Yet, in context, this seems only a muted form of regional glorification as the novel focuses on continuing to chart contemporary social history.

Although Bragg's is the most internal of the three novelists', these uses of Lawrence are only random, referential or partial, not full understandings that seem to incorporate and individually re-shape Lawrence into an extension and revivification of a literary tradition. A much more intrinsic, and perhaps a much more conscious, use of Lawrence as a shaping force is visible in much of the fiction of Alan Sillitoe, David Storey and Doris Lessing. For Sillitoe, the use of Lawrence is certainly conscious. Sillitoe, from a similar working-class background in and around Nottingham, a region combining the industrial and the agricultural, has written directly of Lawrence's influence. In an essay entitled "D. H. Lawrence and His District" (in a volume called *D. H. Lawrence: Novelist, Poet, Prophet*, edited by Stephen Spender in 1973), Sillitoe recalls that, on first reading, the opening paragraphs of *The Rainbow* "electrified me." He goes on to illustrate the attitude he shares with and defines through Lawrence, the combination of love and hatred for the mixed beauty and ugliness of rural and industrial Nottinghamshire, "half town and half country, slum and mansion, pitstock and folly, red brick and priory ruins, lime-kiln and green glen, farmhouse and ironworks."

In his own way, Sillitoe describes the landscape with a map-like accuracy reminiscent of Lawrence, for at least until the mid-1960s it was easily possible to get around much of Lawrence country with copies of the early novels in lieu of road maps. Sillitoe's descriptions, like those of Lawrence, generate emotion through their specificity, although some of Sillitoe's evocations of the spirit of "place" sound slightly more conventional: "Place is everything—soil in the throat, under the feet, in the hands, the nostrils clouded with soot and pollen, the first smells and sounds of life still immediate." Nevertheless, both writers share a sense of the importance and the overwhelming physicality of place. In both, too, history is constantly visible, the locality invariably echoing its past in its present. Yet history and class are also accounts of change. In this essay, Sillitoe recalls how much Lawrence's England changed during the First World War, how Lawrence himself was persecuted and thought the spirit of "old England" had turned into the insensitive and insular "John Bull." Sillitoe quotes Lawrence's description in *The Lost Girl* of Alvina leaving England by ship and looking back at the cliffs of England "a long ash-grey coffin slowly submerging." For Sillitoe, too, the First World War, in historical retrospect, permanently altered and crippled England.

As he suggests in this essay and argues more extensively in *Raw Material* (1972), a volume detailing his background and memories, Sillitoe thinks the war destroyed the social fabric of England, became a needless struggle in which the upper classes sent millions to their deaths in order to preserve their own mindless privilege: "Before 1914 a unity could have been possible, and the men might then have tried it. Joining up to fight was, in a sense, their way of saying yes, but the old men used this affirmation to try and finish them off." Afterwards, Sillitoe's England is locked in class conflict, an intense, unbridgeable division seen comically in *Saturday Night and Sunday Morning*, but more often in the Lawrencean context of a national disaster or death. Lawrence's characters after 1918, like Sillitoe's after the early 1960s, feel intensely (although sometimes ambivalently) the need to survive by leaving the sinking ship.

Influence is not imitation, and Sillitoe is in some ways different from Lawrence. Something of Sillitoe's Lawrence-like alternating incorporation and rejection of Lawrence, beyond the regional and class similarity that neither wears as a badge of permanent identification, is visible in Sillitoe's trilogy about Frank Dawley that began in the mid-1960s (*The Death of William Posters*, 1965, *A Tree on Fire*, 1967, and *The Flame of Life*, 1974). Frank Dawley, a Midlands working man and union official, quits job, class function, wife and children to wander England, just as Lawrence's Aaron Sisson did after the First World War. Frank's motives, like Aaron's, are initially not very clear, can only be discovered through activity and defiance. Frank expresses his rebellion in William Posters, his fictional image of working-class man, intransigent, persecuted, hounded by society but never finally caught, using violence against others and himself indiscriminately and self-destructively, a myth he has derived from notices that read "Bill posters will be prosecuted." As Frank leaves, he looks over the few books that have meant something to him. One is *Sons and Lovers*, although "*Lady Chatterley's Lover* should have been there, but he'd thrown it on the fire in anger and disappointment." Through his wanderings in the novel, Frank learns to incorporate *Lady Chatterley's Lover*, to apprehend sensual experience, as he also learns the connections between sexuality and violence, "war" or "religion" within himself. The physical and mental or spiritual are constantly intertwined.

Like Lawrence, Sillitoe satirizes the conventional mass of people apart from his central figures, sometimes labelling them, as Lawrence did, the "bourgeoisie," more often referring to them as "The Rats," the title of Sillitoe's long 1960 poem and a diffuse, scornful reference to the greedy and unthinking majority he often uses as quick shorthand in all the novels. Through Frank's friend, a working-class painter named Albert Handley who becomes suddenly successful, "The Rats" of the London art and intellectual world are vilified. At the end of the novel, Frank, with his pregnant mistress, Myra, herself in revolt from "The Rats" of the middle classes, needs to get out of moribund England. They leave for Spain, then Morocco, Frank determined to find "purpose," exercise his internal violence politically, and exorcise the sterile and static image of William Posters by running guns to the rebellious FLN in Algeria.

Other elements in Sillitoe's perspective seem less distinctly Lawrencean. The reiterated emphasis on what people can become, on how they develop, seems standard Romantic equipment from the nineteenth-century novel. The explosion of the repressed, the fact that Myra's husband tries to run down Frank and Myra with his car when he learns they are leaving, is done in a way more reminiscent of Dickens than of Lawrence. But the depictions of England and class, the growing complexities of sexual experience, and the geographical movement of the plot strongly echo *Aaron's Rod*.

In the second novel of the trilogy, Frank stays in Algeria to aid the revolution, while Myra returns to England with her new son. As in Lawrence's fiction, one child may be the sign of a satisfactory relationship, but more than one, as in *The Rainbow*, is clutter that deflects human energy from significant focus. Handley, still in England with his wife and large, diverse family, illustrates the problem. Handley's attractive, promiscuous oldest daughter, who wants to drive fast sports cars on the new motorway, reads Huxley and Lawrence with their "slow winded lies." For the boy she later marries, "to swoon and rapturise over wild flowers" is the "false crap" of Lawrence, John Cowper Powys and Henry Williamson. References like these are not the quick, dismissive, general cultural tags of Waterhouse or Wain. Rather, Sillitoe is using different attributes of Lawrence to define different characters and elements in his own world; he is also, with a feisty directness, working out what of Lawrence he can and what he cannot use. In either case, Sillitoe's identification with Lawrence, however uneasy and ambivalent, is conscious and thorough.

Frank's "purpose" in Algeria is no more achieved than is Aaron's in Italy, but, at this point, Sillitoe's plot breaks away from the Lawrencean model. Frank, defeated, his best friend and fellow rebel–outsider killed, returns to England and becomes friendly with Handley's brother, a former army signal officer who was imprisoned by the Japanese in Malaya and is also a class spokesman for the horrors of 1914. He sits at his radio, an emblem of the attempt to survive and control all the rage within the self through technology. But this control is also unsuccessful, for the brother goes mad and starts the fire that burns Handley's house. The implicit rage, the "fire" of the title, devours the "tree," the standard organic symbol for England.

The metaphor is continued in the final novel of the trilogy, *The Flame of Life*, which poses the question of what can be done with the human and social energy represented by the "flame." The "fire" and the "flame" may be echoes of Lawrence's frequent use of "flame" as transforming states of matter in all his apocalyptic imagery, or an answer in an implied dialogue with Lawrence. Yet similar forms of metaphorical combustion are so centrally part of the tradition of English novels, from George Eliot through Bennett, that a singular Lawrencean origin is doubtful. Sillitoe's flame could potentially transform, and he begins the novel assembling all the surviving characters into a commune, almost as if he is testing Lawrence's Rananim vision of a commune of the elect. An authentic Lawrencean complexity is apparent in making up the commune from diverse social and racial strains and in the relationships, as Handley speculates about the material and physical in love (earlier, he had simply been an energetic trophy hunter). Sillitoe gives the relationship with his wife a convincingly interior love–hate treatment, a combination of talk, attraction and "the mud of this matrimonial Passchendaele." But the commune dissolves in a plethora of farce, action, melodrama, politics, deception and attempted murder, as if Sillitoe is wildly severing any connection with Lawrence and dissipating both the force and concept of the novel. The son of William Posters suddenly appears, a hash-peddling teen-ager who will not work and then goes to Turkey with Handley's wife. Some couples marry, other people run off. At the end, only Frank and Myra remain, now married, Frank still nourishing the "flame" that will now support himself, Myra, and their children, a thoroughly bourgeois form of stasis.

Sillitoe's complicated identification with and separation from Lawrence continues in his later fiction. In one novel, *Storyteller* (1979), he dramatizes various uses of fiction through tracing the career of a poor Nottingham boy who escapes schoolyard beatings by telling stories, developing this art into a career as a storyteller in pubs. At times, running out of material, he tries various novels he has read as sources for the stories he improvises. His audience threatens him after he uses *Sons and Lovers*; a tougher audience breaks his arm in response to his version of *The Plumed Serpent*. His later success as a storyteller allows him to escape England with a job on a cruise ship. As he thinks back on an England he now consistently denigrates, welcoming his new stability through the clear metaphors of control and longitude attached to the functioning ship, he "couldn't imagine England consisting, industrially, of little more than a rash of push-bike and wind-up gramophone workshops in rural backyards, while D. H. Lawrence strode about in an Indian poncho under the greenwood tree." Lawrence, both as influence and as icon, to be both assimilated and rebelled against, still functions centrally in Sillitoe's imagination. But so do the cartographic representations of the mathematical and the military, the latter, in Sillitoe, an institution that can potentially control human violence.

In the best of his later fiction, the experience suggested by these metaphors of precision combines with a Lawrencean treatment of sexual relationships. In *The Widower's Son* (1976), a miner's son becomes a career soldier during the First World War. His son, following the chain of class, becomes an army officer, accidentally heroic at Dunkirk. After the war, he meets a brigadier's daughter, and, although he is initially inhibited about sex, they marry. Sillitoe is at his best in describing the strains, complexities and triumphs of the marriage through all the love, the edges of violence, struggle and control, and the continuing abrasions of class issues. Although the marriage finally does not work, Sillitoe uses it deeply and effectively as the metaphor for human and social relationship.

In *Her Victory* (1982), a woman rebels against her husband, a violent and possessive man who has been successful economically in his rise from the working classes. Before the woman, Pam, leaves her suburban life for an unknown London, she has already demonstrated her worth by defending Lawrence's fiction, in a course given by the Worker's Education Association, from the instructor's charge that Lawrence was an Edwardian snob who hated workers because he did not depict them as entirely virtuous proletarians. Alone in London, Pam attempts suicide and is rescued by a former naval man who lives by maps, routines and carefully calibrated assertions against the jungle and chaos of human emotions. They make love on Lawrencean terms: "Because they felt foreign to each other she sensed that it still might be possible to love and yet keep their separate identities." Although their ensuing relationship is stormy, even violent, and is not seen as conclusive or permanent (Pam is also strongly attracted to a bisexual woman who lives with them), he teaches her some capacity to give her life conscious direction and control while she helps him discover a partial Jewish identity that leads him to Israel. He keeps the

Star of David he discovers he has inherited, commenting that its six points and twelve directions make it a geometrical as well as a religious symbol. Pam at least temporarily commits herself to following him to Israel. Sillitoe's theme of the relevant discovery of a Jewish past, in contrast to the rootless nature of contemporary London, may owe more to the tradition of Eliot's *Daniel Deronda* than to anything in Lawrence.

This use of tradition and Sillitoe's sense of order achieved through charts, calibrations and equations do not really reach as far as or substitute for Lawrence's attempt to create whole new myths and religions to explain and sustain the human being. Sillitoe's kind of order does not create as originally or penetrate as deeply. But muted echoes of the metaphysically creative Lawrence may also operate in Sillitoe, as well as the similar approaches to class, history and sexuality. One thinks of Birkin in *Women in Love* explaining to Ursula that a fuller love requires a relationship of control or "direction" as well as one of intensity: "If you are walking westward . . . you forfeit the northern and eastward and southern directions." For Lawrence, as for Sillitoe, love is always in motion.

David Storey's identification with Lawrence is less a matter of plot and activity than Sillitoe's, more a matter of description, situation and interior intransigence. Immersing his early fiction in his own origins, the child of a miner in the provinces (Yorkshire rather than Nottinghamshire), Storey responds to all the details of the environment. He is also, as was Lawrence, a painter, and builds his descriptions with a meticulous visual specificity. One of his early novels, *Flight into Camden* (1960), begins with the funeral of an old miner, the narrator's grandfather. Storey describes the drizzle, the miners in their black, the dead flowers, the adjacent mill and the smoke. In the midst of this grim, static landscape, Storey places an image of being:

> Two graves away, behind my father's back, a blackbird was standing in a puddle on the grass verge, its feathers puffed up, raising a small flurry of water. Its body seemed to spin round in its cloud of spray. Suddenly it stiffened, its feathers like quills, its head bobbing up and its beady eye darting. Then its feathers collapsed, and it hopped on to the far grave. Looking round, it turned its eye up towards the sky;

then crouched and flung itself into the air, flying low over the gravestones with its warning chatter. The small crowd broke up.

The specific, concrete, visual depiction of the environment and life within it gives Storey's prose power and energy. Like Lawrence, he frequently uses this kind of direct, physical description that is also metaphor, although Storey's develops slowly whereas Lawrence's is quick, Storey's a series of smouldering coals rather than a flame. The prose in Storey's early novels is distinguished by its physicality, its evocation of feeling, its tactility. Although he never refers to Lawrence—his prose is almost entirely devoid of literary or cultural reference—he seems, both in setting and in style, to be slowly developing a condition of prior Lawrenceanism.

As he explained in an interview in the early 1960s, Storey's first novels followed a consciously worked-out scheme. *This Sporting Life* (1960), the novel of the young man from the working classes who plays professional rugby, depicts the world of the body, the atmosphere of physicality in both players and spectators. The next novel, *Flight into Camden*, depicts "soul," describes the hard spiritual independence of the miner's daughter who defies family to live with her feckless and artistic married lover in London. The third novel, *Radcliffe* (1963), presents the body–soul conflict as simultaneously the conflict between the vital, physical, working classes and the enfeebled, deracinated remnants of an aristocracy in a Yorkshire town. The conflict is dramatized in two young men, both growing up in close proximity and alternately attracted to and repelled by each other. Storey, through his characters, combines the religious, social and personal dimensions of the body–soul controversy, keeps his metaphors consistent and presents the issues with a fierce emotional intensity. But he also pushes his characters to the point where the intense, narrow focus and the representational quality explode into melodrama. Storey had, at this point, planned a fourth novel in which body and soul were to be reconciled, both within an individual and as a metaphor for the reconciliation of social classes, but the novel was apparently never written. The conclusive violence and melodrama of *Radcliffe* was itself an indication of the abstract nature of the scheme, which was unsuitable for further speculation about human beings and social class.

It is tempting to think of the scheme itself as Lawrencean, although Lawrence never depicted the body–soul controversy as a final split except in so far as it characterized the history of nineteenth-century England (the middle generation in *The Rainbow*, Gerald's parents in *Women in Love*). In Lawrence's novels, his landscapes, significant pressures, characters and author's point of view push toward the unification of body and soul. No Lawrence novel explodes into the kind of locked and simplified melodrama *Radcliffe* represents. In addition, the sense that nineteenth-century English social history could be dramatized as the body–soul conflict was hardly unique to Lawrence. Hardy, for example, in the Preface to *Jude the Obscure*, itself a different metaphorical culmination of nineteenth-century religious and social history, mentioned the "deadly war waged between flesh and spirit," which he substantially qualified within the novel.

Storey, whatever the origins of his scheme, whether too simply Lawrencean, dependent on some other source or more generally a response to the visible puritanical past in the English class system and provincial life, had to abandon the abstract scheme and start over again. He turned to drama, writing plays that echo Lawrence's world and themes much more intimately. He also, at about this time, directed for the BBC a television documentary on Lawrence's origins entitled *Death of My Mother*. Some of the plays seem almost directly transposed Lawrencean situations: the three brothers from different corners of the contemporary classless world who return to the mining village, with its strains and limitations, for their parents' anniversary in *In Celebration*; the similar return of the rebellious son to the agricultural home his sisters have never left, in which the complex familial alliances and conflicts are more explicitly sexual, in *The Farm*. Other plays echo characteristic Lawrencean themes: the anxieties of moving from one class to another, dramatized in metaphors of construction and de-construction in *The Contractor*; the ways in which artists project themselves into their art and the non-literal ways in which life and art connect in *Life Class*. Written in prose that is both compressed and evocative, these and almost all of Storey's plays express a Lawrencean fear of chaos, a sense that individuals, families and societies are breaking down, fragmenting, and only some kind of extraordinary effort, often unimaginable in terms of the specific play, can preserve the individual or society from disintegration.

After nine years without publishing a novel, Storey returned to the more ruminative form of fiction while continuing to write plays. Storey's fullest novel is *Saville* (1976), the long, slow, painstaking development of the sensitive miner's son, Colin. (As in a number of Storey's treatments, the situation parallels Lawrence's: Colin had an older brother who died suddenly just before he was born—the cause in one instance "a case of galloping perfection.") For the first time in Storey's fiction, the parents are not just a single representation of region and class, but are contrasted as emotional and social types, shaped into a conflict that makes integration by the child all the more difficult. Although the novel contains no direct references to Lawrence, Colin follows the pattern of Lawrence's early novels. Colin is always conscious of the physical, interested in all forms of careful construction, like shelters, athletic games and poetry. His education at the grammar school, where he is bullied by some of the masters because of his class, is minutely described. In his intense way, he tries to bring together his interests in football and poetry, his early versions of the body–soul dichotomy. At times, in his physical directness and slowly evolving sensitivity to what he cannot rationally understand, Colin resembles the first Tom Brangwen searching for a kind of life different from anything he has known. His first serious relationship with a girl-friend introduces Lawrencean themes of the limitations of consciousness and the differences between men and women, the latter, like Ursula in *The Rainbow*, often closer than men to a fuller recognition of their own being.

When Colin and his girl-friend are talking about possible careers, he assumes that anyone who creates art, in rebellion from his origins, is self-generated, needing no encouragement and following only half-conscious drives and impulses to articulate. She complicates both the situation and the idea of consciousness: "I'm afraid you're too set in your ways to understand what I've been saying.... It's the unconscious element in a woman that inhibits or prevents her from doing these things, that *organically* restrains her." Storey has moved into Lawrence's sexual territory, as he also moves into

Lawrence's social territory in a scene in which the girl, the daughter of a doctor, comes to tea at the house of Colin's parents. The scene has a Lawrencean texture in which "the air was still" with the thickness of all the social and class implications. The pair eventually break up, Colin becomes a teacher at a grubby and inadequate lower-class school and, eventually, leaves both the school and another woman to escape to London. The plot, however, is less important than the Lawrencean texture of the novel: all the polarities of love–hate, identification with and resentment about class, rebellion–guilt about family, football–poetry as a mirror of body–soul. And none of these polarities can be resolved or transformed.

Unlike Sillitoe's conscious dialogue, his identification with and separation from Lawrence, Storey's connection is never explicitly present in reference or concept. Storey's relationship could depend on a determination to work out the implications of similar sources entirely independently; it could also be a partially unconscious internalization of Lawrence. Yet the similarities to the early Lawrence's world continue to be deep and striking, as in *A Prodigal Child* (1982), a more compressed and finely written novel than *Saville*. In *A Prodigal Child*, Storey is able, like Lawrence, to establish regional history quickly through the evocative description of landscape. In this novel, Bryan, the boy growing up, is made the son of a feckless agricultural worker whose wife resents his drinking. But other influences operate on Bryan as well: the family on the farm where his father works; a childless, middle-class, sensitive woman who sends him to school; the school itself. Bryan, never losing his initial physicality, his responsiveness to the visual and tactile, becomes an artist. As in Lawrence's early world, the background through and against which the artist gains consciousness is agricultural as well as industrial, sophisticated as well as simple, composed of a number of intersecting classes, and creatively as well as destructively sexual. Confronting all these polarities (his less sensitive younger brother wants only to become a boxer), Bryan is able to become a sculptor and shape his identity through his art.

Storey's prose, always suggesting the tactile, becomes itself more sculptural:

Bryan didn't hear Mrs. Corrigan's voice: his gaze was fixed

on her figure, on the downward curve of her cheek with its tint of rouge and its layer of powder, on the outward curve of her lashes as she blinked over her sewing and, beneath this attenuated profile, on the projection of her hips, the bunching of her thigh, the extension of her ankle, and the insertion of her foot inside her heelless slipper.

Although attracted to each other for years, despite differences in age and class, Bryan and Mrs. Corrigan make love only once, while swimming on holiday, dissolving the customary and cultivated shapes of being. Through most of the rest of the novel and in its conclusion, Bryan, connecting his art with his life, uses his art as a bastion against chaos, as a conscious intellectual and emotional form to stave off the fragmentation and dissolution of contemporary experience. Many of the problems and paralyzing dichotomies, as well as the emotional response to them, resemble Lawrence's; the resolution, however, is Storey's own, laboriously and convincingly brought to consciousness.

As the origins in place and class drift further from Lawrence than those of Sillitoe and Storey, the kinds of influence or connection are likely to become more abstract—not less interior or less profound, but more of shared conviction or shared consciousness worked out. Doris Lessing, perhaps more deeply than any other contemporary writer, represents this kind of incorporation. Her classes and places, colonial Africa just before and during the Second World War and the London of writers, artists, immigrants and drifters since 1950, are far from those of Lawrence, although she does invest place and class with a similar importance. Her few references to Lawrence are likely to be generalized into tradition. She mentions him, along with Huxley and Joyce, as one of the "great central lights" in "intellectual and bohemian circles" of the 1920s, as the background, a generation earlier, for one of her two "free women" in *The Golden Notebook* (1962).

When Lessing uses regional accents, as in *The Good Terrorist* (1985), she makes them into poses, as when her characters in the amorphous world of contemporary London use Cockney to cover the "basic BBC correct" that disguised some earlier region or generation. Yet she often describes characters in a way reminiscent of Lawrence's, especially when introducing them, mixing the physical detail of the subject with the physical response the subject generates. The blue (or fiction of fictions) notebook in *The Golden Notebook* has many descriptive introductions like the following:

> His rather rough black hair was thinning at the crown, and his very white, slightly freckled skin was incised sharply around his eyes. These were blue, deep, rather beautiful; eyes both combative and serious, with a gleam in them of uncertainty. A nerve-hung face, she decided, and saw that his body was tense as he talked, which he did well, but in a self-watchful way. His self-consciousness had her reacting away from him, whereas only a moment ago she had been responding to the unconscious warmth of his smile.

Lawrence's Hermione, on first meeting, was "full of intellectuality, and heavy, nerve-worn with consciousness." In both writers, these physical manifestations of interior states of being yield a distinctive identity to almost every character described. The characters are not inhabitants of existential worlds in which roles or poses convey a simulacrum of an identity that does not exist. Lessing explains in *The Golden Notebook*:

> We're told so often that human personality has disintegrated into nothing under pressure of all our knowledge that I've even been believing it. Yet when I look back to that group under the trees, and recreate them in my memory, suddenly I know it's nonsense. Suppose I were to meet Maryrose now, all these years later, she'd make some gesture, or turn her eyes in such a way, and there she'd be, Maryrose, and indestructible. Or suppose she "broke down," or became mad. She would break down into her components, and the gesture, the movement of the eyes would remain, even though some connection had gone. And so all this talk, this anti-humanist bullying, about the evaporation of the personality becomes meaningless for me at that point when I manufacture enough emotional energy inside myself to create in memory some human being I've known.

For both Lessing and Lawrence, the independent identity is a pre-condition for experience or relationship.

In both writers, the independence is constantly visible in sexual relationships, in Lawrencean terms, none of this "mixing and merging," but the connection of two independent beings. The woman is intrinsically and substantially different from the man, although, in Lawrence's world, the grounds for the difference vary so much from character to character and novel to novel that, in contemporary discourse, examples can justify both charges of arrant sexism and praise for deep understanding of the separate identity of the female. Lawrence's depiction of sexual relationships finds its closest contemporary corollaries in fiction written by women, sometimes even in the apparently different mode of Elizabeth Jane Howard.

Lessing's presentation of sexuality provides many parallels, beginning with the conviction, apparent in a character like Ursula in *The Rainbow*, that women are more honest with themselves about sex, more likely to recognize and express vulnerability and self-doubt. For both Lawrence and Lessing, "self-doubt" has nothing to do with self-sacrifice, the kind of passive self-immolation that precludes a significant relationship. Rather, as Lessing depicts sexual relationships, in different degrees of fictionality in *The Golden Notebook*, the woman is active and passive simultaneously, conscious of both control and acceptance more immediately and intrinsically than the man. The control is in the selection, the choice of "free women"; the acceptance, equally physically and instinctual, is in the orgasm. *The Golden Notebook* contains a number of discussions about various kinds of orgasm, dissociated physical response or "emotion." All of them, however, seem to center on the statement of one of the fictional characters in the fictional notebook: "For women like me, integrity isn't chastity, it isn't fidelity, it isn't any of the old words. Integrity is the orgasm. That is something I haven't any control over." For Lessing, this is not a final statement about sexuality. As Lawrence's Birkin and Ursula in *Women in Love* need to go "beyond" orgasm, need to find direction consciously, Lessing's various women need to balance the "integrity" of the orgasm with all the choices and responsibilities in the incompletely "free" contemporary world.

For both writers, sexuality represents the most intense and

intimate version of the complexity of all human connection, which always reveals both an impulse to control or assert and an impulse to accept or submit. The varieties are multiple: the marriages that combine love and hatred, the people tied by mutual need to assert different dependencies, the women tied to males who cannot recognize their own physical virtues or their incapacities, the way women sometimes project their own emotions on to their men and sometimes reflect the diverse relationship back into themselves as "this feeling of being alien to my own body." Both Lessing and Lawrence also connect the possibility or absence of complex and complete sexuality with time and place, history and geography. For Lawrence, sexuality as relationship was destroyed by the puritanical controls of Victorian England's religiosity, the female turned into pure body, bearing children, and the male consciousness into disembodied "soul." In *The Golden Notebook*, all the numerous American males, divided from their country by politics in the 1950s, from the point of view of either the right or the left, are unable to accept relationship at all, are only conscious of themselves sexually in a momentary assault. They are incapable of the kind of suspension in complexity that "free" women can manage. Anna in *The Golden Notebook* can write simultaneously in one of her notebooks of her momentary desire to fling herself out of the window, imagining her blood and brains scattered on the pavement, and her need to shop for "a pound and a half of tomatoes, half a pound of cheese . . . and a quarter of tea."

For both Lessing and Lawrence, fiction is directly connected to experience—not as literal recording or reductively complacent "realism," but as constant commentary on the world outside of fiction. Lessing establishes her most explicitly fictional as "the most truthful of the notebooks." This is her equivalent of Lawrence's contention in "Why the Novel Matters" that the novel is "the one bright book of life," concerned with "*all*" of living human experience. Both writers frequently attach themselves to past literary tradition as well as to historical and contemporary place. In Lessing's terms in *The Golden Notebook*, "we read novels for information about areas of life we don't know—Nigeria, South Africa, the American army, a coal mining village, coteries in Chelsea. . . . We read *to find out what is going on*." We also read for "philosophical statements" in an imaginative patterning that does not preclude varieties of formal experiment and new ways of looking at human experience. Both writers design the enclosures of fiction to radiate outward as counters against the enclosures of self. This balance is reflected in the conclusions of their novels, the edgy, incomplete, ironic integrations of their protagonists with larger experience, like Anna's tonal objection to acceptance, to being "integrated with British life at its roots," or Aaron's wondering to what he must "submit."

In their careers, as in their fiction, Lawrence and Lessing seek successive groups of metaphors outside the self to which they can "submit" or commit the self. Lawrence restlessly went from place to place looking for an authentic cultural metaphor with which to align himself, and Lessing has successively involved herself with Communism, Jungian or Laingian psychology, eastern Sufism and futuristic thought. For both, however, commitment is never subscription, never an immolation of the self. At an elementary level, in Lessing's *The Golden Notebook*, for example, "the really deadly skeleton in the communist closet" is that every one of the old comrades "has that old manuscript or wad of poems tucked away." In aligning themselves with various social and cultural groups and ideas (both physically and abstractly, although never permanently), Lawrence and Lessing berate other groups, those they see as more familiar, complacent and unconscious. By the middle or end of the twentieth century, the attack on what Lawrence meant by the "bourgeoisie" has itself become complacent. Lessing carefully and successively refines her targets to entities like the media adapters who turn all fiction into familiar formula, in *The Golden Notebook*, or the bland, liberal permissiveness of unmoving accommodation that surrounds and infiltrates the squatters in *The Good Terrorist*. The house-squatters are a contemporary version of Lawrence's Rananim, the commune, riddled with contradiction and impossible to sustain, established as a potentially vital group in defiance of the complacent mass of society. For Lessing, as for Lawrence, the influence of place, the grounding of community or potential connection in an identifiable group or culture, gives rebellion a meaning and a self-definition that is not simply solipsistic or self-enclosed.

Although the communes never work, their establishment represents a ceaseless activity, an attempt of consciousness to transform experience. In *The Good Terrorist*, Lessing quotes as the axiom of the complacent: "Against—stupidity—the gods—themselves—contend—in vain." Lawrence's and Lessing's metaphorical surrogates always contend, risk the pretense and failures of gods. They try implicitly to create new forms of being that both radiate out from the individual and help define the individual, forms that are social, racial and religious, public entities constantly changing, the meaning of human history itself. Part of the process is conscious, part not (and the unconscious is often represented in the genetic transmission of human local, social or racial qualities—one of the bases for the importance of sexual experience), with the effort of fiction always to bring more of the hitherto unconscious into conscious and perhaps controllable experience. Both Lawrence and Lessing constantly consider the creation of new forms of racial amalgamation and new forms of religion.

For Lessing, in *The Golden Notebook*, the creation of new social and racial forms in Africa in the 1940s is a vast extension from the evolutionary process visible in lower forms: "Before many hours are out, these insects will have killed each other by fighting, biting, deliberate homicide, suicide, or by clumsy copulation. Or they will have been eaten by birds which even at this moment are waiting for us to remove ourselves so that they can begin their feast." Lawrence is sometimes more likely to emphasize the other end of the evolutionary scale, the one "beyond" humanity, as in *Women in Love*:

> If humanity ran into a cul-de-sac, and expended itself, the timeless creative mystery would bring forth some other being, finer, more wonderful, some new, more lovely race, to carry on the embodiment of creation. The game was never up. The mystery of creation was fathomless, infallible, inexhaustible, for ever. Races came and went, species passed away, but ever new species arose, more lovely, or equally lovely, always surpassing wonder ... new forms of consciousness, new forms of body, new units of being.

For Lawrence, as for Lessing, these forms never crystallize in actual human experience, despite all the efforts of human consciousness. To crystallize permanently would be to violate human history. The new forms of being, constantly created, destroyed and questioned, are coherent only within the active imagination, within fiction that is simultaneously a reflection of self and not-self.

Sillitoe, Storey and Lessing echo different aspects of Lawrence's fiction. Sillitoe's is closest in reflecting the ambivalence toward the particular locality and the condition of England; Storey's is closest in tracing similarities in apparent genesis and in the independent physical response to environment; Lessing's most resembles the correlative functions of fiction and ideology. Yet these similarities, in the absence of more rigorous and extensive analysis of the fiction or more revealing confirmation from biographical sources, are suggestive rather than definitive, likely parallels rather than chains of certain influence. In addition, the similarities can all be qualified by Lawrence's diffusion into the general literary culture, by the way he has become part of the apparatus through which a critic or a reader responds to fiction, part of the derivative critical fiction that we use to interpret experience. Specific references, like those in the fiction of Waterhouse and Wain, are more certain signals, but those indicate little more than the fact that Lawrence has become part of the literary culture. They diffuse and domesticate Lawrence, become simplified counters to mark the shoals of literary history. The more internal and significant, although less easily demonstrable, partial re-creations of Lawrence in Sillitoe, Storey and Lessing (Bragg falls somewhere between the two categories, which are not mutually exclusive) prevent total domestication. The deeper incorporations, changing and adapting, preserve the vitality of Lawrence within the literary tradition, perpetuate something of what Lawrence represents. The deeper incorporation, as it changes and re-creates experience, is the "stuff" of literary history itself.

CHAPTER THREE

Lawrence and English Poetry

WILLIAM M. CHACE

In his celebratory study of Etruscan culture, D. H. Lawrence speaks of their "natural flowering of life," the way in which, as he imagines them, the Etruscans possessed a "conception of the universe and man's place in the universe which made men live to the depth of their capacity." Lawrence believes that "to the Etruscan all was alive; the whole universe lived; and the business of man was himself to live amid it all."[1] Such an assertion—many another could serve as well—issues from the heart of everything Lawrence, for the whole of his career, felt and did. He believed that his rightful claim on the attention of his time, and the attention of posterity, was his assertion that the proper ambition for human beings, Etruscans, Englishmen, was to "live to the depth of their capacity."

What the Etruscans represented for Lawrence was associated with his extraordinary desire to achieve "blood consciousness," to recover the deepest wellsprings of unified being by asserting the primacy of feeling and desire over the claims of the intellect. "My great religion is a belief in the blood, the flesh, as being wiser than the intellect," he wrote in a well-known letter to Ernest Collings, adding that "we can go wrong in our minds. But what our blood feels and believes and says is true. The intellect is only a bit and bridle. What do I care about knowledge?"[2] These attitudes and beliefs, seen as lamentably anti-intellectual by some readers and as vitally inspirational by others, lie at the foundation of any understanding of how Lawrence's achievement helped to define the enterprise of poetry for several important writers after him.

Lawrence's considerable influence as a writer is connected to a central nerve of literary and cultural history. That nerve was inflamed in his time; it is still feverish today. It is felt whenever any writer urges a return to "authenticity," whenever we are rhetorically asked that "since feeling is first/who pays any attention/ to the syntax of things," whenever there is a plea to recover "the force that through the green fuse drives the flower" or a desire to shake off the corrupt artificialities of modern life. For Lawrence, the fascination with this nerve of true being was sustained through his entire literary career. He thought of his own poetry as an effort to revive a literature of "the immediate present," to write in harmony with "the insurgent naked throb of the instant moment." In his introduction to the American edition of *New Poems* (1918), Lawrence set forth the spirit in which his poetry had been written and in which he hoped it would be approached:

> The whole tide of all life and all time suddenly heaves, and appears before us as an apparition, a revelation. We look at the very white quick of nascent creation. . . . Tell me of the mystery of the inexhaustible, forever-unfolding creative spark. . . . Give me the still, white seething, the incandescence and the coldness of the incarnate moment: the moment, the quick of all change and haste and opposition: the moment, the immediate present, the Now.[3]

Caught in this plea and in the extraordinary language with which it is presented is a contradiction that must be appreciated if Lawrence's situation as a poet is to be grasped and if his effect on later poets is to be evaluated. Lawrence is promoting, in argumentation of the most effusive kind, the idea that argumentation—rationality, analysis and logical procedure—is foreign to his needs. With his mind, and with the instrument of his prose, he defends the notion that poetry must be written out of something other than mind and its feeble instruments. Like Eliot's Sweeney, he knows he must use words to talk to us, but he does not want those words, the logical structures out of which their meaning comes and the human and historical contexts in which they must be understood, to denature the unique reality of sensation and meaning that his poetry is meant to reveal.

Lawrence's situation, then, is more complicated than that of the Romantics with whom he is often compared and in whose tradition he is often seen. Wordsworth believed that "One impulse from a vernal wood/May teach us more of man,/Of moral evil and of good,/Than all the sages can." Lawrence would concur, adding, however, that the invasive powers of mind and intellect must constantly be thrust aside if language is to do its work. Yet language, against whose power Wordsworth had no complaint, is of course inextricably linked with those powers of mind. Thus Lawrence's endless efforts to ground the sensation and meaning of experience in experience alone are constantly disabled by his own knowledge, which he cannot suppress, that he cannot limit himself to experience. Words are words, experience experience. He knows that cerebration, the sense of argumentation, the taste for polemic, the wounded and yet hostile Lawrencean sensibility—all make their presence felt in everything he does, and produce a strong self-consciousness on his part. He constantly struggles with that irresistible self-consciousness, impatient that he must fight it with words and all that their use implies.

In the essay *On Naive and Sentimental Poetry* (1795), Friedrich Schiller gives the classic description of the kind of situation faced by Lawrence. For Schiller, the "naive" poet is in perfect harmony with nature; the "sentimental" poet is estranged from it by his history as a civilized and sophisticated man of the world. Schiller imagines Homer and the ancients to have written as "naive" poets, while modern poets have inevitably become "sentimental." In the earlier poetry, the individuality of the poet was not apparent, for he was at one with the nature surrounding him; in the later, the author is omnipresent, saturated in self-consciousness.

"The poet," says Schiller, "either *is* nature or he will seek her. The former is the naive, the latter is the sentimental poet."[4] The "sentimental" poet, unlike his opposite, "*reflects* upon the impression that objects make upon him, and only in that reflection is the emotion grounded which he himself experiences and which he excites in us.... The sentimental poet is thus always involved with two conflicting representations and perceptions."[5] Fundamental to Schiller's observation is the fact that *naïveté* has become impossible for any literate person for the last thousand or so years. We wish to love nature, and to be at one with it, but we cannot do so. Distanced from the intimacy with nature that we desire, we are compelled to be our self-reflexive selves. We will never be as the ancients once were: "they felt naturally; we feel the natural."[6] And, in words that reflect on Lawrence's situation, Schiller adds: "Our feeling for nature is like the feeling of an invalid for health."[7]

Another helpful gloss on the situation that Lawrence faced, and on his compulsively straining to rid himself of the intellectual and rational powers of mind that he believed were damaging to both his poetry and his human well-being, is provided by Joyce's *Ulysses*. In "Scylla and Charybdis," Stephen Dedalus struggles to free himself of his mind's discipline, the very discipline giving him the brilliance he so dramatically puts on show in that episode. Dedalus, as clever and knowing as he is in the National Library, must at last break out in laughter amid the startled and amazed company "to free his mind from his mind's bondage." After he laughs, he suggests to his listeners that his plight as a mind-burdened young intellectual is like the situation faced by Shakespeare, who had to create many opposing characters in order to resolve in his plays a fundamental tension of his life—between passionate intensity and deliberate intellection. "His unremitting intellect is the hornmad Iago ceaselessly willing that the moor in him shall suffer."[8]

Schiller and Joyce can help us see Lawrence as a writer whose poetry was an effort to resist what he thought were the deadly terms of self-understanding, the very terms he knew were always about to swarm into his poems. Lawrence would be naive if only he could be, but he knows he is, in Schiller's term, sentimental. In one of his best-known poems, "Snake," we are, at the end, brought back from the "otherness" of the serpent and from the wonderful *Einfühlung* achieved by Lawrence. We are brought back to the poet himself and to his internal distress. Immediately after throwing a log at the snake and missing it, Lawrence says:

> And immediately I regretted it,
> I thought how paltry, how vulgar, what a mean act!
> I despised myself and the voices of my accursed human
>   education.
>
> And I thought of the albatross,
> And I wished he could come back, my snake.

For he seemed to me again like a king,
Like a king in exile, uncrowned in the underworld,
Now due to be crowned again.

And so, I missed my chance with one of the lords
Of life.
And I have something to expiate;
A pettiness.

Lawrence's attitudes towards Whitman, a mixture of touching praise and witty condescension, reveal the same awareness on his part, a knowledge that he and Whitman *cannot* be at one with the otherness of living things. As much as he admired Whitman, Lawrence felt that the American poet aspired to impossible mergings:

> As soon as Walt *knew* a thing, he assumed a One Identity with it. If he knew that an Eskimo sat in a kyak, immediately there was Walt being little and yellow and greasy, sitting in a kyak....
>
> Walt wasn't an Eskimo. A little, yellow, sly, cunning, greasy little Eskimo. And when Walt blandly assumed Allness, including Eskimoness, unto himself, he was just sucking the wind out of a blown egg-shell, no more....
>
> Oh, Walter, Walter, what have you done with it? What have you done with yourself? With your own individual self? For it sounds as if it had all leaked out of you, leaked into the universe.[9]

What Lawrence knew, and what he feared Whitman did not know, is that, as much as we love the otherness of nature, and as much as we might want to become "naive" in our poetry, we are condemned to be "sentimental." Schiller wrote that "to be naive it is necessary that nature be victorious over art, whether this occur counter to the knowledge or will of the individual or with his full awareness."[10] Yet Lawrence's knowledge and his awareness were so considerable that they made it impossible for him to achieve the victory of nature over art. In short, he could not overturn the weight of his self-consciousness and could not establish the supremacy of the nature that he saw over the art that he practiced.

With these tensions in mind, it makes sense to trace Lawrence's relationship to certain later poets by noting the ways they encountered and dealt with the situation in which the poet desires to affirm an unmediated connection with the otherness of the world but is perpetually forced to cope with the presence—sometimes welcome, sometimes not—of his own mediating sensibility. To the degree that their achievement is deeply bound up in that struggle we may say that such poets are truly "Lawrencean."

There are other ways, of course, to trace Lawrence's legacy in the achievement of later poets. Sandra Gilbert lists those modern poets—Robert Bly, Ted Hughes, Denise Levertov, Joyce Carol Oates, Adrienne Rich—who are like Lawrence in their engagement with the structures of myth and with Orphic symbolism.[11] And Marjorie Perloff, giving her own list—Charles Olson, Robert Duncan, Robert Creeley, Allen Ginsberg—says that the legacy is known by the degree to which the later poets are like Lawrence as a rhetorician and as an adopter of a "performative stance."[12]

These approaches are sensible, and one values the kinships they suggest. But the signs by which they identify these kinships may well be based on incidental or superficial points of comparison. Many poets since Lawrence (and before him) have employed myth (Robert Graves, to choose one notably non-Lawrencean example), and, indeed, much of twentieth-century poetry after the impact of Ezra Pound and T. S. Eliot has been strenuously engaged in the employment of mythic structures. But that poetry has not deferred to Lawrence as its only, or most important, progenitor. As for poets who have adopted a "performative stance," it is difficult to think of any poets who have not done so, any poets who have evaded the enormous pressure to assume a kind of mask or persona in the development of their identities. That pressure has come from Whitman, from Yeats, from Pound, from the poets involved in the scruples of New Criticism, and even from the lessons of someone now as "dated" as Robert Browning. Because the elaboration of rhetorical postures is pervasive in the poetry of this century, there is reason to believe it would be there with or without the lesson of Lawrence.

I. INFLUENCES ON LAWRENCE

There are general reasons to be cautious in arguing the influence of a given writer on the writers of later generations. Not only is influence notoriously difficult to demonstrate in a precise or scientific way, but it is also true that some writers seem little engaged in negotiating strong relationships to their literary past. As an emerging poet, Lawrence himself apparently responded to few influences: the poetry of the Bible, of Blake, of Thomas Hardy and of Whitman.[13] And, even there, the connections are not as strong as is sometimes alleged. In tracing "influences" and "connections," we should be sobered by the fact that the putative mover of others was more or less unmoved himself. Lawrence shows no interest in Blake's intricate mythic, symbolic and religious–political inventions. He had no taste for Hardy's elegiac dejection, his sense of settled bleakness, his calm provincialism. As for Whitman, Lawrence's skeptical disbelief in "Walter's" oceanic powers of identification has already been noted, and we may now add to it his incredulity in the face of everything represented by Whitman's bardic expansiveness. W. H. Auden points to the tenousness of the Whitman–Lawrence connection:

> On no other English poet . . . has Whitman had a beneficial influence; he could on Lawrence because, despite certain superficial resemblances, their sensibilities were utterly different. Whitman quite consciously set out to be the Epic Bard of America and created a poetic *persona* for the purpose. . . . On the other hand it is doubtful if a writer ever existed who had less of an artistic *persona* than Lawrence. . . . Whitman looks at life extensively rather than intensively. No detail is dwelt upon for long; it is snapshotted and added as one more item to the vast American catalogue. But Lawrence in his best poems is always concerned intensively with a single subject, a bat, a tortoise, a fig tree, which he broods on until he has exhausted its possibilities.[14]

It is the dramatic difference in *sensibilities*, as Auden says, that must be appreciated if the true distinctions between a Whitman and a Lawrence are to be understood. Those sensibilities control all other apparent similarities and distinctions between poets.

II. W. H. AUDEN

This principle can be tested with the example of Auden himself, who seems to bear strong similarities to Lawrence. As Humphrey Carpenter has shown, Auden fell under Lawrence's spell in the 1920s and spoke favorably of him then, but it was not Lawrence the poet who attracted Auden.[15] Rather, it was the author of *Fantasia of the Unconscious*. The undergraduate Auden responded warmly to Lawrence's proclamations in that book that spontaneity is preferable to constraint and cerebration. He relished the explorations into that which was hidden and mysterious in the creation of personality. He appreciated the "burrowing" and secretive understanding of life that Lawrence conveyed. But such exposure and teaching (reinforced by a contemporaneous reading of Georg Groddeck and Homer Lane) had no known effect on Auden's practice, early or late, as a poet. Indeed, Auden was many years later to recall that Lawrence's "message" was once important to him, but the poetry never: "When I first tried to read it, I did not like it; despite my admiration for him, it offended my notions of what poetry should be. Today my notions of what poetry should be are still, in all essentials, what they were then and hostile to his."[16]

Auden was always charitable to Lawrence, and was even to respect his "genius" by remarking, for example, in 1947 that "Lawrence's answers do not mean much to us any more; his questions still disturb a great deal. His genuine visions of plants, of animals, of certain passionate states will be treasured even if and when all his questions and ours, being truly answered, have ceased to vex."[17] This same indulgence is elsewhere mixed with searing criticism:

> As an analyst and portrayer of the forces of hatred and aggression which exist in all human beings and, from time to time, manifest themselves in nearly all human relationships, Lawrence is, probably, the greatest master who ever lived. But that was absolutely all that he knew and understood about human beings; about human affection and human charity, for example, he knew absolutely nothing. The truth is that he detested nearly all human beings if he had to be in close contact with them.[18]

Auden is clearly unfair here to the complexity of Lawrence's sensibility, and the heat of his language reveals the intensity of his desire to distance himself from the earlier poet. The most trenchantly dissociative of Auden's remarks about Lawrence firmly establish their profound differences in both sensibility and artistic means: "Reading Lawrence's early poems, one is continually struck by the originality of the sensibility and the conventionality of the expressive means.... He is content to versify his thoughts; there is no essential relation between what he is saying and the formal structure he imposes upon it."[19] Auden, of course, was a poet for whom expressive means and formal structures existed as a never-ending challenge to his imaginative and playful mind. He was, his biographer tells us, the poet who once challenged his young students to attempt versification in the manner of the *cywydd*, the classical Welsh medieval meter. He had such abundant technical facility that the critic Clive James has said that Auden had "a Shakespearian gift, not just in its magnitude but in its unsettling—and unsettling especially to its possessor—characteristic of making anything said sound truer than true."[20] Such gifts can slide into decadence, but Auden never chose to throttle these gifts by practicing the regular and monochromatic music into which Lawrence's passions, as a poet, continually fell.

The essential difference between the poet Lawrence and the poet Auden is that the latter is supremely conscious of the effect of his dexterity with language. Moving from psychological insight to moral urgency to light verse to pastiche to memorable maxim, and from salutes to Hardy, Eliot, Pound, Wilfred Owen, Henry James and Rilke to modes ranging from the whimsical to the politically engaged and the religiously transcendental, Auden exhibited an easy mastery of whatever medium seemed appropriate to the occasion or the decade. But, as R. G. Cox has remarked, this "technical facility, indeed, comes to seem Auden's chief danger henceforward. Poem after poem contains brilliant or powerful lines but is less successful as a whole because he has not been able to resist the irrelevant elaboration, the chasing of too many hares at once, the smart epigram, or the multiplication of self-conscious ironies."[21]

It is this *knowingness*, this happy yielding to the superiority of *art* over *nature*, that distinguishes the sensibility of Auden from that of Lawrence. In Schiller's terms, it makes of Auden a comfortably *sentimental* poet, one free of the illusion that he could sustain an unmediated connection to the natural world around him. With lines like "Anxiety receives them like a grand hotel," "Events not actual/In time's unlenient will," "Death's coercive rumour" and "the luscious lateral blossoming of woe" studding Auden's verse, we approach his work with an understanding that his virtuosity stands between us and everything else. His lack of *naïveté* is all the more apparent when we recall the bold cynicism of celebrated lines like: "For poetry makes nothing happen: it survives/In the valley of its making where executives/Would never want to tamper." That cavalier sloughing-off of the prophetic claims of poetry, delivered in a voice that has played with the notion of prophecy in its own time, is an echo of nothing to be found in Lawrence.

III. DYLAN THOMAS

The situation is different when one turns to the poetry of Dylan Thomas. The fact that Lawrence and Thomas shared a Nonconformist religious background, and in that environment were steeped in both the language and the prophetic strains of the Bible, gives them a common foundation in life as well as in art. But acknowledging that fact does not take us very deeply into the issue of their respective poetic practices and sensibilities. There must be more to the question of one's "Lawrencean" character than a grounding in church experience and a familiarity with some of the most prominent religious teachings in Western culture. The question turns on what the two poets shared after the obvious biographical issues have been put aside.

One of the most apparent characteristics of Thomas's poetry (one at the center of the controversy that has continually surrounded him) is that his language and diction—odd, surprising, lyrically and stunningly opaque—succeed in thrusting his inventive and rhapsodic mind directly in front of us. This language—"The planet-ducted pelican of circles/Weans on an artery the gender's strip," "In the groin of the natural doorway I crouched like a tailor/Sewing a shroud for a journey/By the light of the meat-eating sun," "When, like a running grave, time tracks you down,/Your calm and cuddled is a scythe of hairs,/Love in her gear is slowly through the house,/Up naked stairs, a turtle in a hearse,/Hauled to the dome"—tends to be crafted, cerebral and abstrusely shaped. Constantly calling attention to itself, it is nothing if not a reminder of the lengths to which the instrument of language can be pushed to make a kind of poetry never heard before. The self-referentiality and the thrice-cooked quality of that poetry owe nothing to Lawrence, any more than the fact that Thomas, like Auden, easily concedes that his connection to nature is through the medium of language. That connection certifies a lack of immediacy and spontaneity in confronting the "other" world. Thomas' immediacy rests with the immediacy of his poetry.

John Bayley's early and resourceful defense of Thomas in the face of the charges of incoherence brought against him addresses this very question of the immediacy of his poetry. Noting that the poet is seen by some readers as "a careless genius often blessed with good luck," and by others as "a laborious craftsman obsessed with the ways in which language can be brought more and more directly into contact with feelings and things," Bayley concedes that "the critical uncertainty which must still be felt about Thomas's real status as a poet arises from the fact that we still do not know whether language is capable of what he tried to do with it; or rather whether the consciousness of the receiver can adapt itself to such a variety of linguistic uses and such a multiplicity of verbal stimuli."[22]

Since the limits of language are a central issue in any proper evaluation of Thomas' achievement, it follows that Thomas stands at a great distance from Lawrence. Lawrence willed to give prominence not to the medium, but to his prophetic urgencies and to what he hoped would be the perfect marriage of those urgencies and the words momentarily recruited as their means of conveyance. Lawrence would have found distracting and "unvital" Thomas' darkly brooding and infatuated preoccupation with the limits of language. Certainly Lawrence's latter-day champions and defenders did; among the voices raised in strong objection to Thomas were heard those in *Scrutiny*. Following the line laid down by F. R. Leavis, they announced that Thomas was a master of confusion.[23]

From two other points of view, however, the distance between Lawrence and Thomas is small. The first has to do with Thomas' recurrent sense of innocent wonder before the humming splendor of life, and his preoccupation with the ways to reclaim that wonder. The second has to do with his views of society, particularly industrial society. In poems such as "Fern Hill," Thomas is able to relax the pent-up possibilities in language and to write poetry that does not seem feverishly excited about itself: "Now as I was young and easy under the apple boughs," "And as I was green and carefree." Furthermore, in poems such as "When All My Five and Country Senses See," he is able to evoke an understanding of how sensation can, through synaesthesia, be brought to a perfect arousal and provide a Lawrence-like union of self and surroundings: "My one and noble heart has witnesses/In all love's countries, that will grope awake;/And when blind sleep drops on the spying senses,/The heart is sensual, though five eyes break." At these moments, Thomas does seem to have what Lawrence called a "greater, enkindled awareness" in which imagery becomes "the body of our imaginative life."[24]

Were these moments sustained in his poetry, and were they the primary signatures of his accomplishment, he would be a very different poet from the one he is. He would be closer to Lawrence. But, as Bayley reminds us, the Thomas we actually encounter is, for the most part, compulsively interested in "the single word as thing." He is a man who, in a moment of considerable self-recognition, said: "I'm a freak *user* of words, not a poet."[25] The result is that "multiplicity of verbal stimuli" that we, and Bayley, find:

> My Egypt's armour buckling in its sheet,
> I scrape through resin to a starry bone
> And a blood parhelion.
>
> Turning a petrol face blind to the enemy
> Turning the riderless dead by the channel wall.
>
> The chitterlings of a clock. . . .
>
> Though the town below lay leaved with October blood.
>
> My busy heart who shudders as she talks
> Sheds the syllabic blood and drains her words.[26]

These notes, predominant in Thomas and at the core of his accomplishment, obliterate the Lawrencean responsiveness to sensation in his poetry.

But what of the young South Wales writer who, looking at the life around him and seeing its destructive squalor, came to political opinions very much like those of Lawrence? In *Quite Early One Morning*, Thomas said of his native landscape:

> There were poets who were beginning to write in a spirit of passionate anger against the inequality of social conditions. They wrote, not of the truths and beauties of the natural world, but of the lies and ugliness of the unnatural system of the society under which they worked—or, more often during the nineteen twenties and thirties, under which they were not allowed to work.... [They wrote] in ragged angry rhythms, of the Wales *they* knew: the coal tips, the dole-queues, the stubborn bankrupt villages, the children, scrutting for coal on the slag-heaps, the colliers' shabby allotments, the cheap-jack cinema, the whippet races, the disused quarries, the still pit-wheels.[27]

This is unmistakably a Lawrence-like voice, rancorous with disgust about the "ugly, ugly, ugly" quality of modern industrial life, particularly the life of coal-mines and third-grade provincial culture. But it is not a voice echoed in the poetry Thomas wrote. There, society, politics, the life of toil and the viciousness of exploitation vanish, replaced by the resurrection of childhood appareled in innocence, or nature surging in mystical plenitude, or sexuality mysteriously dangerous, or death omnipotent. But to note this fact about Thomas also compels one to note it in Lawrence. Neither poet, as poet, is interested in the grittiness of specific social issues; neither writes with ideological polemics chiefly in mind. But this is hardly a fact of much force or consequence. Many writers indeed have been apolitical. We are still left with a Lawrence straining to liberate himself from the weight and consequence of words, the verbal reality he knew he had to use, and a Thomas happily intoxicated with words and the extremes of originality to which he could drive them. The former is a poet profoundly ill at ease with his self-consciousness; the latter is one for whom throbbing self-consciousness was an incentive to exult in language.

IV. SEAMUS HEANEY

What to make, however, of the Lawrencean influence on a contemporary writer such as Seamus Heaney, a poet close to the natural world of Northern Ireland, its farms, animals, rituals and violent reminders of precious living amid terrible dying? Heaney is aware of his Antaeus-like instincts, looking earthward always, rooted in the feel of things as they are found, Wordsworthian, rural and honest:

> I cannot be weaned
> Off the earth's long contour, her river-veins.
> Down here in my cave
>
> Girdered with root and rock
> I am cradled in the dark that wombed me
> And nurtured in every artery
> Like a small hillock.
> "Antaeus"

Heaney is also the poet who, early in his career, seemed to be registering his loyalty to Lawrence in many ways (for instance, "Blackberry-Picking," a poem in the true and naive Lawrencean manner). And, in "An Advancement of Learning," Heaney's memory of an encounter with a rat, and his embarrassed analysis of his self-conscious reactions, appear to owe almost everything to "Snake":

> The tapered tail that followed him,
> The raindrop eye, the old snout:
> One by one I took all in.
> He trained on me. I stared him out
>
> Forgetting how I used to panic
> When his grey brothers scraped and fed
> Behind the hen-coop in our yard,
> On ceiling boards above my bed.
>
> This terror, cold, wet-furred, small-clawed,
> Retreated up a pipe for sewage.
> I stared a minute after him.
> Then I walked on and crossed the bridge.

Like Lawrence, Heaney is, in this poem, uncomfortably aware of his sensibility. He is not simply a passer-by, but a passer-by equipped with perceptions enforcing the differences between himself and a representative of the natural world. Virgilian and pious though he might be, he *knows* he is Virgilian and a student of his own piety. In "Digging," an early poem that has served as his credo, the easy naturalness of his father's and grandfather's digging for turf is at once a metaphor for his own poetic craft and a reminder that he is no farmer at all, but a writer whose connection to the world is verbal:

> My grandfather cut more turf in a day
> Than any other man on Toner's bog.
> Once I carried him milk in a bottle
> Corked sloppily with paper. He straightened up
> To drink it, then fell to right away
> Nicking and slicing neatly, heaving sods
> Over his shoulder, going down and down
> For the good turf. Digging.
>
> The cold smell of potato mould, the squelch and slap
> Of soggy peat, the curt cuts of an edge
> Through living roots awaken in my head.
> But I've no spade to follow men like them.
>
> Between my finger and my thumb
> The squat pen rests.
> I'll dig with it.

If we think of Lawrence as a poet straining at every nerve to become at one with the world that was *not* himself, but forced again and again to accept the heavy burden of his considerable self-consciousness, we find in Heaney the same concern. In this important sense, Heaney is Lawrencean. Indeed, Heaney's awareness of himself as a poet, and all the discomfiture that fact provides, gives to some of his poems their celebrated curtness. They are fetchingly laconic, immediate and direct, almost "unpoetic" in their seeming avoidance of any devices that would heighten the rhetoric or expose the artificiality of his endeavors:

> Yet for all this art and sedentary trade
> I am incapable. The famous
>
> Northern reticence, the tight gag of place
> And times: yes, yes. Of the "wee six" I sing
> Where to be saved you only must save face
> And whatever you say, you say nothing.

Blake Morrison has said that the cumulative effect of such poems suggests that "as a young poet Seamus Heaney found himself in the position of valuing silence above speech, of defending the shy and awkward against the confident and accomplished, of feeling language to be a kind of betrayal. This might be thought a somewhat paradoxical position for a poet to take up."[28] But such a "paradox" is, in fact, the one experienced by Lawrence. Language and all it could do was, for the earlier poet, the problem, the source of a corrupting sophistication which, generating poetry, also generated the distance between naive mind and simple thing. The shovel become a pen is the farmer become a poet, the sensual life become the cerebral life. The prognosis, as Lawrence would have it, is therefore one of increasing disease, for linguistic dexterity inevitably replaces the possibility of an unmediated vision. In a later Heaney poem, the situation is similar:

> Late summer, and at midnight
> I smelt the heat of the day:
> At my window over the hotel car park
> I breathed the muddied night airs off the lake
> And watched a young crowd leave the discotheque. . . .
>
> A girl in a white dress
> Was being courted out among the cars:
> As her voice swarmed and puddled into laughs
> I felt like some old pike all badged with sores
> Wanting to swim in touch with soft-mouthed life.
>
> "The Guttural Muse"

"Soft-mouthed life" and all it represents is what can never be touched, by Lawrence or by Heaney. Between them and it falls the shadow of language, of mind, of design and control. But, if the awareness of this problem is what the two poets share, their different responses divide them. Lawrence was incapable of resting easily with the fact that he was, after all, a man of words, a man empowered by the artificiality of language while confined by it. In all his writing he aims ultimately to discover a way to discard the impediment of the words streaming from him so as to embrace the Truth. Heaney, on the other hand, is inclined to recognize that the nature he greets with such reverence is inaccessible to him save through the language he assembles, workmanlike, on the page:

> Take hold of the shaft of the pen
> Subscribe to the first step taken
> from a justified line
> into the margin.
>
> "The First Gloss"

Heaney begins "from a justified line," from writing and all the self-consciousness it promotes. "Soft-mouthed life" is conceded to lie somewhere beyond his real grasp, perpetually out of reach and yet forever his subject. "Oysters," the first poem in *Field Work*, is Heaney's acknowledgement of his own incarceration in language. It begins in delight at the succulence of the oysters:

> Our shells clacked on the plates.
> My tongue was a filling estuary,
> My palate hung with starlight:
> As I tasted the salty Pleiades
> Orion dipped his foot into the water.

But it ends with the confession that the oysters can serve only to reveal Heaney's ulterior purposes to himself; the "frond-lipped, brine-stung/Glut of privilege" is but an incentive to something else, something poetic and not oyster-like at all:

> I ate the day
> Deliberately, that its tang
> Might quicken me all into verb, pure verb.

Lawrence and English Poetry

The loyalty to language, to the resources of "verb, pure verb, is deep in Heaney. He has never denied the injunction he sees coming to him from his cultural past, an injunction exposed in the poem "North":

> Lie down
> in the word-hoard, burrow
> the coil and gleam
> Of your furrowed brain.
>
> Compose in darkness.

V. TED HUGHES

The poetry of Ted Hughes seems to fall almost perfectly into the patterns of sensibility set by Lawrence. Hughes is a poet of nature, a writer provoked to writing by the startling distinctiveness of the *otherness* of life, a sensibility little concerned with the feeble interferences thrown up to the strong imagination by civility, urbanity, politeness and custom. He knows, as Conrad's Kurtz knew, the horror existing just below the surface of the skin—a horror beautiful in its predatory rapacity. Edward Lucie-Smith, noting the similarities between Lawrence and Hughes, remarks that "it is not merely that the poetic method is the same in both . . .—a slow, almost groping progression, a *feeling into* the life of the creature—but there is, in addition, an insistence on the mystery and darkness to be found at the heart of the experience."[29]

With Hughes, however, the inwardness, the intimacy of sympathetic understanding about the nature of life in the *other* habitually becomes a fascination with the death of the other. In "Pike," for instance, what begins as awed scrutiny of the characteristics of the living fish ends as fascination with how those fish kill and are themselves killed:

> Pike, three inches long, perfect
> Pike in all parts, green triggering the gold.
> Killers from the egg: the malevolent aged grin.
> They dance on the surface among the flies.

Or move, stunned by their own grandeur,
Over a bed of emerald, silhouette
Of submarine delicacy and horror.
A hundred feet long in their world....

Three we kept behind glass,
Jungled in weed: three inches, four
And four and a half: fed fry to them—
Suddenly there were two. Finally one.

With a sag belly and the grin it was born with.
And indeed they spare nobody.
Two, six pounds each, over two feet long,
High and dry and dead in the willow-herb—

One jammed past its gills down the other's gullet:
The outside eye stared: as a vice locks—
The same iron in this eye
Though its film shrank in death.

As it is with the cruel fish, so it is with the equally cruel otters, animals uniquely destructive in life, destined to ravage and then be ravaged:

> Underwater eyes, an eel's
> Oil of water body, neither fish nor beast is the otter:
> Four-legged yet water-gifted, to outfish fish;
>   With webbed feet and long ruddering tail
>   And a round head like an old tomcat....
>
>   The heart beats thick,
> Big trout muscle out of the dead cold;
> Blood is the belly of logic; he will lick
> The fishbone bare. And can take stolen hold
>
> On a bitch otter in a field full
> Of nervous horses, but linger nowhere.
> Yanked above hounds, reverts to nothing at all,
> To this long pelt over the back of a chair.

"An Otter"

The power of observation is Lawrencean: precise, keen, reverential, but what Hughes adds, as he moves closer to the object of his attention, is the sudden twist of interest on his part in the savage end of all things in nature. Everything, after a bloody encounter, finds itself dead and is rendered "nothing" (a word omnipresent in Hughes). The contrast with Lawrence is unmistakable: the earlier poet, while well-acquainted with death and lovingly, even morbidly, fascinated with it, embraced it poetically but then subsumed it in a larger world of understanding:

> Now it is autumn and the falling fruit
> and the long journey towards oblivion.
>
> The apples falling like great drops of dew
> to bruise themselves an exit from themselves.
>
> And it is time to go, to bid farewell
> to one's own self, and find an exit
> from the fallen self. . . .
>
> Wait, wait, the little ship
> drifting, beneath the deathly ashy grey
> of a flood-dawn.
>
> Wait, wait! even so, a flush of yellow
> and strangely, O chilled wan soul, a flush of rose.
>
> A flush of rose, and the whole thing starts again.
>
> "The Ship of Death"

Lawrence knows the fall toward oblivion and the seductive powers of "nothingness," but he is circular and redemptive in the pattern of his imagination: "a flush of rose" will return. Hughes, by contrast, is vertical, reaching downward always, plummeting towards annihilation and ecstatic horrors. His brilliantly bleak and remorseless landscape is, as his fellow poet Heaney has said, "King Lear's heath which now becomes a Yorkshire moor where sheep and foxes and hawks persuade 'unaccommodated man' that he is a poor bare forked thing, kinned not in a chain but on a plane of being with the animals themselves . . . and the poet is a wanderer among the ruins, cut off by catastrophe from consolation and philosophy."[30]

No more than Lear alone on the heath is Hughes able to blame nature for the cruelties it constantly inflicts ("I tax not you, you elements, with unkindness"). There is nothing other than nature, and nature will prove unkind. Thus the meaning of *Crow*, and everything it compulsively emphasizes, and everthing it omits. In Hughes there is no room for human mind and human redemption, not even the pathetic grace eked out by a Lear who has also seen, in his own way, the nothingness of life, but has not lost the sweetness of small human connections: "Pray you, undo this button. Thank you, sir."

For Hughes, the human and the human intellect are equally negligible, equally flimsy in the face of nature, which to him is a Darwinian universe made contemptibly malign. All that humans can ever do is to foul the proper design of things; "poetry is nothing if not that," Hughes has said, "the record of just how the forces of the Universe try to redress some balance disturbed by human error."[31] This is the Lawrencean animadversion upon intellect made complete. The history of Hughes's obsession with everything that can be found to be murderous, even the mind that murders, has no parallel with Lawrence's history of often finding, where least expected, the goodness of the human:

> Things men have made with wakened hands, and put soft
>   life into
> are awake through years with transferred touch, and go on
>   glowing
> for long years.
> And for this reason, some old things are lovely
> warm still with the life of forgotten men who made them.
>
> "Things Men Have Made"

What Calvin Bedient has rightly called the "monstrous marriage of nihilism and vitality"[32] in Hughes' poetry, and the disaffection in Hughes' sensibility with everything the poet might modestly *make*—in contrast to the destructive processes he might everywhere chronicle—is an extension of self-conscious Lawrencean uneasiness. Mind is nothing for Hughes, and must quickly be brought to heel if it anywhere tries to assert itself. "Crow," a force and not a man, destroys all before it, "flying the black flag of himself."

The invention of "Crow" is Hughes' most ambitious attempt to rid himself of the encumbrance of a stable poetic self-consciousness. "Crow" is not a persona for the poet, but rather an expulsion of everything meant by "selfhood." As "Crow" speaks and acts, we are in the presence of implacable and destructive energy, energy devoid of all the variousness and possibility of the human. Inventing "Crow," Hughes provides a dismaying answer to the problem faced by Lawrence, of wanting to overturn the weight of self-consciousness and to assure the supremacy of "nature" over "art." With "Crow," the revenge against art is complete: lines and words huddled and tossed together, diction broken, conventions trashed ("songs with no music whatsoever, in a super-simple and super-ugly language,"[33] as Hughes himself said). As Bedient remarks, "Hughes seems to lay about for phrases, not to care much about the words themselves.... There is great cynicism in the style, which is slung out like hash. At this stage of case-hardened disillusion ... words will all taste the same anyhow.... A master of language who tosses words on the page—can any aesthetic justify this?"[34] The answer is that the justifying aesthetic is one in which the victory of nature over art will be guaranteed, fixed at any cost. Hughes will try to recover, as Lawrence tried to recover, a *naïveté* from which all contaminations of the "knowing" and the sophisticated will be removed. In Hughes, however, the attempt is coarse, willed and, in the end, stylized. He forces his constructive powers to establish, in *Crow*, expressions of brutishness that are formulaic and melodramatic:

> So finally there was nothing.
> It was put inside nothing.
> Nothing was added to it
> And to prove it didn't exist
> Squashed flat as nothing with nothing.
>
> Chopped up with a nothing
> Shaken in a nothing
> Turned completely inside out
> And scattered over nothing—

> So everybody saw that it was nothing
> And that nothing more could be done with it
>
> And so it was dropped. Prolonged applause in Heaven.
>
> It hit the ground and broke open—
>
> There lay Crow, cataleptic.
>
> "Conjuring in Heaven"

Sinister-seeming and yet bogus, this is a poetry that, in avoiding the traditionally poetic, avoids the self-reflexive powers of mind that make the human sensibility humane. Wanting to be "primeval" and pre-human, it succeeds only in calling attention to the fact of its constitution: a working poet, in a willful stupor of self-escape, conceived of its sing-song rhythms and childish beat. The spectre of Lawrence hovers nearby, but it is Lawrence of only limited dimensions, a Lawrence reduced and *voulu*.[35]

VI. POETIC INFLUENCE AND THE QUESTION OF TECHNIQUE

Like Auden, the poet Stephen Spender was, as a young man, much impressed by Lawrence and his passionate sensitivity to the "otherness" of the natural world. Lawrence showed Spender the narrowness and sterility of academic and "clubby" life; he also made Spender aware of how great the dimensions of emotional and sensual existence could be:

> Lawrence, despite his artistic defects [Spender said], wrote poetry and prose which turned outwards from himself towards men and women, and towards nature.... He had a sense that the distinctions between outer and inner are sacred: that whilst the inner life should meet the outer, the outer world should not become the inner world of the writer.... No attempt to resume Lawrence's ideas can explain the influence he had over me. This was an immediate reaction when I read a page of his descriptive prose, or one of his poems. At once I

was aware of nature as a life-and-death force, existing independently of man's existence but containing energies capable of renewing him.[36]

Both the praise and the criticism must be noted here. Spender reports on his early admiration but also remarks on the most serious failure of Lawrence's poetry—its "artistic defects." In Lawrence's case, such defects are obvious and unforgettable, and they are what provoked R. P. Blackmur's famous denunciation of the poet. But, more importantly, they seem to have been the very Lawrencean characteristics that later poets, including those enamored of his philosophy and vision, seemed most anxious to avoid. Blackmur noted that Lawrence wanted to carry his vision without the support of the necessary and appropriate technical structure, and that, as a consequence, his unstructured words had to do too much work:

> On the one hand he rejected the advantages of objective form for the immediate freedom of expressive form, and on the other hand he preferred the inspiration of immediate experience to the discipline of a rationally constructed imagination.... Since he willfully rejected as much as he could of the great mass of expressive devices which make up the craft of poetry, the success of his poems depends, not so much on his bare statements, as upon the constant function of communication which cannot be expunged from the language.... He used language straightforwardly to the point of sloppiness, without ever willfully violating the communicative residue of his words.[37]

Not even A. Alvarez's brilliantly sympathetic treatment of Lawrence's poetry can ignore the many artistic things that Lawrence, as a poet, simply did not do. Defending Lawrence with great resourcefulness and skill, Alvarez nonetheless agrees that "he was not interested in surface polish; his verse is informal in the conventional sense.... Lawrence's controlling standard was delicacy: a constant, fluid awareness, nearer the checks of intimate talk than those of regular prosody. His poetry is not the outcome of rules and formal craftmanship."[38] One may add that Lawrence's art, as it matured, became minimalist in its construction; so severely handicapped, Lawrence inevitably ran great risks as a poet.

These risks have not been assumed by later poets. For example, Edwin Muir, cited as "Lawrencean" in his devotion to the life of primitive agricultural communities and to the sacredness of their daily and seasonal rituals, encases one of his most "Lawrencean" poems—"Horses"—in wholly traditional rhythmic and stanzaic patterns:

> Those lumbering horses in the steady plough,
> On the bare field—I wonder why, just now,
> They seemed terrible, so wild and strange,
> Like magic power on the stony grange.
>
> Perhaps some childish hour has come again,
> When I watched fearful, through the blackening rain,
> Their hooves like pistons in an ancient mill
> Move up and down, yet seem as standing still. . . .
>
> Their eyes as brilliant and as wide as night
> Gleamed with a cruel apocalyptic light.
> Their manes the leaping ire of the wind
> Lifted with rage invisible and blind.
>
> Ah, now it fades! it fades! and I must pine
> Again for that dread country crystalline,
> Where the blank field and the still-standing tree
> Were bright and fearful presences to me.

And the South African Roy Campbell, also "Lawrencean" in his robust vitalism and his lyrical interest in the natural world, is remarkably unlike Lawrence in the rigid strictures of his versification and the precision of his heightened diction:

> With breath indrawn and every nerve alert,
> As at the brink of some profound abyss,
> I love on my bare arm, capricious flirt,
> To feel the chilly and incisive kiss
> Of your lithe tongue that forks its swift caress
> Between the folded slumber of your fangs,
> And half reveals the nacreous recess
> Where death upon those dainty hinges hangs.

> Our lonely lives in every chance agreeing,
> It is no common friendship that you bring,
> It was the desert starved us into being,
> The hate of men that sharpened us to sting:
> Sired by starvation, suckled by neglect,
> Hate was the surly tutor of our youth;
> I too can hiss the hair of men erect
> Because my lips are venomous with truth.
>
> "To a Pet Cobra"

Whether it is the diction of "nacreous recess," or the alliteration of "Sired by starvation, suckled by neglect," or the metaphorical inventiveness of "Hate was the surly tutor of our youth," or the inversions and elaborateness of later lines, this is a poetry standing at a far technical remove from Lawrence's. Whether it is a better or worse poetry is not the question; the issue is influence, not inherent quality. And the Lawrencean influence has been, in the case of both Muir and Campbell, direct but severely attenuated.

VII. CONCLUSION

Thus we return, by the telling example of Hughes and others, to the central fact of Lawrence's poetry: his extraordinary protestations of a kind of "pre-verbal" innocence, his implicit yearning for a poetry that does not call attention to itself as poetry. To become "art" was, for Lawrence, to become disengaged from the exterior and important reality that could, in its power and splendor, release human beings from themselves and from their solipsism. But these aims and protestations, while apparently understood by later poets, have not generally been sustained by them. Even in the work of Hughes, the employment of an overwhelming technical arsenal, designed to promote the "primeval" and annihilate the genteel self, serves only to illuminate the plight of a writer who cannot escape himself and the peculiar ingenuities of his art. Muir and Campbell admired the felicities of wholly traditional technique far more than any lessons they might have learned from Lawrence. Heaney seems to confront the challenge laid down by Lawrence (and the success of his writing), but his stubborn common-sense, and his brilliant virtuosity, compel him to address the fact that he is a word-user and not a digger of peat. For good or for ill, he is compelled to dig with his pen. In his most recent volume, *Station Island*, he digs with the shadowy presences of Dante, William Carleton, Patrick Kavanagh, Horace, St. John of the Cross and James Joyce nearby; there is little likelihood of *naïveté* in that company.

The lesson of this historical survey is clear. The spread of poetic influence is substantially more dependent on the transmission of technique than on the transmission of philosophy or vision. From Auden to Thomas to Heaney to Hughes (and with Muir and Campbell as minor examples), little resistance can be found to the essential and deeper Lawrencean principles of life. Indeed, most of these poets willingly accepted much of what Lawrence believed about the sacred, the passionate and the "alive." But that acceptance was weakened by many important qualifications and conditions when they began their individual acts of writing. Some of them recognized the heroism of Lawrence's ambition to escape the trap of language and the self-consciousness it necessarily promotes. Others offered no explicit recognition of the problem, but proceeded to write as if they knew escape was futile. In no instance did any of them fail to reach out to the enormous and vital provisions of technique that poetic language, an artificial construct, was constantly able to offer to them. The slender diet on which Lawrence so brilliantly survived was not one to which any later poets returned. Richer sustenance was available; it was taken.

CHAPTER FOUR

Lawrence and Travel Writers

JEFFREY MEYERS

I

Lawrence's greatest contribution to the travel-writing tradition was to shift the center of interest from the external world to the self. His books on Italy and Mexico seemed to be spontaneous revelations of his own feelings and thoughts. He defined himself in relation to landscape and people, and showed the response of an extraordinary personality to the "spirit of the place."[1] His physical journey also had intellectual goals. Lawrence's works described both an escape from the "hateful homogeneous world-oneness"[2] of industrial countries, and a search for a climate and culture that would nourish an ideal society and reveal a new mode of consciousness.

The classical travel books on Italy—Dickens, Ruskin, Butler, Gissing, James and Douglas—evoked antiquarian, aesthetic and cultural associations. Lawrence, much more subjective and impressionistic, saw the natural world with his imagination as well as with his eye. He was influenced by the travel books of Melville and Stevenson, and tested himself against writers who were primarily interested in people and landscape rather than in history and art. He tried to go "back towards the past, savage life,"[3] to recapture a traditional culture, even if the actual place could no longer satisfy his nostalgia for the past or sustain the civilization he hoped to find there.

Lawrence's aesthetic of travel influenced most of the writers who came after him. He preferred a rough rather than a formal journey, popular rather than high culture, colloquial rather than mandarin style. Excited by change and movement, he wished to go to geographical as well as emotional extremes of temperature, altitude and distance. He sought a natural rather than a man-made world, was attracted to traditional people who knew nothing of the machinery of modern civilization, and craved contact with scenery that still retained its savagery. Travel for Lawrence was a relief from and incitement to writing, a means of inner exploration and a source of immediate inspiration. Travel intensified his sense of being English at the same time that it removed him from England and allowed him to see his own country more clearly.

Lawrence believed that "a new place brings out a new thing in a man,"[4] and his lifelong credo was: "when in doubt, *move*."[5] When he seemed to be running out of places to see, he wanted to stretch the globe and exclaimed: "I wish I were going to Thibet—or Kamschatka—or Tahiti—to the Ultima ultima ultima Thule. I feel sometimes, I shall go mad, because there is nowhere to go, no 'new world.' "[6]

Unlike most of his predecessors, who romanticized and glorified their experience, Lawrence was engagingly frank whenever he suffered backward and brutal people, boring journeys and self-created torments. Despite enthusiastic letters to friends, he was forced to admit: "Travel seems to me a splendid lesson in disillusion—chiefly that."[7] *Twilight in Italy* was a lament for a lost life, its lyricism radically undermined by its portrayal of "the hideous rawness of the world of men, the horrible, desolating harshness of the advance of the industrial world upon the world of nature."[8] In his review of H. M. Tomlinson's *Gifts of Fortune*, Lawrence confirmed that though the pattern of his travel books moved from enchantment to disillusion, the quest itself was still valid: "We travel, perhaps, with a secret and absurd hope of setting foot on the Hesperides, of running our boat up a little creek and landing in the Garden of Eden. This hope is always defeated. There is no Garden of Eden, and the Hesperides never were. Yet, in our very search for them, we touch the coasts of illusion, and come into contact with other worlds."[9]

On setting out for Australia, Lawrence noted: "one suffers getting adjusted—but that is part of the adventure. . . . I love trying things and discovering how I hate them."[10] But he felt the excitement more than balanced the sinister aspects of the journey, willingly endured the "incidental beastliness of travel" and knew that the worst trips made the best reading. *Sea and Sardinia*, inspired by a powerful compulsion expressed in the opening sentence, "Comes over one an absolute necessity to move," expressed his psychology of travel and portrayed the traveler as victim.

Lawrence did not follow a specific literary tradition, but he created one. His influence can clearly be seen in the writers who shared his attitudes, interests, mode of travel, and followed his innovative example. Auden, MacNeice, Isherwood, Greene, Miller, Durrell and Gerald Brenan were all (like Lawrence) expatriate writers whose lives were characterized by movement and whose works emphasized the importance of place. Like Lawrence, they charged their books with curiosity and energy, combined description and interpretation with social criticism and political commentary, and expressed the dominant themes of their books in symbolic scenes. All these authors employed Lawrence's techniques and repeated his themes: the escape from a mechanical to a natural life, the quest for inspiration, the idealistic search for a personal connection with ordinary people, the vital response to landscape and culture, the imaginative rather than realistic view of the world, the self-exploration and self-revelation. As these travel writers ranged from the ecstatic to the horrific and moved from the extremes of Europe—Iceland, Spain, Greece and Cyprus—to China, Mexico and the Andes, they also reflected Lawrence's honest portrayal of discomfort, disillusionment and despair.[11]

II. W. H. AUDEN AND LOUIS MACNEICE, *LETTERS FROM ICELAND* (1937)

Lawrence—who had died in 1930, whose *Letters* appeared in 1932 and who was the subject of ten memoirs published between 1931 and 1935[12]—was very much on Auden's mind as he traveled through Iceland from June to September 1936. Auden's ideas were influenced by Lawrence's *Fantasia of the Unconscious* and *Apocalypse*, particularly by his Romantic belief that "to act on one's deepest impulse is to be happy and virtuous, immune to neurosis . . . a living beacon to the tormented and the ill."[13]

In *Letters from Iceland* Auden acknowledged his intellectual debt to Lawrence:

> I met a chap called Layard and he fed
> New doctrines into my receptive head.
> Part came from Lane, and part from D. H. Lawrence;
>   Gide, though I didn't know it then, gave part.
> They taught me to express my deep abhorrence
>   If I caught anyone preferring Art
> To Life and Love and being Pure-in-Heart.[14]

Auden praised Lawrence's power to evoke the spirit of the place through a muddled but quite brilliant transformation of reality into personal vision: "Landscape's so dull/if you haven't Lawrence's wonderful wooziness." And he sided with Lawrence by preferring a traditional open hearth fire to a mechanical means of warmth:

> Preserve me, above all, from central heating.
> It may be D. H. Lawrence's hocus-pocus,
> But I prefer a room that's got a focus.

Auden also contrasted Lawrence's notable fluency (exaggerated in Norman Douglas' account of Lawrence's work habits in Florence)[15] with his own perplexity about how to proceed with the Iceland book:

> I know I've not the least chance of survival
>   Beside the major travellers of the day.
> I am no Lawrence who, on his arrival,
>   Sat down and typed out all he had to say.

And Auden contrasted Lawrence's innovative approach with commonplace travel books in which "the actual events are all extremely like each other—meals—sleeping accommodations—fleas—dangers, etc., and the repetition becomes boring. The usual alternative, which is essays on life prompted by something seen, the kind of thing Lawrence and Aldous Huxley do, I am neither clever enough nor sensitive enough to manage." Though Auden seemed unwilling to compete with Lawrence, his technique was actually quite close to the Master's. For Auden said that his poetic letter to Lord Byron—an avatar and kindred spirit of Lawrence: both came from Nottinghamshire, were exiles, traveled continuously in the remote corners of Europe, rebelled against the social code, had a scandalous life and a notorious literary career[16]—"will have very little to do with Iceland, but will be rather a description of an effect of travelling in distant places which is to make one reflect on one's past and one's culture from the outside."

As Conrad observed in *Under Western Eyes*, the crucial question for the traveler, artist, adventurer, exile and criminal was: "Where to?" Auden was drawn to the rural north by a claim of Icelandic ancestry, a childhood love of the Sagas ("With northern myths my little brain was laden") and a lifelong interest in geology that inspired "In Praise of Limestone." But his remote genealogy was dubious, the "gangster virtues" of the Sagas not quite civilized, his passion for rock essentially subterranean and industrial. For the aspiring mining engineer: "Tramlines and slagheaps, pieces of machinery, / That was, and still is, my ideal scenery." Auden's nostalgia for industrial landscapes could only be felt by someone who had never been trapped there.

Auden's background, outlook, temperament and physique led to an almost Calvinistically predestined disillusionment when his romantic preconceptions were shattered by the reality of Iceland. "There is not much to be said for Reykjavik," whose tourist sights included four of its more interesting inhabitants and a museum the fastidious would want to miss. Akureyri was a nicer town: "Unfortunately there is a fish factory to the north and to-day the wind is blowing from the north." There were no trees, trains or architecture, few fruits and greens, limited culture: "no drama, and little knowledge of painting or music." The oldest church in the country was "squat and turf covered, like a shaggy old sheep with a ball round its neck." The sculpture was the worst he had ever seen in his life.

The food at the surly breakfasts and crude suppers was even more appalling. There were three particularly horrible soups: "one of sweet milk and hard macaroni, one tasting of hot marzipan, and one of scented hair oil." The dried fish varied in texture: "The tougher kind tastes like toe-nails, and the softer kind like the skin off the soles of one's feet." Owing to its smell, the half-rotten shark, tough as an old boot, had to be eaten outdoors.

This left the somber landscape, the main attraction of the place and staple of the travel books. But the dead craters, angled crags, jungles of lava, crinkled fjords, dense scrub and stony desert were "like the uninteresting and useless débris of an orgy"; the stones "not big enough to impress and not small enough to negotiate." They were "absolutely unpicturesque and absolutely non-utilitarian," like rocky rubbish and dry bones out of an Eliot poem. Auden's response to Kaldidalur, a clammy and rheumatic showpiece of scenery wedged between glacier and geyser, was characteristic: "There is no point in staying in this particular little swamp a minute longer than we need."

The distance between the real and ideal seemed impassable.[17] Since Auden had accepted a commission to write a travel book about the country of his choice, with expenses paid by his publishers, he had to devise a way to transform his disappointment, discomfort and boredom into a competent and saleable book. Negative travel books would satisfy the public's appetite for vicarious experience and, at the same time, reassure them about the virtues of their own society. The self-conscious mode of the work allowed a glimpse of his struggle with the problem: "I've been here a month and haven't the slightest idea how to begin to write the book. [The publisher, Victor] Gollancz, told me before I left that it couldn't be done, and he's probably right. Still the contracts are signed and my expenses paid, so I suppose it will get done." A little later he hit upon the ideal solution: "I suddenly thought I might write [Byron] a chatty letter in light verse about anything I could think of, Europe, literature, myself. He's the right person, I think, because he ... disliked Wordsworth and that kind of [sentimental] approach to nature." The five-part verse letter to Lord Byron, which threaded the narrative like a dolphin leaping through the sea, was essentially digressive and discursive. But it solved the problem by establishing the jaunty mood and avoiding the dreary subject.

In his autobiography, *The Strings Are False*, MacNeice conceded that their "travel book was a hodge-podge, thrown together in gaiety."[18] But the apparently centrifugal *Letters from Iceland* was held together by the Byronic tone, the epistolary form and the haphazard trail of the journey round the island. The Byronic voice—lively, sophisticated, ironic, gossipy, familiar, flippant, civilized, humorous, even campy—mixed satire with serious reflection:

> I like your muse because she's gay and witty,
>   Because she's neither prostitute nor frump,
> The daughter of a European city,
>   And country houses long before the slump;
>   I like her voice that does not make me jump:
> And you I find sympatisch, a good townee,
> Neither a preacher, ninny, bore, nor Brownie.

Just as Lawrence, in *Etruscan Places*, compared the ancient Romans to the modern Fascists who threatened the traditional way of life, so Auden revealed how the rise of totalitarianism threatened even the Scandinavian sanity of remote Iceland. Auden remarked "the Nazis have a theory that Iceland is the cradle of the Germanic culture," and noted the great excitement on the island when Alfred Rosenberg and Goering's brother arrived for an official visit. In the Epilogue that concluded the book, MacNeice revealed that the Spanish War broke out while they were traveling in the far side of the continent:

> Down in Europe Seville fell,
> Nations germinating hell,
> The Olympic games were run—
> Spots upon the Aryan sun.

Auden observed that "we are too deeply involved with Europe to be able, or even to wish to escape" and lamented the grim future:

The news from Europe [is] interwoven with our behaving.
The pleasant voice of the wireless announcer, like a consultant
  surgeon, [says]
"Your case is hopeless. I give you six months."

Auden's technique and themes were both Lawrencean: his rejection of a conventional for an idiosyncratic travel book as well as his discomfort and disillusionment in a country he had hoped would match the ideal image of his childhood. The satiric undercurrent that masked Auden's anger and expressed his sense of loss was strikingly similar to passages in *Sea and Sardinia* where Lawrence bitterly observed that Cagliari was "rather bare, rather stark, rather cold and yellow" and Mandas freezing cold with nothing to do: "one goes to bed when it's dark, like a chicken."[19]

III. W. H. AUDEN AND CHRISTOPHER ISHERWOOD, *JOURNEY TO A WAR* (1939)

In his review of *Letters from Iceland*, Isherwood remarked: "Poets never seem to notice anything; it is a pity there was no novelist in the party."[20] He soon remedied the situation by accompanying Auden on a trip to China during February–June 1938 and providing "the impersonal eye of the camera/Sent out by God to shoot on location,"[21] which Auden had mentioned in the Iceland book.

Though *Journey to a War* was more serious, the two travel books had a good deal in common. Both were co-authored and written in verse and prose, both emphasized the discomfort of the journey, both had photographs to enhance the words. But the images of China were far superior and included Chiang Kai-shek and his wife, Chou En-lai, the photographer Robert Capa and the journalist Peter Fleming (brother of Ian) as well as "Train parasites" (an old lady begging for food) and ironically paired contrasts: "Children in Uniform: With Legs and Without," "The Innocent" (blinded civilians) and "The Guilty" (dismembered Japanese soldiers).

Both travel books used public-school humor, and adopted a satiric attitude to the country and its food. Auden and Isherwood mocked and loathed the bound feet of the women, the endless expectoration, the rat's-nest hotels, the intolerable stench, the revolting folk medicine ("the warm intestines of a freshly-killed chicken are a favourite Chinese antiseptic"[22]) and the embarrassment of being carried by coolies on "The Bad Earth." Cheng-chow smelled of disease, Sian smelled of murder. Isherwood relished the disgusting details, and the food provided some of the best jokes. The markets sold "the filthiest parts of the oldest and most diseased animals; stodgy excrement-puddings; vile, stagnant soups and poisonous roots ... an orange which tasted of bitter aloes and contained, in its centre, a large weevil." In the shops, "Auden gazed in horror at the edible black-beetles, I at the tubs of live swimming snakes. If I had to eat a snake, I said, I thought I should really go mad. Auden determined to trick me into doing so at the first possible opportunity."

Both books contained self-portraits of the authors. In *Journey to a War* the foreign devils, W. H. "Au Dung" and Christopher "Y Hsaio Wu" were naive though observant muddlers who tried to amuse each other on the interminable train trips by "screaming with laughter at mysterious jokes, singing in high falsetto or mock operatic voices, swaying rhythmically backwards and forwards on their seats, reading aloud to each other." They also discussed questions like "Does a man become a different person in a different place?," which was lifted straight from *Aaron's Rod* when the hero asks Lilly: "Shall *you* be any different in yourself, in another place?"[23] Unlike Osbert Sitwell, Edmund Blunden, Harold Acton, William Empson and Julian Bell, who had lived in China and written about the country, Auden and Isherwood were not profoundly affected by their experience in an alien culture.

The spirit of Lawrence hovered over both works. A horribly uncomfortable journey, after the fashion of *Sea and Sardinia*, was called a "D. H. Lawrence *Todesfahrt*." Their chauffeur reminded them "of a character in a novel by D. H. Lawrence—the groom in *St. Mawr*, or one of those 'dark,' sinister Mexicans in *The Plumed Serpent*." And in Sian they even met Lawrence's Swiss doctor, who described his medical examination after the near-fatal hemorrhage: "Dr. Mooser examined Lawrence and told him that he was suffering from tuberculosis—not from malaria, as the Mexican doctor had assured him. Lawrence took it very quietly. He only asked how long Mooser thought he would live. 'Two years,' said Mooser. 'If you're careful.' That was in 1928 [i.e., 1925]."

The travel diary that formed the core of the book was written by Isherwood from separate journals kept by both authors. But, unlike Orwell's *Homage to Catalonia*, it did not do justice to its tragic subject. Their reportage, which is now historical rather than topical, seems insubstantial. They spoke no Chinese, had no special knowledge of Far Eastern affairs, had unreliable informants and frankly admitted their limitations: "We can only record, for the benefit of the reader who has never been to China, some impression of what he would be likely to see, and what kind of stories he would be likely to hear." Isherwood's clearer focus inspired better reviews than *Letters from Iceland* had received.

The literary reputations of the authors and the propagandistic value of their book allowed the celebrities easy access to everyone they wanted to see. Auden and Isherwood interviewed Madame Chiang Kai-shek, who asked if poets like cake. Chou En-lai, organizer of the 1927 Shanghai insurrection that Malraux had portrayed in *Man's Fate* (1933), believed the struggle against Japan created national solidarity. Though Chiang had turned against his Chinese allies, killed them or driven them into exile, Chou felt "the longer the war continued the more complete would be China's victory, and the closer would be the understanding between the Communist Party and the Kuomintang. What he feared most was a compromise peace between the Kuomintang and Japan at the Communists' expense."[24]

Lawrence would have agreed with Isherwood that "the ideal travel book should be perhaps a little like a crime story in which you're in search of something and then either find it or find that it doesn't exist in the end."[25] *Journey to a War* began with Auden's poem "Whither?" and pessimistically suggested that the unreal excitement of the journey was like a fever. The Lawrencean quest for a Rananim—for a Good Place and a just life—was doomed to disappointment.

During the thirties Auden and Isherwood had idolized the heroic T. E. Lawrence, who died in a motorcycle crash in 1935 and inspired the mountaineer Ransom in *The Ascent of F-6*. In China, their own more modest heroic quest focused on the search for war. But they traveled protected, as in a bell jar. Like Auden in Spain, they were near the front-line fighting for only a few days of their fifteen weeks, saw gunfire but not battles, and escaped from Meiki before the town fell to the Japanese. Their "offstage" war was "untidy, inefficient, obscure, and largely a matter of chance."

A dream-like quality pervaded the book and the unreality was symbolized by Isherwood's theatrical dress. He tried to look stern and martial in "his new riding-boots and his beret and his turtleneck sweater," but his Hollywood director's costume was merely a "symptom of an amateur's stage-fright." The foolish or mysterious "stage-Chinese" were merely cardboard figures. The artillerymen did not shell the Japanese because they did not want the enemy to know they had big guns. Even the Long Bar at the Shanghai Club seemed too short. The British-owned river-boats near Canton were never bombed by the Japanese, though they "playfully aimed their machine-guns at our heads." The authors put on dark glasses and watched a spectacular air-raid—during which five hundred civilians were killed—from the Consulate lawn in Hankow. And they finished up at a hotel called "Journey's End," an escape from an escape, an illusory bit of Chinese Switzerland in the Yangtze Valley.

Some requisite reality entered the narrative when they met the flamboyant Peter Fleming. He was married to an actress, sported (like Isherwood) a Gent's Tropical Exploration Kit and seemed a living parody of the pukka sahib. But he was also a tireless traveler and indefatigable professional who understood the labyrinth of oriental politics and could penetrate the vague, polite, optimistic answers to some vital questions: when would the Chinese attack? what would be the outcome of the war?

Like the threat of industrialism in *Twilight in Italy* or of Fascism in *Etruscan Places*, the threat of war in Europe was depressing: "History opposes its grief to our buoyant song,/To our hope its warning." *Journey to a War*, like *Women in Love*, portrays the effect of war on civilians rather than on combatants. The Civil War was still raging in Spain, and in March 1938 the authors learned that Germany had annexed Austria. Auden observed that during the ominous years "When Austria died, when China was forsaken,/Shanghai in flames and Teruel retaken"—"Only the man behind the rifle had free-will." The rest were merely victims. Auden's exclamation that "civilization hasn't advanced an inch!" recalled Lawrence's lamentation in November 1915, which foreshadowed the cataclysmic opening of *Lady Chatterley's Lover*: "I am so sad, for my country, for this great wave of civilisation, 2000 years, which is now collapsing, that it is hard to live. So much beauty and pathos of old things passing away and no new things coming . . . the winter stretches ahead, where all vision is lost and all memory dies out."[26]

IV. CHRISTOPHER ISHERWOOD, *THE CONDOR AND THE COWS* (1949)

From September 1947 to February 1948 Isherwood journeyed with his current lover, Bill Caskey—who took the fine photographs and drew the endpapers of Cuzco—from La Guaira, Venezuela, through Colombia, Ecuador, Peru and Bolivia to Buenos Aires. He did not know Spanish; but he traveled as a well-known author and collaborator of Auden, and had many useful introductions. Though oppressed by the need to gather facts, he dutifully provided a certain amount of economic, political, historical and cultural information. But his concluding remarks on the continent were familiar and facile. And his travel diary was essentially subjective, impressionistic and "frankly personal, with S. America in the background of my thoughts and meditations in the foreground."[27]

Though Lawrence was not specifically mentioned, his influence pervaded the book. It opened abruptly, like *Sea and Sardinia*, with: "First morning at sea." Isherwood's modes of travel—by river-boat, car and bus—were deliberately rough. Most visitors went to Ecuador by train; Isherwood hired a car that broke down on a road which was "no more than a neglected trail, boggy and rough, with a big rocky hump in the middle."[28] He continued the journey on a "racing bus [that] creaks and rolls like a boat amidst its clouds of dust" and took thirteen uncomfortable hours to go 175 miles. He satirized the grimly devout American tourists who followed the via dolorosa "over the mountains from Lima to Buenos Aires—gasping in the high altitudes, vomiting and terrified in planes, rattled like dice in buses, dragged out before dawn to race along precipice-roads, poisoned with strange foods, tricked by shopkeepers, appalled by toilets." But he also suffered similar experiences.

In Sardinia, Lawrence wrote, "sights are an irritating bore. Thank heaven there isn't a bit of Perugino or anything Pisan in the place: that I know of. Happy is the town that has nothing to show."[29] Isherwood, who wrote more interestingly on the country than the city, also tried to avoid tourist attractions. He found it much more pleasant to drink beer on the hotel balcony than to see Curaçao, and perversely decided to walk around the dirty, shabby little port of La Guaira than to travel twenty miles inland to Caracas. Bogotá was hideously ugly, the mud-thick streets of Puerto Berrío cheerful and alive. Easily tired by the splendor of churches and palaces, he thought the slums of Guayaquil looked beautiful. He provided only a perfunctory description of the astonishing Inca ruins of Machu Picchu and gave up entirely on the great colonial town of Peru: "There is no sense in my trying to describe Cuzco; I should only be quoting from the guide-book."

Just as Lawrence had said that he "couldn't live [in Sardinia]—one would be weary-dreary. I was very disappointed,"[30] so Isherwood was severely disenchanted by his journey. It never had a *raison d'être* and failed to satisfy his need for a goal. The irony of travel, Isherwood bitterly observed, was that "you spend your boyhood dreaming of a magic, impossibly distant day when you will cross the equator, when your eyes will behold Quito. And then, in the slow prosaic process of life, that day dramatically dawns—and finds you sleepy, hungry and dull. The equator is just another valley; you aren't sure which and you don't much care."

"The truth is that South America *bored* me," he explained to friends, "and I am ashamed that it bored me, and I hate it for making me feel ashamed. . . . I should really have approached it in the spirit of [Henry Miller's] *The Air-Conditioned Nightmare*, but my fatal politeness gripped my pen."[31] The suppression or omission of Isherwood's true feelings, the loss of spontaneity and honesty, the tantalizingly brief description of Jorge Luis Borges and the vagueness about his previous sexual relations with Berthold Szczesny (who had become a prosperous businessman in Argentina), made *The Condor and the Cows* a less successful book than *Journey to a War*.

In *Sea and Sardinia* Lawrence focused on the unpleasant aspect of the journey. Messina was dismal and horrible; Palermo windy and desolate. The ship was late, the cabin smelly, the food disgusting. Trapani, which looked so lovely from a distance, was filthy and crude. In *The Condor and the Cows*, Isherwood also wrote a kind of anti-travel book. He described his psychological discomfort in Bogotá and his negative mood in La Paz: "In the mornings I feel tense, restless and uneasy; in the afternoons lazy, exhausted and sad. . . . We had grown weary, weary to the bone, of those inhumanly gigantic mountains, that sombre plateau haunted by its Incaic ghosts, that weird rarefied manic-depressive atmosphere." He dwelled on his diarrhea and vomiting as well as on his altitude sickness: "waking, suddenly breathless, at about 3 a.m.—you lean out of the window and gasp for air; palpitations, gas-pains and causeless anxiety." The travelers' tension inexplicably erupted when Caskey, drunk on Pisco Sours, leaned over and slapped Isherwood's face.

Just as Lawrence used the contrast between the lemon gardens and the mechanical door, the peasant Paolo and the worker Giovanni, the self-absorbed spinner and the regimented monks to symbolize his attitudes in *Twilight in Italy*, so Isherwood suggested his revulsion from the cruelty and violence (which Lawrence had experienced in Mexico) in a series of symbolic anecdotes. There were alligators on the edge of the water, "their mouths slightly open with an air of contented depravity"; shrunken heads "prepared by medical students from cadavers in the dissecting-room"; bodies that writhed convulsively, eyes that bulged and stared during shock-treatments in a madhouse; Indians who had sexual intercourse with syphilitic llamas; would-be suicides at the Falls of Tequendama, protectively handcuffed to a policeman, who "try to drag him with them into the water"; condors that peck "the eyes out of cows and then drive them with their wings off the edge of a cliff."[32]

V. GRAHAM GREENE, *THE LAWLESS ROADS* (1939)

Conrad's menacing mood and Stevenson's melodramatic adventures were the main influences on Graham Greene.[33] But Greene also learned a good deal from Lawrence, who adopted many of the characteristics of Stevenson's travel books.[34] Lawrence lamented: "We have lost the art of living." But he believed the Etruscans, by their still vivid example—their "profound belief in life, acceptance of life"[35]—could restore their precious gifts to modern man. In *Journey Without Maps* (1936), Greene too tried to discover what had gone wrong in the modern world by seeking man's primitive origins in Liberia: "when one sees to what unhappiness, to what peril of extinction centuries of cerebration have brought us, one sometimes has a curiosity to discover if one can from what we have come, to recall at which point we went astray."[36]

In the spring of 1938 Greene, who knew little Spanish, was

commissioned to write a book on religious persecution in Mexico. He traveled in a circle from Laredo on the American border, south to Monterrey, San Luis Potosí and Mexico City; east to Vera Cruz on the Gulf of Mexico; by boat to Frontera in the southern state of Tabasco; and through the state of Chiapas to Tuxtla. From there he flew north to Oaxaca (where Lawrence had written *The Plumed Serpent*) and to Mexico City. He saw Puebla, Taxco and Cuernavaca; and left by ship, traveling third class, from Vera Cruz.

Greene's reaction to the violence and brutality of the country resembled the fear and scorn which Lawrence had expressed in letters from Mexico City in November 1924 (quoted with approval in *The Lawless Roads*):

'This city doesn't feel *right*—feels like a criminal plotting his next rather mean crime,' and again, 'I *really* feel cynical about these "patriots" and "socialists" down here. It's a mess,' underlining his words like Queen Victoria. 'You know, socialism is a dud. It makes just a mush of people: and especially of savages. And 70 per cent of these people are real savages, quite as much as they were 300 years ago. The Spanish-Mexican population just rots on top of the black savage mass. And socialism here is a farce of farces: except very dangerous.'[37]

A consumptive in the car to Puebla had "a black Lawrence beard." And the burning of the saints and statues during the auto-da-fé in Salto de Agua was similar to the "Auto da Fé" chapter in *The Plumed Serpent* (1926)—except that Greene lamented and Lawrence celebrated the replacement of the Dead Christ by the dark gods of the Aztecs: "The crowd scattered in the wind, rebozos waving wildly, leaves torn, dust racing. Sayula was empty of God, and, at heart, they were glad."[38]

Greene's book reeked of propaganda and piety. He mentioned neither the social progress and land reform that took place during the Mexican revolution nor the exploitation and oppression practiced by the Catholic Church. He referred to Díaz, Villa, Madero, Huerta, Carranza, Cardenas and the Cristeros, but did not give a clear picture of the historical background.[39] He unconvincingly compared the martyred Father Miguel Pro to the brilliant Renaissance martyr, Edmund Campion, and claimed that "President Calles had begun the fiercest persecution of religion anywhere since the reign of Elizabeth." The fact that Greene traveled openly as a Catholic and as a foreigner investigated the "war for the soul of the Indian" seriously undermined this claim.

Other statements were also extremely dubious. Greene mocked rumors of a Stalinist plot against Trotsky, who was murdered in Mexico the following year by one of Stalin's agents. He stated that Mexican education was Fascist, rather than Socialist. And he insisted that "the only body in the world to-day which consistently . . . opposes the totalitarian State is the Catholic Church"—though it had consistently cooperated with Mussolini and actively supported Franco in the Spanish Civil War. As in *Letters from Iceland* and *Journey to a War*, also written in the late 1930s, the references to the fighting in Spain and the *Anschluss* in Austria emphasized the menace of Fascism and the threat of global war. The Mexican Catholics in Las Casas, like the volunteers in Greene's cabin on the Nazi ship from Vera Cruz, were all pro-Franco.[40]

Greene also seemed as gullible and superstitious as the Mexican Indians. He illogically argued: "Even if it were all untrue and there were no God, surely life was happier with the enormous supernatural promise." He believed that in 1531 a peasant had a vision of the Virgin of Guadalupe. And he searched for a miraculous speaking image in Sanoyo, which turned out to be "a little hollow head made, I think, of lead like a toy soldier."

Mexico was a perfect subject for Greene, who specialized in squalor. He soon developed a pathological hatred for both the country and the people that surpassed the most rabid ravings of Lawrence. Greene began with the familiar Lawrencean illusions about travel and observed: "There is always something exhilarating about moving inward from the sea into an unknown country," but he quickly lapsed into disappointment and despair. Mexico, he felt, was even more horrible than the African bush. The food was tasteless and repellent. The dingy hotels had dead beetles and smelled of urine. The side streets of Laredo "were ankle-deep in mud, and there was nobody to talk to." Mexico City had the sick smell of sweets and a legion of lottery sellers. The market in Orizaba was filled with flies and ordure, and its river stank of a rubbish dump. "One's standard in Mexico," Greene remarked, "falls with brutal rapidity."

The atmosphere and people matched the place. The hostility to foreigners intensified after the government expropriated the foreign oil companies.[41] Law was non-existent, corruption rampant, human life cheap. Idealism quickly degenerated into brutality, which emanated from the evil Aztec soil. All monuments in Mexico commemorated violent deaths.

Greene's book became considerably more interesting—and more horrible—when he traveled to the primitive and repressive regions of Tabasco and Chiapas, "the only two states left where Catholics cannot receive the Sacraments of their faith except secretly." He was repeatedly warned about the sea trip to Frontera. One man said: "I wouldn't go in one of those boats for a thousand dollars"; another told him: "Nothing will ever make me go on that boat again." Greene remained sceptical. As he recklessly bought his ticket, they talked about him with pity and amusement. The boat was far worse than he had ever imagined or feared. Breakfast, he said, was "a plate of anonymous fish scraps from which the eyeballs stood mournfully out. I couldn't face it, and rashly made my way down to the only privy: a horrible cupboard in the engine-room with no ventilation, no flushing, and the ordure of I don't know how many days and voyages."

The fourteen-hour mule ride to the ruins of Palenque matched the boat trip. It was one of the worst days Greene had ever experienced—the worst boredom, fear and exhaustion. He would raise his damp cardboard sun hat for coolness and then lower it for fear: "So one always starts a journey in a strange land—taking too many precautions, until one tires of the exertion and abandons care in the worst spot of all." When he reached Palenque, he was too weary to see the ruins.

Marooned for a week in remote Yajalon, waiting for a plane that never arrived, Greene caught fleas and listened to the rats in his room: "It was like the grave, the earth taking over before its day." After reaching Las Casas, the farthest point and real object of his journey, he was too tired, disgusted and depressed to enjoy the rare happy moments—the amazing beauty of northern Chiapas, the bosky squares of Oaxaca, the wounded beauty of Puebla—which stood out like plums in a vomit.

VI. HENRY MILLER, *THE COLOSSUS OF MAROUSSI* (1941)

In *The Wisdom of the Heart*, Henry Miller wrote: "The world of Lawrence seems to me like a strange island on which for a number of years I was stranded."[42] He considered Lawrence "an artist worthy of being put alongside Dante or Shakespeare or Goethe."[43] Miller was attracted to the primitive, passionate, orgiastic, orgasmic aspects of Lawrence. He admired in the modern Greeks what Lawrence had admired in the Etruscans and the American Indians: "their dark, passionate, mysterious and powerful qualities. Anti-mechanical, anti-scientific, anti-logical." For Miller, Lawrence was "the symbol of life because he has made the supreme identification with life. ... His message was: 'enjoy all experience to the fullest.' "[44] Miller identified with Lawrence's eccentric view of things, his spontaneous response to experience and his opposition to conventional values.

Miller absorbed more and learned less from Lawrence than any other travel writer. He exalted rather than described Greece in an indiscriminate series of effusive passages: "This is where I begin to exult. ... Nobody can explain anything which is unique. One can describe, worship and adore."[45] And he carried Lawrence's mannerisms and idiosyncrasies—egoism, enthusiasm and muddled mysticism—to absurd extremes. In Corfu, "the palate itself became metaphysically attuned: the drama was of the airs, of the upper regions, of the eternal conflict between the soul [body?] and the spirit." At Epidaurus, he "felt a stillness so intense that for a fraction of a second [he] heard the great heart of the world beat." At Thebes, there was "an invisible corridor of time, a vast, breathless parenthesis which swells like the uterus and having bowelled forth its anguish relapses like a run-down clock." Miller lacked Lawrence's art; and his badly written, repetitive, formless book shows the *negative* influence of the master.

Lawrence and Miller were both influenced by Whitman,[46] whom Miller praised as "the only great writer we ever had." Miller's book was characterized by a Whitmaniac quest for experience: "I want to see the sky, the big birds, the short grass, the waves of blinding light, the swamp mist rising over the plain," and ended with an effective catalogue of the things he loved best in Greece. Like Lawrence in *Etruscan Places*, Miller was aware that "the earth is sown with the bodies and relics of legendary figures." But, unlike Lawrence and other travel writers who read up on their subject and made a serious attempt to provide historical background, Miller actually boasted about his ignorance. He admitted that he could never bring himself to read a line of Homer, that he had "but the scantiest knowledge of Greek history and even that is thoroughly confused."[47] Like Lawrence, who wrote, "Comes over one an absolute necessity to move," Miller could not explain his sudden departure from Thebes—"except that best of all reasons, imperious desire." Shackled prisoners gratuitously appeared at the beginning and end of *Colossus*. But Miller did not, like Lawrence in *Sea and Sardinia*, transform them into figures who had a thematic purpose, symbolized absolute evil and should have been "hung at once."[48]

Following Lawrence, Miller condemned the "blight called Christianity" and rejected contemporary European civilization. He contrasted the vitality of Greece to the soulless, mechanical existence of America,[49] which had given him so many shocks and bruises. But he kept meeting materialistic Greeks who were desperately eager to go—or return—to America, who wanted to acquire "more machines, more efficiency, more capital, more comforts."[50]

In *The World of Lawrence*, Miller observed: "All longing for travel, adventure, exploration, is based on a desire to experience life more fully. It is a protest, or admission therefore, against the flatness, exhaustion of the customary stale routine."[51] From July to December 1939 Miller took a long vacation and abstained from writing. He traveled to Athens and to Corfu; to Nauplia, Epidaurus, Mycenae and Mistras in the Peloponnesus; to the islands of Poros, Hydra and Spetsai; to Delphi and to Crete. He drifted and took what came along, tried to see everything "as if for the first time," maintained his keen expectations and sense of adventure. Like Lawrence, he avoided dreary churches, palaces, libraries, museums and public statues. Like Greene at Palenque he did not even bother to see the magnificent Byzantine ruins at Mistras. Miller found the "man-sized" landscape healing and soothing, and felt: "The light of Greece opened my eyes, penetrated my pores, expanded my whole being."

The Colossus of Maroussi, like all books by Miller, was more about himself than his ostensible subject. The three most potentially interesting characters—his friend Lawrence Durrell, the Greek poet George Seferis and the eponymous colossus, George Katsimbalis—were mere extensions of Miller and did not come alive. Miller's literary persona was *faux-naïf*, intellectually pretentious and banal: "Nature can cure only when man recognizes his place in the world ... the link between the natural and the divine." Miller rhapsodized about the enthusiastic, curious, passionate, direct, approachable, generous, "open, frank, natural, spontaneous, warm-hearted" Greeks, who lived in harmony with their surroundings. But the principal impression conveyed by the book is that the natives were simple people who admired Miller enormously.

The war theme appeared in Miller's book as it did in the works of Auden, MacNeice, Isherwood and Greene. Miller mentioned the massacre of the Greeks at Smyrna in 1922 and the destruction of Shanghai during the Sino-Japanese War. He was unexpectedly forced to leave Corfu when war threatened and the Greek army mobilized. War broke out when he was in Athens and the American Consul ordered him to return home immediately. But, unlike Lawrence and his committed followers in the 1930s, the solipsistic and irresponsible Miller was "thoroughly and completely indifferent to the fate of the world." As Orwell observed of Miller in "Inside the Whale": "He believes in the impending ruin of Western Civilisation much more firmly than the majority of 'revolutionary' writers; only he does not feel called upon to do anything about it. ... He has performed the essential Jonah act of allowing himself to be swallowed, remaining passive, *accepting*."[52]

VII. LAWRENCE DURRELL, *BITTER LEMONS* (1957)

Lawrence Durrell and Gerald Brenan were the only travel writers in the Lawrence tradition who spoke the language of the country and resided in rather than journeyed through the places they described. Durrell had lived in Corfu, Athens, Cairo, Rhodes, Belgrade (and Buenos Aires) from 1936 to 1952 and acquired a thorough knowledge of the eastern Mediterranean. *Bitter Lemons*, his "impressionistic study of the moods and atmospheres of Cyprus during the troubled years 1953–6,"⁵³ continued his excellent series of island books. *Prospero's Cell* (1945) concerned Corfu; *Reflections on a Marine Venus* (1953) described Rhodes.⁵⁴

In his correspondence with Henry Miller, Durrell discussed the personal and political aspects of his life on Cyprus. He wrote that the island, "a piece of Asia Minor washed out to sea . . . has the lazy moist sensuality of the Eastern Levant."⁵⁵ He called the troubled years "a very queer and thrilling period, sad, weighed down with futility and disgust," and was critical of the short-sighted British policy: "Clearly we can't go on being a great power if our political grasp of things is so elementary."⁵⁶ We learn from Durrell's letters, though not from his book, that his mother was looking after his house and caring for his baby, Sappho, because his wife Eve was recovering from a nervous breakdown in England; and that Durrell met his second wife, Claude, on Cyprus. Though he first taught English for thirty hours a week in Nicosia and then worked even longer hours as Press Adviser to the Government, he was also writing *Justine* (1957), which brought him international fame.

In *Spirit of Place*, whose title was borrowed from Lawrence, Durrell recalled his method in *Bitter Lemons* and observed that the travel writer's "task is to isolate the germ in the people which is expressed by their landscape. . . . But how few they are those writers! How many can write a *Sea and Sardinia* or a *Twilight in Italy* to match those two gems of D. H. Lawrence?" Durrell qualified his praise by criticizing Lawrence's great strengths: "Genius that he was, he carried too much intellectual baggage about him on his travels, too many preconceptions; and while the mirror he holds up to Mexico, Italy, England is a marvellous triumph of art, the image is often a bit out of focus."⁵⁷ Despite his reservations, Durrell, more than any other travel writer, came closest to recapturing brilliantly Lawrence's spontaneous response to people and places, his vivid style, his organic structure and his symbolic scenes.

Durrell's lyric and tragic book was structured by his search for and symbolic rebuilding of an old Turkish house in the Greek village of Bellapaix. The constructive progress of the house and destructive outbreak of political violence ran parallel. Though Durrell had Irish parentage, was born in India and led an expatriate life, he was completely loyal to the British. He was forced to leave the village to work in the capital. And the insurrection of the Greek Cypriots, who wanted to break away from British rule and become united with Greece, made it impossible for him to return to Bellapaix and finally drove him off the island. The great and moving theme of *Bitter Lemons* was paradise lost.

Durrell provided the little-known historical background of the island—which had been governed by Crusaders, Venetians, Turks and British—as well as learned epigraphs, bibliography and index. He did not want to live the deformed and refined suburban life the British had established in the northern port of Kyrenia. He wished to learn about the island by "sharing a common life with the humble villagers of the place . . . to expand [his] field of investigation to its history—the lamp which illumines national character—in order to offer [his] live subjects a frame against which to set themselves."

Durrell was fortunate to find Bellapaix, in the hills above Kyrenia, which was so idyllic that he feared he would never do any work there. The village had a spectacular view, honey and nightingales, silkworms that sounded like a crisp forest fire, a ruined Gothic abbey with a church still in use, balconies spanning the narrow conversational streets, a huge Tree of Idleness under which the villagers gathered to drink and gossip, and an atmosphere of guileless joy.

Durrell did not "make the 'big gentleman.' " But he adopted local manners as protective coloring, manipulated the naive villagers and got what he wanted by a rhetorical yet cunning mode of flattery. He convinced Sabri to find him a house by saying: " 'You are obviously a Turkish gentleman, and I feel I can confide myself entirely in your care. . . . I have nothing to offer except gratitude and friendship. I ask you as a Turkish gentleman to assist me.' . . . I could see that I had scored a diplomatic stroke in throwing myself completely upon the iron law of hospitality which underpins all relations in the Levant." He won the friendship of Morais, a hostile nationalist villager, by declaiming: " 'I have come to live with you. I know what Greek hospitality is. I want you to know that I am always ready to be of service to my neighbour. I have heard praise of you everywhere in the village as a fine and honest farmer.' " And he obtained precious water rights from Pallis by stating: " 'My dear fellow, no Greek would charge that. . . . You astonish me'. . . . I brought him to his knees by comparing the Greek sense of 'philoxenia' with the Cypriot. He melted like an ice."

Durrell's Eden was penetrated and the air of suffocating inertia disturbed when the agitation for Enosis (union with Greece) led to strikes, demonstrations, shootings and bombings. The narrow-minded British Colonial Office, which ignored the views of both Athens and Ankara, offered an unsatisfactory constitution that was promptly and predictably rejected. Troops opened fire at Limassol, wounding three youths, but the atmosphere remained charged with a carnival air. Arms and dynamite were sent to the rebels from Greece, but the police captured the caique with cargo and crew. While waiting at dawn for the arms to appear, Durrell ironically combined rhapsodic and disgusting descriptions of the beach at Paphos, on the southwest coast, to convey the bittersweet mood of the book. He listened "to the oldest sound in European history, the sighing of the waves as they thickened into roundels of foam and hissed upon that carpet of discoloured sand." And he watched a lean dog dig out and feast on the decomposed entrails of a sea-turtle that lay dead on the beach.

As synchronized explosions erupted around the island, Durrell realized that the British were facing two kinds of enemies: idealistic schoolboys and mountain bandits. It was extremely difficult to maintain control and to gather evidence against these criminals. The Turks, outnumbered five to one, urged more repressive measures. Durrell defended the British decency and democracy, though it weakened their hold on the island, and rejected the German or Russian solution: a series of mass murders and deportations that would have solved the Enosis problem in half an hour.[58]

After failure at the London Conference and the United Nations, the unreal atmosphere became normal. The flavor of terrorism produced intangible fears that reminded Durrell of war in the Western Desert, of fighting in Kenya and Malaya. Durrell borrowed a pistol; Field Marshal Sir John Harding arrived to restore public order and strengthen the weakest link in NATO.

In the midst of all this, Durrell and his schoolmaster friend Panos escaped into the mountains to gather wild flowers. But their idyll was interrupted while they were eating and drinking among the butterflies. They heard a shot and were startled by the hostile approach of a man with a gun. Panos cursed "at the humiliation of having to feel afraid in the presence of an unknown man—a sensation so foreign to Cyprus as to be quite frightening in itself." They were relieved to recognize the stranger as an old friend. This symbolic scene revealed how Durrell learned from Lawrence to express, subtly and effectively, the complex themes of *Bitter Lemons*.

Panos and Durrell returned from the mountains to learn that Karaolis, who had committed murder for the cause of Enosis, had been sentenced by the British to hang. Durrell believed that this decision, though judicially correct, was politically disastrous. He felt he had achieved nothing during his two years as a servant of the crown, took four months' leave and was glad to depart the island. Though his old neighbor Michaelis admitted, "we were happy enough before these things happened. . . . the sight of an Englishman had become an obscenity on that clear honey-gold spring air." Durrell never came back to reside on the island, and on March 26, 1957, he bitterly wrote to Richard Aldington: "[I] bought and made over a ravishing Turkish house in Cyprus which is now too dangerous to live in, and under present circum[stance]s unsaleable! I should have moved into France and Italy while I had a little capital."[59]

VIII. GERALD BRENAN, *SOUTH FROM GRANADA* (1957)

Gerald Brenan's journey to Spain in 1919 was clearly influenced by Lawrence's life and art. Like Lawrence, Brenan was rebelling against middle-class existence and an England "petrified by class feeling and by rigid conventions." He wanted to find a society which was not "conditioned by the rhythm of its machines . . . which put the deeper needs of human nature before the technical organization that is required to provide a higher standard of living."[60]

South from Granada was an account of Brenan's seven years in the remote Spanish village of Yegen. He portrayed himself as simple, rough, earnest, independent; a bit muddled, careless with money and extremely poor. He was curious, self-educated and somewhat pedantic, interested in nature and common folk as well as in botany, geology, archeology, history and poetry. In *Personal Record* he wrote: "I was immune to lonelinesss so long as I had books to read, mountains to climb and Spanish country people to talk to."[61] In that book he also described his turbulent love affair with a village girl and revealed that he had a daughter by his second maid, the "White" Maria.

The style and structure of *South from Granada* matched Brenan's character. He was engagingly casual and informal ("But where shall I begin?"); combined anecdote with history, experience with learned references. He explained what he was doing as he went along ("I have now put down what I can remember of my life at Yegen up to the spring of 1924") and urged his readers to skip the potentially boring pages on geography and prehistory. He chose not to describe the visits of Roger Fry and Bertrand Russell, as he had vividly described those of Lytton Strachey and Virginia Woolf, because his book was "coming to an end."

Brenan wrote that in the fall of 1919 "I had just been demobilized and was looking for a house where I could live for as long as possible on my officer's bounty." He went to Spain to educate himself and to write, and has spent most of his life there. Like Durrell, he became deeply attached to the serene and timeless atmosphere of the village and to its magnificent view that sometimes included the Atlas mountains, across the Straits of Gibraltar in Morocco. He expressed his feelings about Yegen—which was fifty-seven miles from Almeria, stood 4,000 feet high and had 1,000 inhabitants—in an epigraph from Horace's *Odes* (II.6), which I translate as:

> Every corner of that land beyond smiles at me,
> Where the honey equals that of Hymettus,
> And the olive vies with the green of Venafrum.
> Where Jupiter provides a long spring and a mild winter.

His book described Yegen's "customs, its folk-lore, its festivals, and a certain number of its more striking characters with their quarrels and love affairs."

The main, Lawrencean attraction of the village was the sense of ritual in the life of the people. During the 1920s, when Lawrence lived in Italy, the pagan and primitive elements in the religious rites confirmed his belief that traditional life was superior to the industrialization of the modern age, and put him back in touch with essential emotions that had been lost in contemporary society. He saw the tragedy of modern existence in the lack of physical vitality, the emptiness in the lives of civilized people. The peasants provided a way for Lawrence to mediate between mechanized humans and the non-human world of animals and flowers. For the same reasons and in the same way, Brenan admired the self-contained life of his village. It had "just the proper degree of isolation and strength of tradition to draw out the lively and human qualities of the inhabitants as far as they would go." The village had a "primitive community feeling" and everyone who lived there "felt assured of possessing a niche in society which was his by right."

Lawrence particularly praised the Mediterranean peasants, who provided a standard of masculine behavior that made his fellow Englishmen seem repressed and even impotent. The warm, extroverted people worshipped the mother, were devoted to the family, and maintained clear sexual divisions between men and women—a notable contrast to the cocksure women and hensure men in the "more advanced" society of England. Brenan criticized Lawrence's belief that "the sexual life of these peoples . . . was stronger or more free from guilt than that of the Anglo-Saxons." But he entirely agreed with Lawrence about the value of strongly defined sexual roles: "from childhood men were taught to put their pride in being as manly as possible, and women to put theirs in being womanly. . . . How different to the state towards which we seemed to be moving in England in which, in the name of justice and equality, men and women were to be as like one another as possible!"[62]

Lawrence admired and translated the works of the Sicilian novelist Giovanni Verga. Verga's characters—like Lawrence's Italians and Brenan's Spaniards—had a strong family sense, a bond with the rural community, a vital relation to the changing seasons and a connection to the landscape that seemed to exist as an independent force. Lawrence emphasized the heroic stature of Verga's Mastro-don Gesualdo by relating the modern Sicilians to the classical Greeks, who had colonized the island before the age of Theocritus. He asserted that Gesualdo had the old Greek impulse toward splendor and self-enhancement, and might really be a Greek in a modern setting: "He has the energy, the quickness, the vividness of the Greek, the same vivid passion for wealth, the same ambition, the same lack of scruples, the same queer openness."[63] Brenan made precisely the same comparison in *South from Granada* when he observed: "Those who have lived for long in villages in the south of Europe will have noticed how many of the petty dramas of peasant life recall those of classical Greek tragedy. The Fates, the Furies, catastrophic lusts and hatreds, examples of hubris and of demonic possession all find their place ... in these communities."

Brenan's visit to a half-crazy Scots neighbor, a rare change from the isolation of village life, provided a striking contrast of character. The drunken, spendthrift, scandalous MacTaggart, who loathed the Spaniards and had never bothered to learn their language, had lost his dignity and forfeited their respect. MacTaggart exclaimed: "The people of this country are very untrustworthy. . . . Their nerve has gone, there's nothing left of all their past pride and spirit." But Brenan, unlike the Scotsman and all the other travel writers in the Lawrence tradition, never became disillusioned. He remained loyal to Spain throughout his life, became the leading English authority on the country and still lives there. *South from Granada*, the best book on Spain, was an affectionate and moving tribute to "a pattern of living which, though rude and primitive was worth preserving."

IX

Lawrence influenced these seven travel writers in different ways. They all adopted his focus on the exhilaration and discomfort, on the personality and ideas of the narrator; his desire to escape; his attraction to traditional culture; his criticism of industrial society; his hostility to Fascism. These writers acutely felt the threat of European war. But, in fleeing from it, Auden, Isherwood, Greene, Durrell and (later on) Brenan ironically encountered civil war in China, Mexico, Cyprus and Spain.

The success of the travel books was largely determined by their original inspiration, by whether they were commissioned or (as Lawrence's works always were) spontaneous. Auden and his co-authors, MacNeice and Isherwood, did not particularly like the countries they visited, and took their journey and their books as a lark. Isherwood and Greene felt boredom in and hatred for South America and Mexico. They dutifully followed their itinerary, fulfilled their obligations and—almost relishing their misery—completed their rather depressing books.

Miller, the least intelligent and most muddled of these writers, drifted into Greece and adored the country with indiscriminate enthusiasm. He was overwhelmed rather than inspired by Lawrence and exaggerated Lawrence's worst characteristics. Durrell and Brenan, who spent years in Cyprus and in Spain, best learned the lesson of the master. They subtly absorbed Lawrence's sensitivity and style, his recreation of character and landscape, his selection of detail and symbolic scenes, his primitivism and vitalism. Durrell and Brenan admired the Cypriots and Spaniards as Lawrence had admired the Etruscans. To these people, "all was alive; the whole universe lived; and the business of man was himself to live amid it all. He had to draw life into himself, out of the wandering huge vitalities of the world."[64]

CHAPTER FIVE
Lawrence and American Poetry

ROBERTS W. FRENCH

I

Although D. H. Lawrence occupies a uniquely important place in the development of modern American poetry, his role is often obscured. He was English; and those who have sought the major influences behind the innovative poetry that has become, over the last twenty-five years, the dominant American mode have gone to American poets: to Walt Whitman, William Carlos Williams and Ezra Pound.[1] The fact remains, however, that Lawrence is, in his way, a part of the American poetic tradition. By far the most important influence on his own poetry was Whitman, and it was in large part through Lawrence that Whitman was brought into the twentieth century, for Lawrence was the first major poet to make extended use of Whitman's stylistic discoveries. Because Lawrence was a pioneer in developing a distinctly American mode of writing, many American poets have looked to him for direction and encouragement. In general, those who acknowledge the influence of Whitman, Williams and Pound in shaping their poetry also acknowledge Lawrence.

While Lawrence has significantly influenced American poetry, in his relationships with American poets he remained, characteristically, the outsider. Of the major figures of his time—Pound, Eliot, Williams, Frost, Stevens—he met only Pound, and only for a few times in 1909 and 1910. Their first meeting left Lawrence impressed. In a letter to Louie Burrows he described Pound as "a well-known American poet—a good one. He is 24, like me," Lawrence continued, "but his god is beauty, mine, life. He is jolly nice: took me to supper at Pagnani's, and afterwards we went down to his room at

Kensington. ... He is rather remarkable—a good bit of a genius, and with not the least self-consciousness."[2]

Although Pound disliked Lawrence personally, he nevertheless recognized the value of his work. When Pound reviewed *Love Poems and Others* in 1913, he called it "the most important book of poems of the season," adding that "Mr Lawrence has attempted realism and attained it. He has brought contemporary verse up to the level of contemporary prose, and that is no mean achievement."[3] Pound's comments about Lawrence in his letters were equally laudatory, despite his personal hostility. "Detestable person," he wrote to Harriet Monroe in 1913, "but needs watching. I think he learned the proper treatment of modern subjects before I did."[4] It was the accuracy of perception that mattered most to Pound at this time. The poems had the ring of truth about them; as Pound said in his review, "The characters are real."

T. S. Eliot wrote no reviews of Lawrence's poetry, and in his published writings we have only a scattering of references to Lawrence, none earlier than 1927. On Lawrence's side the story is quickly told: although he and Eliot shared a number of mutual acquaintances, and although they moved, for a time, in somewhat similar circles (the Cambridge–Bloomsbury group in particular), they never met, and Lawrence seems hardly to have been aware of Eliot's existence. He does not refer to him in his critical writings or in the extensive posthumous collections of *Phoenix* and *Phoenix II*; and in the several thousand pages of published correspondence there is only one reference to Eliot. That comes late, in 1929, when Lawrence says in his last letter to John Middleton Murry, rejecting Murry's overtures of friendship, "The animal that I am you instinctively dislike—just as all the Lynds and Squires and Eliots and Goulds instinctively dislike it."[5] Robert Lynd, J. C. Squire and Gerald Gould had written unfavorable comments on *The Rainbow*. The inclusion of Eliot is a little harder to explain, but a possible cause—apart from anything that Lawrence may have heard from mutual acquaintances—is Eliot's first published commentary on Lawrence (the only one Lawrence could have seen), an article entitled "Le Roman Anglais Contemporain" that appeared, in French, in *La Nouvelle Revue Française*, May 1, 1927. In the English text of this article Eliot said about Lawrence, among other generally unappreciative (and sometimes uninformed) comments:

> Mr. Lawrence is a demoniac, a natural and unsophisticated demoniac with a gospel. When his characters make love—or perform Mr. Lawrence's equivalent for love-making—and they do nothing else—they not only lose all the amenities, refinements and graces which many centuries have built up in order to make love-making tolerable; they seem to reascend the metamorphoses of evolution, passing backward beyond ape and fish to some hideous coition of protoplasm.[6]

If Lawrence showed little concern for Eliot, however, Eliot was considerably bothered by Lawrence, particularly after the mid-1920s, when he had become a Christian convert (1927) and, increasingly, a spokesman for orthodoxy and tradition. Eliot's strongest attack on Lawrence appeared in *After Strange Gods*, where Lawrence was described as "an almost perfect example of the heretic."[7] Nevertheless, Eliot saw Lawrence as an ally as well as an enemy: an ally because he had, like Eliot himself, spoken out frequently against "the living death of modern material civilisation"; an enemy because Lawrence represented "individuality" in all its dangerous excesses rather than the stability of tradition which Eliot considered essential for the spiritual health of civilized culture. As Eliot explained, "The point is that Lawrence started life wholly free from any restriction of tradition or institution, that he had no guidance except the Inner Light, the most untrustworthy and deceitful guide that ever offered itself to wandering humanity." Lawrence was, Eliot concluded, "spiritually sick."[8] Whatever Lawrence may have thought—and there is no reason to believe that he would have been any more sympathetic toward Eliot than Eliot was toward him—Eliot saw him as representing attitudes that were opposed to and irreconcilable with his own.

While Lawrence was distant from Eliot, he had much in common with William Carlos Williams; it is unfortunate that the two never met or exchanged correspondence. For a brief time the possibility was there: in 1926 Lawrence favorably reviewed *In the American Grain* for the *Nation*, and Williams responded by sending Lawrence a laudatory letter, which was never answered. Actually, Lawrence may not have known much about Williams; throughout the review he refers to him as "Mr." Williams, rather than "Dr.," and does not mention him again, either in the published correspondence or in the critical writings.

Most significantly for the development of modern poetry, Lawrence shared with Williams a stylistic freedom and inventiveness that promoted the use of free verse. In this respect, both looked to Whitman as the poet who opened the doors of liberation; and it was Whitman who brought Williams and Lawrence together as major influences behind much recent American poetry. As Karl Shapiro observed in the late 1950s, when the new poetry was emerging from the conflict with formalist tradition, "With D. H. Lawrence, Williams is the leader of what authentic American poetry is being written today."[9] Shapiro's view of Lawrence as a leader of "authentic" American poetry reveals how thoroughly the English poet had been adopted by Americans as an artistic model.

Williams and Lawrence developed independently of each other, so there could be no question of Lawrencean "influence." Still, one might surmise from Williams' "Elegy for D. H. Lawrence" that the English writer was for him, as for so many others, a long-time source of strength and encouragement, an example of passionate energy committed to battle against forces of negation, sterility and death. The opening lines summarize Williams' attitude:

> Green points on the shrub
> and poor Lawrence dead.
> The night damp and misty
> and Lawrence no more in the world
> to answer April's promise
> with a fury of labor
> against waste, waste and life's
> coldness.

There is not much to be said of Lawrence's relationship with Frost, whom he mentions only once in his published correspondence. The reference is slighting. "I believe," he wrote to Eunice Tietjens in 1917, "in America there is the courage of ultimate truth—which in Europe there is *not*—But your

Sandburgs and Untermeyers, even your Edgar Lee Masters or Robert Frosts—the vanity ticklers—no, they are not to be borne."[10] Frost, on the other hand, responded enthusiastically to his discovery of Lawrence. As he wrote to Edward Garnett in 1915, "I'll tell you a poet with a method that is a method: [D. H.] Lawrence. I came across a poem of his in a new Imagiste Anthology just published here, and it was such a poem that I wanted to go right to the man that wrote it and say something."[11] Frost does not comment further, but one might guess that it was Lawrence's terse realism that he, like Pound, found so effective.

And finally, about Wallace Stevens Lawrence says nothing at all, nor, apparently, does Stevens have anything to say about Lawrence. These two great and original poets remain eternally distant from each other, as though to demonstrate the possibilities of twentieth-century Romanticism.

For poets of succeeding generations, however, Lawrence has remained as a challenging resource and a representative of artistic possibility. Stanley Kunitz, for example, includes Lawrence among eight moderns who were "Explorers at the frontiers of the creative intuition. Their images," Kunitz adds, "brought us news."[12] A true Romantic, Lawrence wanted to break out of the prisons that restrain and repress, including, in poetry, the restraints of form. Always he sought authenticity; and he knew that, in order to be authentic, he had to be free to state his feelings of the moment, to be spontaneous, to speak out of instinct and intuition, to allow the voice of the self to be heard over the clamor of conformity. The emphasis on truth-saying remained central; as various critics have pointed out, Lawrence may be intemperate, he may be absurd, he may be embarrassing, but he is never pretentious or dishonest. It is this distinct quality of voice, direct and open, free to say what it must, free to speak what it *feels*, that is one of his most important legacies to many American poets. Robert Duncan, to name one, has spoken of the important development of freedom in the voice of poetry, "the freedom which is essentially the freedom of a created 'I' that can do anything in a poem." He finds such freedom in Whitman, in the Pound of *Personae*, in the Williams of *Spring and All*, and particularly, among moderns, in Lawrence: "Lawrence has it all the way through, of course."[13]

II

Ultimately, freedom in poetry meant, for Lawrence, free verse. His introduction to the American edition of *New Poems* (1918) celebrates free verse with all the excitement of discovery. "Much," he remarked, "has been written about free verse. But all that can be said, first and last, is that free verse is, or should be, direct utterance from the instant, whole man. It is the soul and the mind and body surging at once, nothing left out."[14] Free verse broke the chains; it was not poetry as *art* that mattered, but poetry as *expression*, unfinished though it may appear.

In a time when free verse is widely practiced, it is important to remember that, until recently, poets hesitated to use other than traditional forms. "As late as the 1950s," Louis Simpson (born 1923) has testified, "American poets were expected to write in meter and rhyme."[15] The broad acceptance of free verse was a long time coming. "I can remember," writes Marvin Bell (born 1937), "having to defend my practice of 'free verse' in workshops. Someone might raise an eyebrow and say, 'This appears to be written in free verse.' 'Oh no,' I'd reply, 'it's written in sprung accentuals with variant lines.' " Poetry has changed, Bell adds, "because we have gone back to thinking of poetry as something more than a bundle of techniques."[16]

As poets in the 1950s and 1960s increasingly felt the limitations of traditional forms, many looked for a way out. In an interview of 1961, Robert Lowell described both the situation of the time and his particular problems as a poet:

> Poets of my generation and particularly younger ones have gotten terribly proficient at these [tightly compressed, metrical] forms. ... Yet the writing seems divorced from culture somehow. It's become too much something specialized that can't handle much experience. It's become a craft, purely a craft, and there must be some breakthrough back into life.[17]

The emphasis on craft that Lowell came to find repressive unquestionably influenced attitudes toward Lawrence as a poet. Writing in 1957, A. Alvarez noted that

Our modern poetry began with a vigorous attack on outworn conventions of feeling and expression. But the emphasis has gradually gone so much on the craft and technicality of writing that the original wholeness and freshness is again lost. One sort of academic nullity has been replaced by another: the English "gentleman-of-letters" conceit, which prevailed at least until the end of the Georgians, has gone under. In its place is a Germanic *ponderismuskeit*, a deadening technical thoroughness. Lawrence's demon is as out of place in that as it was in the old port-and-tweed tradition.[18]

Partly because Lawrence's poems *were* "out of place" and offensive to orthodoxy, they had distinctive value for many American poets, particularly in the late 1950s. Karl Shapiro suggests the nature of this value in a curious and stimulating essay published in 1959.[19] Shapiro argues that, if he could take only one book of poems with him to a desert island, he would take Lawrence's. This is an odd choice, since Shapiro admits that by any objective standards, including "originality, suitable intensity, applicability, ability to transport, re-readability, contemporaneity," there are better poets, such as Eliot, Pound, Stevens, Yeats and Auden. Furthermore, Shapiro adds, "Lawrence misses the mystery of language-making in his passion for his own ideas," which, he concedes, are all wrong. Nevertheless, Shapiro believes "that Lawrence in his sincerity, fool that he was, broke through the façade of artistry and literary affectation and stood at the doorway of poetry."

Shapiro's answer suggests one of the most widely appealing features of Lawrence's poetry. Lawrence at his best can seem beyond poetry in that he rejects conventional notions of what acceptable poetry is, including demands of craft and technique, and yet his works still stand, impressive and moving. In his dismissal of formal embellishments, Lawrence, like Whitman before him, appears to be approaching essence, to be arriving somehow at the thing itself.

Standing firmly outside the tradition of English poetry, Lawrence asserted rebellious possibility. Not surprisingly, he aroused opposition; and, over the years, it was the opposition of the New Critics that proved most persuasive. Valuing tightly structured, complex, allusive poems, seeking the play of wit and intelligence in poetry, demanding intricate craftsmanship in rhyme and meter, the New Critics could not, for all their great contributions to poetic analysis, adequately deal with such poets as Whitman and Lawrence. Richard Blackmur—whose views can be taken as representative of the New Criticism—dismissed Lawrence by saying, "you cannot talk about the art of his poetry because it exists only at the minimum level of self-expression." Lawrence's poems, Blackmur went on to say, illustrated "the fallacy of the faith in expressive form . . . that if a thing is only intensely enough felt its mere expression in words will give it satisfactory form, the dogma, in short, that once material becomes words it is its own best form."[20]

Blackmur's description, it should be noted, is less than fair to Lawrence, who would never say that intensity of feeling was of itself sufficient for successful poetry; he *would* say, however, that without that intensity no poem could succeed. Often in his letters, when he comments on another's poems, it is the lack of passionate feeling that he singles out as the major weakness. In a letter of 1917 Lawrence had commented, "Art itself doesn't interest me, only the spirit content"[21]—which is not to deny the art, but rather to indicate the standard by which art is to be judged. The art that would stifle the "spirit content" cannot be good art, no matter how elaborate and polished it may be. Lawrence knew what he was about, and he has always appealed to those poets who value the energy of passionate speech over the finish of technique. Robert Bly, for example, has commented,

> Lawrence was a novelist. He doesn't seem to be taken seriously as a poet. He is without "skill" and yet when his poems come out, one out of fifteen or one out of twenty of them is marvelous. If a man has experienced certain things, I'm not sure how much craft is necessary in order to do something that's really . . . marvelous . . . that really has psychic energy. If the craft kills that, obviously we're worse off than we were before.[22]

Bly's paradoxical suggestion, that Lawrence was somehow a successful poet who lacked art, recurs elsewhere in various forms. It is as though readers knew from their responses that the poems worked, were surprised that they did, suspected that they should have failed, and were at a loss to explain their success. Even so astute a reader as W. H. Auden seemed perplexed. "As for [Lawrence's] poetry," he wrote, "when I first tried to read it, I did not like it; despite my admiration for him, it offended my notions of what poetry should be. Today my notions of what poetry should be are still, in all essentials, what they were then and hostile to his, yet there are a number of his poems which I have come to admire enormously."[23]

The mystery—that Lawrence succeeds even while violating the reader's standards of acceptable poetry—suggests that Lawrence discovered a power not attainable in traditional forms. While there are effects open to the traditionalist that he cannot achieve, his successes indicate that he has found the forms sufficient for his uses, thus demonstrating, like other innovators, that the boundaries of poetry extend more widely than custom would allow. Tradition showed what *had* been done; it did not show what *could* be done, and it was the realm of possibility that Lawrence chose to explore.

III

Lawrence's insistence on the spontaneous and expressive nature of poetry was important to many American poets, representing as it did a demonstrable alternative to T. S. Eliot's often-repeated assertions about the impersonality of art. "The progress of an artist," Eliot wrote in his most famous essay (published in 1919), "is a continual self-sacrifice, a continual extinction of personality." About poetry in particular Eliot stated, "Poetry is not a turning loose of emotion, but an escape from emotion; it is not the expression of personality, but an escape from personality."[24] Lawrence stood firmly on the other side: if poetry was not the expression of personality, what could it be? How could it be *authentic* if it did not represent the deepest feelings of the poet?

To many poets who found the dominant poetics dry and academic, Lawrence's emotional force and personal involvement were strongly appealing. Among these poets was Kenneth Rexroth, a major force (not altogether to his pleasure in later years) behind the Beat Generation of the 1950s and their successors, the Hippies of the 1960s and 1970s. Through him, Lawrence's influence reached many to whom Lawrence himself was only vaguely known.

In his comments on Lawrence, Rexroth was always careful to keep his distance, as though to preserve his independence from a poet with whom he had so much in common. Although much about Lawrence displeased him, including the politics ("anti-humane") and the personality ("a rather disgusting man"),[25] Rexroth acknowledged Lawrence to be "certainly one of the major poets of the twentieth century, along with Guillaume Apollinaire and William Carlos Williams."[26] Rexroth followed Lawrence in writing poems that were direct, personal, unpretentious and unadorned, poems that emphasized expressiveness rather than craft.

As early as the 1920s Rexroth was developing the autobiographical mode that Lawrence had made available in his first books, especially in *Look! We Have Come Through!* Rexroth was to become one of the major love poets in American literature, a genre in which Lawrence's influence is particularly significant. While reading Rexroth, one is often reminded of Lawrence: there is the same frankness, the unashamed sensuality, the openness to experience, the free expression of personal feeling, the autobiographical focus, the sense of immediacy, the pressure of memory. While Rexroth is generally more subdued and even-toned than Lawrence, restrained and meditative where Lawrence is energetic and volatile, the fluent ease of his lines—the deliberations of a sensitive man responding to a particular situation—suggests much in the Lawrence of *Look! We Have Come Through!* and of the great *Last Poems*.

In addition to the autobiographical love poetry, Rexroth followed Lawrence in the writing of invective. Like Lawrence, Rexroth could be gentle and sympathetic; he could also be fierce in his denunciations of human brutality, stupidity, pretense and greed. There are poems of Rexroth's that would not be out of place in Lawrence's *Pansies*, *More Pansies* and *Nettles*. Rexroth's "Thou Shalt Not Kill," it should be remembered, has been called the forerunner (and perhaps model) for Allen Ginsberg's *Howl*, and in verbal violence it certainly approaches that poem as well as Lawrence's furious denunciations.

Like Rexroth a poet of love and fury, Sylvia Plath recorded in her journals that she had two masters to whom she went to learn, D. H. Lawrence and Virginia Woolf.[27] Her response to Lawrence was visceral and deeply affecting. After hearing a reading of sections from *The Man Who Died*, for example, she wrote,

> felt chilled, as in last paragraph of "The Dead," as if angel had hauled me by the hair in a shiver of gooseflesh: about the temple of Isis bereaved, Isis in search. Lawrence died in Vence, where I had my mystic vision with [Richard] Sassoon; I was the woman who died, and I came in touch through Sassoon that spring [with] that flaming of life, that resolute fury of existence. All seemed shudderingly relevant; I read in a good deal; I have lived much of this. It matters.[28]

That was not the only time Plath recorded her close identity with Lawrence and his work. She felt that Lawrence was writing her life, that somehow his works anticipated her own feelings, her own situations. While she was teaching at Smith College (1957–58), she read and re-read Lawrence, whom she had assigned for one of her classes. She resented having to share Lawrence with her students. "I don't like talking *about* D. H. Lawrence," she wrote to her brother Warren in the fall of 1957, "and about critics' views of him. I like reading him selfishly for an influence on my own life and my own writing."[29] Her responses continued to be as strong as they were at Cambridge. "Today," she wrote in her journal,

> from coffee till teatime at six, I read in *Lady Chatterley's Lover*, drawn back again with the joy of a woman living with her own gamekeeper, and *Women in Love* and *Sons and Lovers*. Love, love: Why do I feel I would have known and loved Lawrence. How many women must feel this and be wrong! I opened *The Rainbow*, which I have never read, and was sucked into the concluding Ursula and Skrebensky episode and sank back, breath knocked out of me, as I read of their London hotel, their Paris trip, their riverside loving while Ursula studied at college. This is the stuff of my life—my life, different, but no less brilliant and splendid—and the flow of my story will take me beyond this in my way—arrogant?[30]

Plath found in Lawrence a writer to emulate; he encouraged her powerful expression of feeling and appealed to the sensuality evident everywhere in her writing. In her *Journals* she specified what it was in Lawrence that attracted her with such intensity: "the rich physical passion—fields of forces—and the real presence of leaves and earth and beasts and weathers, sap-rich."[31] Lawrence showed Plath how to write in a sensual and emotional way; in his work she found strong feelings and deep sensations that stimulated her own.

Lawrence's poems, especially the later ones, unashamedly represent the expression of a life, direct and open; thus he anticipates the work of the American "confessional" poets. From the beginning, Lawrence was conscious of the strong autobiographical impulse behind his poetry. When he gathered the four volumes of *Love Poems and Others*, *Amores*, *New Poems* and *Bay* into his *Collected Poems* (1928), he noted that he had "tried to establish a chronological order, because many of the poems are so personal that, in their fragmentary fashion, they make up a biography of an emotional and inner life."[32] Even more clearly autobiographical are the poems that Lawrence included in *Look! We Have Come Through!* In his Foreword to this volume, Lawrence indicated that the poems were not isolated lyrics, but rather parts of the same story, held together by the life of one man, referred to in the third person, but clearly the poet. "These poems," he wrote,

> should not be considered separately, as so many single pieces. They are intended as an essential story, or history, or confession, unfolding one from the other in organic development, the whole revealing the intrinsic experience of a man during the crisis of manhood, when he marries and comes into himself. The period covered is, roughly, the sixth lustre of a man's life.[33]

The poems of *Look! We Have Come Through!* are lyrical representations of crisis and discovery; taken together, they constitute something of a notebook or diary of fragmentary realizations. In his way, Lawrence contributes to the development of the modern poetic sequence as it derives from Whitman and Dickinson; the method of *Look! We Have Come Through!* is not, after all, so different from that of Berryman's *Sonnets* and *Dream Songs* or Lowell's *Life Studies*, *History* (in an earlier version called *Notebook*), and—perhaps most comparable—*The Dolphin*, with its focus on marriage and a new beginning in a new land.

Lowell, as has often been noted, passed through extreme formalism to the new style of *Life Studies*, loose, colloquial, flexible, capable of sudden shifts and turns; his development follows, for all its differences, that of Lawrence, who similarly passed through the formalism of his earlier, rhymed poems to the innovative free verse that begins to appear in *Look! We Have Come Through!* What Alfred Kazin wrote in 1959, reviewing *Life Studies*, might well have been said of Lawrence more than forty years earlier: "Here Lowell has achieved the nakedness toward which all good poets yearn—freedom from the suffocating traditions of fine style that in our day have again overcome poetry."[34] In achieving the new style of *Life Studies* Lowell has acknowledged that the free-verse poems of *Birds, Beasts and Flowers* were an essential influence, and ten years after the publication of that work, Lowell still had Lawrence's bird and animal poems sufficiently in mind so as to list them, along with the works of three other poets and some selections from the Bible, as among those poems "that would be thoroughly marred and would indeed be inconceivable in meter."[35]

Lawrence's pioneering was more than stylistic, however; in the range of his moods, and more particularly in the *extremes*, he pointed toward such poetry of intimate revelation as has become prominent in recent years. One feels that Lawrence would say anything, providing that he felt it enough to *want* to say it; he is willing always to take the chance, to pass beyond restraint, beyond decorum, beyond moderation, beyond (it might seem) control. The dangers of such a method, if that is the right word, are obvious, and Lawrence did not always escape them. He can be wordy, flat, dull and pedantic as well as exasperating and offensive; but the point was to keep throwing off poems, to let the energy and passion have its say—to imitate nature in its creative force. Thus Lawrence learned to listen to his demon, the voice within. His poetry chronicles the liberation of the poet.

The theme is Romantic, of course: the freeing of the creative soul from the demands of a destructive and self-denying society so that it may, at last, discover itself, and in so doing take possession of the vast world of its own potential. It is Emerson's theme, and Whitman's as well, but Lawrence brings it into the twentieth century, becoming in time the pre-eminent prophet of spiritual resurrection, proclaiming return to the physical, the consciousness of the body, the primitive and instinctive as the way to recapture vitality and escape the prison of a mechanized commercial society. Following Lawrence in the development of these themes are such poets as Robert Bly, Gary Snyder, Theodore Roethke, Galway Kinnell and Robert Creeley.

Robert Bly has written at length on the biological nature of poetry, and he has argued that in the modern age the mind or intellect has come to dominate body and soul (the unconscious), with the result that "What we're living in is something that would have to be called a 'mind-hell.' "[36] The way to salvation, then, is to return to the body and allow the unconscious to make itself known. Although Bly has developed his own theories of poetry and human development, Lawrence has helped to shape the general outlines of his thought. As Bly remarked in 1974, "I still learn much from Lawrence, not from his poetry, but from the motion that he made away from the intellect and down into the body."[37]

What matters for Bly, as for Lawrence, is the set of the poet's mind or spirit; no amount of craft or technique can be satisfactory if the poet is moving away from the body and the unconscious, or if the poet writes from intellect alone. The true poet, for Bly as for Lawrence, is an explorer, one who penetrates through barriers of the conscious mind in order to reveal the depths and spaces and, it may be, the chaos beyond; the true poet sees through illusion and deception and tradition, through all the false creations of the centuries, to show the realities of human nature and human existence. Bly sounds much like Lawrence when, during an interview, he rejects the word "craft," preferring instead the phrase "letting the animal live."[38] The fact is, however, that we deny this animal life within us because, as Bly argues (following Lawrence), the conscious mind has come to dominate our beings; it has become in the modern world far more powerful than body or soul. And yet, Bly insists—again following Lawrence—it is precisely in body and soul that we can find salvation: "These days the body is fresh, and the unconscious is fresh, and their freshness can act as a balance to this horrifying mind-hell in which people live."[39]

IV

Bly has spoken of three levels of consciousness. The first is that in which most people live, the level dominated by repression, violence and isolation; the second level is that in which the individual moves out from his own ego into the non-human world of plants and animals. According to Bly, Lawrence attained this higher level.[40] In his important essay, "Pan in America," Lawrence notes how man's development of abstract thought, making possible the production of machines, has given him power over nature, with consequent loss: "This was the death of the great Pan. The idea and the engine came between man and all things, like a death. The old connexion, the old Allness, was severed, and can never be ideally restored. Great Pan is dead."[41] Lawrence does not advocate a return to the primitive, and he does not glorify the savage; still, he insists, "civilized man, having conquered the universe, may as well leave off bossing it. Because, when all is said and done, life itself consists in a live relatedness between man and his universe: sun, moon, stars, earth, trees, flowers, birds, animals, men, everything—and not in a 'conquest' of anything by anything." Whatever we are, he concludes, "we can still choose between the living universe of Pan, and the mechanical conquered universe of modern humanity."[42]

The book of poems in which Lawrence is most open to the non-human world is the one generally considered to be his best, *Birds, Beasts and Flowers*. Gary Snyder has spoken specifically about its effect; when an interviewer asked him, "How do you see the role of D. H. Lawrence in the evolution of modern Anglo-American art and aesthetics?," Snyder responded,

> Oh, I have a great respect for Lawrence, great respect, and he was certainly one of my greatest teachers. He was my first modern poetry teacher. It was in my early years of high school when my focus was essentially mountains and nature, when somebody was passing around a copy of *Lady Chatterley's Lover*—wow—so I read that, and I thought: I would like to read some more of this fellow. So I went to the Public Library and I found *Birds, Beasts and Flowers* listed in the catalogue. I read the book and I said: This man knows what he is talking about, and I was converted to the poetry right there, and to modern poetry.[43]

Snyder has written essays as well as poems that center on the relationships of human beings to nature; he has also written on personal relationships. Like Lawrence, he finds in both cases that Western culture has moved in profoundly mistaken directions. His ideas derive from a variety of sources, including studies in Buddhism and the writings of Thoreau, but Lawrence is surely of major importance, particularly since Snyder happened upon him at such an early and impressionable age. In certain basic themes the two writers are very close. Snyder, for example, has written,

> There are many things in Western culture that are admirable. But a culture that alienates itself from the very ground of its own being—from the wilderness outside (that is to say, wild nature, the wild, self-contained, self-informing ecosystems) and from that other wilderness, the wilderness within—is doomed to a very destructive behavior, ultimately perhaps self-destructive behavior.[44]

Lawrence's concern with both kinds of wilderness is evident throughout his writings.

In *Birds, Beasts and Flowers*, the one book that would seem to be, from Snyder's account, most responsible for making him a poet, Lawrence approaches the natural world with profound respect and a sense of dignity, ever conscious of its awe and mystery. Snyder's attitude toward nature—one of the major themes in his poetry—follows directly from Lawrence's. "What," Lawrence has asked, "does life consist in, save a vivid relatedness between the man and the living universe that surrounds him? Yet," Lawrence continues, "man insulates himself more and more into a mechanism, and repudiates everything but the machine and the contrivance of which he himself is master, god in the machine."[45] Snyder also sees the fatal separation of man and his universe: "At the root of the problem where our civilization goes wrong," he writes, "is the mistaken belief that nature is something less than authentic, that nature is not as alive as man is, or as intelligent, that in a sense it is dead, and that animals are of so low an order of intelligence and feeling, we need not take their feelings into account."[46]

Lawrence's best-known poem about the relationship of man to the natural world is probably "Snake," in which the snake is seen, finally, as "a king in exile," "one of the lords of life"; but Lawrence's respect for the natural world is constant. In "Man and Bat," for example, Lawrence admits his feelings of revulsion at finding a bat in his room, but he refuses to kill the intruder. "I didn't create him," he thinks; "Let the God that created him be responsible for his death." His conclusion is deeply reverent toward life:

> Bats must be bats.
> Only life has a way out.
> And the human soul is fated to wide-eyed responsibility
> In life.

Despite his distaste for bats, Lawrence recognizes their claims to a place within the scheme of things; they are created beings, just as he is, and therefore he cannot assume superiority. Lawrence anticipates contemporary environmentalists by refusing to proclaim human beings the crown of creation; humans are, rather, one species of many, and all have their right to existence. What matters, always, is the "live relatedness between man and his universe." Finally, all things connect. This theme of unity is central to Snyder, who asserts it plainly in the lines that close his latest book, *Axe Handles*:

> I pledge allegiance to the soil
> > of Turtle Island,
> > one ecosystem
> > in diversity
> > under the sun
> With joyful interpenetration for all.

More domesticated in his concern with the natural world than Snyder, but also deeply influenced by Lawrence, is Theodore Roethke, whose interest in Lawrence was profound. He did special reasearch in Lawrence while studying for his master's degree at Michigan in 1930, he assigned Lawrence's stories in his classes at Lafayette College, he listed Lawrence among those poets for whom he had "a real enthusiasm," and he frequently referred to Lawrence in his notebooks, along with his other favorites: Blake, Jung and the Bible.[47]

Roethke read widely, and he absorbed many writers for his

own distinctive uses; and yet the Lawrencean note is distinctly heard, in manner as in theme. It is particularly revealing, in view of the attacks on Lawrence as one deficient in craft, that Roethke went to Lawrence to learn about technique. He cites Lawrence (along with Whitman) as a poet who made effective use of "enumeration, the favorite device of the more irregular poem"; and, in discussing general aspects of technique, Roethke singled out his "Elegy for Jane" as a poem that "indicates in a way some of the strategies for the poet writing without the support of a formal pattern—he can vary his line length, modulate, he can stretch out the line, he can shorten. It was Lawrence," Roethke adds, "a master of this sort of poem (I think I quote him more or less exactly) who said, 'It all depends on the pause, the natural pause.' In other words, the breath unit, the language that is natural to the immediate thing, the particular emotion. Think of what we'd have missed in Lawrence, in Whitman, in Charlotte Mew, or, more lately, in Robert Lowell, if we denied this kind of poem."[48]

Of particular importance is Roethke's nature poetry, which often suggests Lawrence's. In both there is the same exact observation combined with intuitive and passionate identification; for Roethke, as for Lawrence, nothing—a mouse, a slug, a towhee—is too small to be noticed, nothing is unworthy or insignificant. "I live/To woo the fearful small," Roethke wrote in "The Small"; "What moves in grass I love." Like Lawrence, Roethke avoids scenes of Romantic grandeur to focus instead on the near and common; he reaches out to the natural life around him, as though to lose himself in it and transcend his own being. The effort, however, despite some apparent successes, must ultimately fail, as human consciousness asserts its identity and feels its limitations. In Roethke's poem "Snake," for example, the reptile is presented as remote and unalterably "other," a representation of "pure, sensuous form" beyond human attainment, though not beyond human desire; and in Lawrence's poem of the same title, the snake, as we have seen, appears as an emblem of divinity, as distant as the stars:

He drank enough
And lifted his head, dreamily, as one who has drunken,
   And flickered his tongue like a forked night on the air, so black,

> Seeming to lick his lips,
> And looked around like a god, unseeing, into the air.

In both Roethke and Lawrence there is a similar probing of the unconscious, the dark springs of human nature. Significantly, Roethke defends free verse by saying, "There are areas of experience in modern life that simply cannot be rendered by either the formal lyric or straight prose."[49] One of those areas, surely, involves the exploration of the mind, which must be allowed to move to its own rhythms and through its own associations. That Roethke thought of Lawrence in connection with his psychic explorations, especially into repressed and mysterious aspects of being, is made clear by a notebook entry:

> For Lawrence and I are going the same way: down:
> A loosening into the dark, a fine-spume drift,
> The touch of waters: the dark whorls, the curled eddies.[50]

The water imagery of these lines, with its suggestion of a descent into unknown modes of being, into the unconscious, becomes particularly important in the meditative poems of Roethke's posthumous *The Far Field*, where (especially in the "North American Sequence") Lawrence's influence has been most thoroughly absorbed. In these poems Roethke is indebted not only to the nature poetry of *Birds, Beasts and Flowers*, but also to the stately meditations on death and darkness in the *Last Poems*. Both poets are looking into the abyss, as though sensing that the end is near, and both find cause for celebration as they achieve, in the knowledge of fast-approaching death, wholeness at last. Roethke concludes "The Long Waters" with this superb vision:

> I, who came back from the depths laughing too loudly,
> Became another thing;
> My eyes extend beyond the farthest bloom of the waves;
> I lose and find myself in the long water;
> I am gathered together once more;
> I embrace the world.

And Lawrence, too, emerges from the depths to find joy in the waters, as he proclaims in "Kissing and Horrid Strife":

> I have been defeated and dragged down by pain
> and worsted by the evil world-soul of today.
>
> But still I know that life is for delight
> and for bliss
> as now when the tiny wavelets of the sea
> tip the morning light on edge, and spill it with delight
> to show how inexhaustible it is.

In the last poems of both Roethke and Lawrence there is a turning away from civilization, a longing for the natural, the primitive, a desire for immersion in a deep order of consciousness beyond the human. The versification, with its loose and flowing irregular lines, apparently as formless and shifting as the water that pervades the poems, and its flexible turnings that follow the rhythm of thought itself, shows what Roethke has learned from his reading of Lawrence, and how far he has moved from the sculptured formalism of his early work.

For all the importance of Lawrence's technical influence, however, it seems clear that for Roethke, as for so many others, Lawrence the man was as important as Lawrence the writer. His courage, his commitment to life and literature, his spirituality, his striving, his energy and vitality, his relentless probing of the mysterious dark areas of human consciousness—these things mattered to Roethke. In the notebook entry quoted above—"For Lawrence and I are going the same way: down"—Roethke seems to have chosen Lawrence as a Virgil to play opposite his Dante, as both descend into the hidden places of the mind. And elsewhere Roethke indicates that Lawrence is with him to offer counsel, as when he exhorts himself in his notebooks, "Be one of those on whom, as Lawrence said, nothing is lost."[51] The note concerns writing, but even more, it concerns *living*. For Lawrence, of course, there was little distinction between the two. Writing was never just a matter of craft; always, it involved the whole being.

Of those poets who have followed Lawrence into the non-human world, into primitive darkness and the deep springs of the mind, Galway Kinnell is among the most important. Kinnell has spoken of the "immense admiration" he has for Lawrence's poetry, and he has said that "Lawrence is among the great germinal poets of modern times."[52] Owing much to the Lawrence of *Birds, Beasts and Flowers*, Kinnell reflects a major concern of that book when he states that "Part of poetry's usefulness in the world is that it pays some of our huge unpaid tribute to the things and creatures that share the earth with us."[53] Certainly *Birds, Beasts and Flowers* does precisely that: responding to the natural world on its own terms, with full awareness of its links with the human as well as of the separate existence that leaves it, finally, mysterious, beyond human knowing. As Aldous Huxley noted,

> Lawrence's special and characteristic gift was an extraordinary sensitiveness to what Wordsworth called "unknown modes of being." He was always intensely aware of the mystery of the world, and the mystery was for him always a *numen*, divine. Lawrence could never forget, as most of us almost continually forget, the dark presence of the otherness that lies beyond the boundaries of man's conscious mind.[54]

And yet, although there was no denying the "otherness," Lawrence's Romanticism impelled him to seek relationship beyond himself, to share in the lives of the non-human world. According to Huxley,

> A walk with him in the country was a walk through that marvellously rich and significant landscape which is at once the background and the principal personage of all his novels. He seemed to know, by personal experience, what it was like to be a tree or a daisy or a breaking wave or even the mysterious moon itself. He could get inside the skin of an animal and tell you in the most convincing detail how it felt and how, dimly, inhumanly, it thought.[55]

In Kinnell's best-known (and distinctively Lawrencean) poem, "The Bear," the speaker actually does "get inside the skin of an animal". He folds himself into the bear's carcass, there to sleep, and in his dreams becomes the bear itself, living through its last moments. When he wakes, he wakes to a world transformed by his experience of life other than his own. In its way, this poem may be seen as a modern version of Keats' "Ode to a Nightingale," with its waking and sleeping, its concern with creative process, its sense of a world beyond human perception, its momentary union with the non-human; and, like the "Ode," "The Bear" ends with a question: "the rest of my days I spend/wandering: wondering/what, anyway,/was that sticky infusion, that rank flavor of blood, that poetry, by which I lived?" There is no answer, and can be none; the mystery remains.

The mystery is crucial. Lawrence and Kinnell are both Romantics seeking to recover, in a mechanized and scientific world, a primitive sense of wonder and mystery. "If the things and creatures that live on earth don't possess mystery," Kinnell has remarked, "then there isn't any. To touch this mystery requires, I think, love of the things and creatures that surround us: the capacity to go out to them so that they enter us, so that they are transformed within us, and so that our own inner life finds expression through them."[56] One finds this sense of mystery everywhere in *Birds, Beasts and Flowers*. In "Fish," for example, Lawrence writes of the nature of fish-life, as he imagines it into being, until finally he is confronted by his own limitations: fish, like so much else in the natural world, must always be beyond him. In some splendid lines, Lawrence describes catching a fish, only to realize that the fish must always, inevitably, escape: *"This is beyond me, this fish,/His God stands outside my God."* Again, the mystery remains.

What Kinnell has said about Lawrence's animal poems—"the animals remain animals yet take on a symbolic character too"[57]—is true of some of his own as well; and it is not just the animals that become symbolic. Like Lawrence, Kinnell seems more than the object before him, for objects have significance; the world is not blank. Lawrence's tones are clearly heard in Kinnell's recent book, *Mortal Acts, Mortal Words* (1980), which includes the distinctly Lawrencean poem, "These Are the Things I Tell No One." With its irregular lines, its varied sections, its personal openness and directness of statement, its union of spiritual and physical, its stately music, its concern with the nature of being itself, and perhaps most important, its affirmation against the darkness, it suggests the Lawrence of the *Last Poems*. The poem concludes:

> Yes, I want to live forever.
> I am like everyone. But when I hear
> that breath coming through the walls,

grace-notes blown
out of the wormed-out bones,
music that their memory of blood
plucks from the straitened arteries,
that the hard cock and soaked cunt
caressed from each other
in the holy days of their vanity,
that the two hearts drummed
out of their ribs together,
the hearts that know everything (and even
the little knowledge they can leave
stays, to be the light of this house),

then it is not so difficult
to go out, to turn and face
the spaces which gather into one sound, I know now,
    the singing
of mortal lives, waves of spent existence
which flow toward, and toward, and on which we flow
and grow drowsy and become fearless again.

Lines like these would be hard to imagine before Lawrence wrote his poems, with their outspoken frankness and their turnings from the sensual and immediate to the eternal and unknown.

Lawrence's manner of reaching out after the mystery has been important to Kinnell, and not only in the poems of nature and meditation. When asked "What sort of thing is it in Lawrence that you find most attractive?," Kinnell responded, "His best love poems move us so far into the mystery. They turn into acts of cosmic adoration. In some of them love of one person passes into worship of sexuality itself, as in the great poem, 'River Roses.' "[58] This particular poem would seem to be one of the central documents for Kinnell; it is one of two he refers to in a discussion that, in the manner of Lawrence, characteristically mixes the physical and the spiritual. "It is curious," he wrote, "that sexual love, which is the only sacred experience of most lives on this earth, is a religion without a Book."[59] While it lacks a Book, Kinnell goes on to say, it *does* have poems, and "River Roses" is one of them.

Kinnell also follows Lawrence in recognizing and protesting

the fragmentation of the modern world: people, he finds, are separated from themselves, from others, and from their universe. His view of the self would seem to derive directly from the assertions of Lawrence. "Somehow it has happened," Kinnell has written, "that the 'mind' got separated from the rest of us. It got specified as the self. In reality, the mind is only a denser place in the flesh. Might we not just as well locate our center in the genitals, or in the solar plexus?"[60]

The quest for integration and wholeness, so central to Lawrence, involves the individual's relationship not only with self, but also with the rest of creation. Lawrence has spoken passionately, in a passage previously quoted, of the need for "a live relatedness between man and his universe: sun, moon, stars, earth, trees, flowers, birds, animals, men, everything"; and Kinnell speaks in much the same terms when he describes the qualities of authentic nature poetry. "The real nature poem," he has stated, "will not exclude man and deal only with animals and plants and stones; it will be a poem in which we men refeel in ourselves our own animal and plant and stone life, our own deep connection with all other beings, a connection deeper than personality, a connection which resembles the attachment an animal has for an animal."[61]

V

Lawrence has from the start been particularly important to the Black Mountain poets, a group that includes Charles Olson, Robert Creeley, Denise Levertov and Robert Duncan. All four have written extensively on poetry, but the major theoretician was Olson, whose essay on "Projective Verse," published in 1950, has been widely influential. This essay asserts as its central aesthetic statement a sentence attributed to Creeley: "Form is never more than an extension of content."[62] The assertion has its antecedents in Coleridge and Emerson, but it suggests also the expressiveness of Lawrence, whom Olson considered to be one of the two major literary figures of the century ("the huge two," he called Pound and Lawrence).[63] While Lawrence has contributed much to the forms of the Black Mountain poets, his most important contribution may have been the way he represented for them a man fully responsive to his time and able to confront it with insight, courage and determination. As Olson has written, Lawrence was "the man who more and more stands up as the one man of this century to be put with Melville, Dostoyevsky and Rimbaud (men who engaged themselves with modern reality in such fierceness and pity as to be of real use to any of us who want to take on the post-modern)."[64] When Olson looked for a person who exemplified total commitment to life as well as to literature, he cited Lawrence—*only* Lawrence, he emphasized; and before him, Dostoyevsky.[65]

An especially close relationship exists between Lawrence and Robert Creeley. "I read Lawrence intensely when I was a younger man," Creeley has said,[66] and it is a quotation from Lawrence's poetry—the final stanza from the "Hymn to Priapus"—that stands as epigraph for Creeley's *Collected Poems*, published in 1982. When asked, "What importance has Lawrence had in your work?," Creeley commented:

> It's very hard for me to think of "my work's" existence apart from Lawrence. His stories especially made clear to me how emotion might be engaged in prose, and no writer I'm aware of has ever been able to convey as intense feelings as he. So he was my model—because, like it or not, feelings were my own basic materials. In poetry, it was really his cadence that fascinated me—as, for instance, the rhythms of those quatrains in "Hymn to Priapus," and the way they shift about half way through that poem. When it came time to cite one writer, almost as measure, pledge, and introduction, for the outset of my COLLECTED POEMS, he and that poem were truly it—because I could not ever forget them.[67]

Responding to the question, "What importance would you attach to Lawrence's *craft* as distinct from his thematic concerns?," Creeley was reluctant to make a distinction. "It's somewhat hard," he said, "for me to separate the two, i.e., contact, immediacy, enactment are each modes of theme and craft in his case. Their importance for me is very great—shared with Williams but with very few others finally." When asked, "What has Lawrence meant to you personally over the years?," Creeley focused on those traits of character he has found in Lawrence's writing: "A measure of integrity, a vision I could depend upon, a vulnerability, perception, commitment, restless human wonder, anger, pride,—he was it."

During the process of discovering his own voice, Creeley valued Lawrence as an alternative to the dominant, Eliot-influenced modes of poetry. In 1950, when Creeley was twenty-four, he was reading *The Waste Land*. His response is preserved in a letter to Charles Olson:

> Read, yesterday, the Wasteland. And then, reading further, every damn thing: beginning that way. That tone. I am sick to death of this deadness. I want not the slightest part of it, Ez [Pound] or any of it. I don't want the remembering. I want the straight thing. The straight open breath of it, the freshness, the love, exact & living. Lawrence is worth 50,000 Pounds in any market.[68]

Two months later, Creeley was reading Lawrence, and he wrote to Olson about it; his letter gives some sense of the excitement and stimulation that he felt: "Reading WOMEN IN LOVE. Flying home. Gone things, like they say, the grooviest. I love, again, that man, still, the most. He is too much."[69]

Creeley's excitement is characteristic of many writers who found Lawrence exhilarating. To American poets he was, above all, a liberating force: in poetic technique, in personal expressiveness, in emotional response, in sensual awareness, in exploration of the self, in penetrating barriers of denial and conformity, in relationships with the natural world, in recognizing the mystery and magnificence of existence, in sexual openness, in asserting the self against convention and authority. Lawrence showed American poets how to write as individuals fully alive in thought and feeling, at all times responsive to the passing moment. Nothing, Lawrence knew, could compensate for deficiencies of spirit; and so he urged people to regard themselves with proper reverence, and further, to express freely, without shame and without repression, their truest beings. Among his many legacies, none is more enduring than that of the spirit.

CHAPTER SIX

Lawrence and American Fiction

EUGENE GOODHEART

Studies in Classic American Literature (1923)[1] is Lawrence's most significant entry into the American literary imagination. The essays on Franklin, Dana, Cooper, Hawthorne, Melville and Whitman may be read as fictions of criticism, reinventions of the classic figures of American literature according to the imperatives of Lawrence's own imagination. *Studies* is a sort of fable about the Americanization of the European colonizers.

They came to America for two reasons:

1. To slough the old European consciousness completely.
2. To grow a new skin underneath, a new form. This second is a hidden process.[2]

The American experience reverses the cycle of growth: "She starts old, old, wrinkled and writhing in an old skin. And there is a gradual sloughing of the old skin, towards a new youth. It is the myth of America."[3] If this is indeed the process of white or European consciousness in America, it is also the process of Lawrence's consciousness almost from the very beginning of his imaginative career—certainly from *The Rainbow* on. In discovering America, his America, Lawrence found already objectified on a national scale his own imaginative process. Disintegration and renewal, death and rebirth: they constitute the narrative principle of his art.

What Lawrence found in American literature and in his own experience of the New Mexican landscape was "a shadow of violence and dark cruelty . . . the aboriginal demon hovering over the core of the continent." A writer like James Fenimore

Cooper was both fascinated and repelled by the demon. The European in him needed to fight the "devilish resistance in the American landscape" in order to survive and to build civilization, but he also wanted the energy and renewal that springs from the landscape. Cooper idealized the landscape in an attempt to neutralize the menace. "Spring coming, forests all green, maple-sugar taken from the trees; and clouds of pigeons flying from the south, myriads of pigeons, shot in heaps; and night-fishing on the teeming, virgin lake; and deer-hunting."[4] Lawrence sees the idealizing defensiveness of Cooper's representation of the American landscape as a phase in the history of American consciousness.

> Cooper . . . glosses over this resistance, which in actuality can never quite be glossed over. He *wants* the landscape to be at one with him. So he goes away to Europe and sees it as such. It is a sort of vision.
>
> And nevertheless, the oneing will surely take place—some day.[5]

How or when the "oneing" will take place Lawrence does not, perhaps cannot, say, but what he has in mind is some reversion to archaic modes of existence (expressed by Indian life), which is not quite the same as a lapse into sheer primitivism.

Did Lawrence discover the process in America or did he invent it? I am not sure how scholarship can answer this question. What is clear from the critical response to Lawrence's *Studies* is that the most thoughtful and perceptive critics of our literature (Wilson, Trilling, Dahlberg, Fiedler, Howe, Kazin among others) have seen the book as representing the deepest penetration ever made into our classic literature. Indeed, critics coming after Lawrence have lived off the capital of this short book. It is as if a European of genius was required for Americans to become aware of their own destiny. What was latent in the American consciousness, Lawrence made manifest.[6]

If *Studies* represents discovery, as the greatest fictions do, then the Lawrencean intervention in both his essays and his novels becomes not so much an influence, an alteration in our consciousness, as a collaboration, an affinity with what is already an ongoing process. For example, in all his work Lawrence used the words "livingness" and "flow" over and over again, words that represented the desire to free the self for change, for continual self-transformation. The desire for fluid identity is deeply embedded in American literature. As Tony Tanner shows in *The City of Words*, it is an expression of a peculiarly American paranoiac fear of entrapping systems.[7] The American novel does not need to know Lawrence to want the freedom of fluid identity. Nor does it need to learn from Lawrence the risks of vertigo and of self-dissolution that a fluid identity incurs. Rather, in knowing Lawrence, it knows itself. Lawrence then is an incarnation of American consciousness, a re-enactment of the greatest of American dramas: the European becoming American. *Studies in Classic American Literature* is itself a fable of American literature.

Edward Dahlberg, a writer whom Lawrence admired, viewed *Studies* as the first serious criticism of American literature.

> Before Lawrence American books on the poetasters in the American wilderness, Anne Bradstreet, the pamphleteer-versifier Freneau and the gothic dunciad Brockden Brown, came from the dreariest academic scriveners. There was not a critical volume from which one could quarry a truth until Lawrence's *Studies* which seeded the work of Sherwood Anderson, Allen Tate, Hart Crane, William Carlos Williams's *In The American Grain* and Josephine Herbst's *The Hunter of Doves*.[8]

In his *Confessions*, Dahlberg shows little admiration for Lawrence's fiction, but he acknowledges his indebtedness to *Studies* in *Can These Bones Live* (1941). Dahlberg reads Lawrence as the great critic (like de Tocqueville or Amiel) of "a democratic commonwealth," who finds in the New World a "negative energy."[9] (One thinks of the fiercely hostile landscape of New Mexico in *St. Mawr.*) The American wilderness proved a perfect foil for the puritan will, a testing ground for its flesh-suspicious spirituality. Lawrence's critique addresses the costs to the spirit of the puritan triumph of the will, a victory at once pyrrhic and incomplete. In *Can These Bones Live*, Dahlberg continues the critique of the "stink" of Puritan repression that Lawrence makes in *Studies* and elsewhere.

Yet knowing Dahlberg's other work, one questions whether "influence" is the route to an understanding of whatever affinity exists between Lawrence and Dahlberg. What Dahlberg did not have to learn from Lawrence was the vatic contempt for American philistinism (Dahlberg's biblical idiom is even more salient than Lawrence's) or the indignant eloquence that was natural to both writers. There is influence of another sort. In the introduction that he wrote to *Bottom Dogs*, Lawrence profoundly affected the reader's perception of the book. Lawrence's understanding was deeper than that of Dahlberg, who seemed to be confused both by what he had accomplished and by Lawrence's understanding of that accomplishment. Dahlberg experienced some revulsion from his own book:

> Determined to expunge sky, grass, sea and trees the robber giants had stolen from the American people, what I had failed to realize was that I was also starving the exieic [a Dahlberg locution] eyes. There was not a drop of water in the novel....
>
> How had I purposed to compose an energetic novel in the corrupt language of inertia?[10]

But Lawrence saw the distinction of *Bottom Dogs* in its very imagination of revulsion from the body and the bodily functions. The novel is the *ne plus ultra* of the "repulsive consciousness," a consciousness endemic to modern life. "And now, man has begun to be overwhelmingly conscious of the repulsiveness of his neighbor, particularly of the physical repulsiveness."[11] He finds the origins of this consciousness in the Great War, which demystified the previous one-hundred-year effort to elevate man above his "baser functions." It is a theme or phase of Lawrence's own art, which he sought to transcend, though not in the spiritual–Christian direction. Lawrence's own imagination of the repulsive consciousness is very powerful. Dahlberg was puzzled by the introduction, calling it a "hectic and cerebrated invective" and wondering why Lawrence "who wished to help an unknown and poverty-stricken author [would] make him the victim of his own theoretical malice."[12] But Lawrence's statement about *Bottom Dogs* has a penetration, a truth to it that Dahlberg's own remarks about the book lack.

For all their differences, what Lawrence and Dahlberg have in common, in varying degrees of genius, is the personal presence of the creative writer who reimagines not only an entire literature, but a continent as well. This is also true of William Carlos Williams' *In the American Grain*. Williams' characterization, for example, of the ambiguous New Worldly character of Benjamin Franklin, as it played itself out in its diplomatic guise in Europe, is not precisely what Lawrence would have written or did write about Franklin, but it is marked by the reductive, demystifying and recreating effort of imagination.

> His mind was ALL out of the New World. Feeling a strength, a backing which was the New itself, he could afford to be sly with France, England or any nation; since, to live, he had to be sly with the massive strength of that primitive wilderness with whose conditions he had been bred to battle: thus, used to a mass EQUAL to them, he could swing them too. So again he asserted his nativity.
> Strong and New World in innate strength, he is without beauty. The force of the New World is never in these men open; it is sly, covert, almost cringing. It is the mass that forces them into praise of mediocrity to escape its compulsions: so there is a kind of nastiness in his TOUCHING the hand of the Marchioness, in his meddling with the lightning, a resentment against his upstart bumptiousness in advising London how to light its stupidly ill-lit streets.[13]

What we hear in this passage is an individual voice, addressing a character derived from history and reinvented by a contemporary sensibility. Williams' Ben Franklin, like Lawrence's, is a live Franklin.

Between Lawrence and American writers there is affinity (or disaffinity) rather than influence. Sherwood Anderson wrote *Dark Laughter* and *Many Marriages* in "the Lawrencean orbit" (in Irving Howe's phrase). Perhaps one can speak of influence there, the effect of which is not salutary. Anderson's novels are poor stuff compared to *The Rainbow* and *Women in Love*. But, in the four stories under the title "Godliness" (in *Winesburg, Ohio*, not written in the Lawrencean orbit), there is a biblical simplicity and elevation of language that recalls *The Rainbow*: "His walking in the fields and through the forests at night had brought him close to nature and there were forces in the passionately religious man that ran out to the forces in nature."[14]

Anderson's memorable portrait of Jesse Bentley combines the natural and the religious in a Lawrencean way. The three generations of Bentleys are a microcosmic analogue to the generations of Brangwens in *The Rainbow*. Like Lawrence in his exaltation of the Brangwen body, Anderson celebrates the life in the Bentley body.

> All over his body Jesse Bentley was alive. In his small frame was gathered the force of a long line of strong men. He had always been extraordinarily alive when he was a small boy on the farm and later when he was a young man in school. In the school he had studied and thought of God and the Bible with his whole mind and heart.[15]

Both works evoke the ethos of the biblical patriarchs.

Like Lawrence, Anderson was a provincial with a special sensitivity to the spirit of the place, but it was a spirit that could not satisfy every need, a spirit that provoked a restlessness, a desire for new places, new worlds. The provincial spirit, more perhaps in Anderson than in Lawrence, pervades all the new places visited by the imagination.

In using him as a perspective for viewing other writers, there is a risk of making Lawrence less interesting and problematic than he is. Irving Howe comments on the differences between Lawrence and Anderson: "Lawrence had a commanding grasp of Western culture when he decided it was not enough, Anderson had only scraps and fragments. Lawrence acted from the strength of secure renunciation, Anderson from the weakness of enforced deprivation."[16] It is true that Lawrence was a novelist of ideas as Sherwood Anderson was not. There is a continuous note of bafflement in the interrogative mode of a novel like *Dark Laughter*. Fred Grey's puzzlement about marriage persists throughout the novel:

> MARRIAGE! Had she intended marriage, had Fred really intended marriage that night in Paris when both Rose Frank and Fred rather went off their heads, one after the other? How did one ever happen to get married anyway? How did it come about? What did people think they were up to when they did it? What made a man, after he had known dozens of women, suddenly decide to marry a particular one?[17]

Sherwood Anderson and his characters face life without confidence.

Lawrence did have enormous confidence in his ideas, but "commanding grasp" tends to block inquiry into questions about the integrity, coherence and value of those ideas. If his culture were contrasted with Freud's, whose grasp would then be the commanding one? Nor is it clear what it means to claim "the strength of secure renunciation" for Lawrence. The phrase evaporates the dialectical struggle in his life and thought. Howe goes on to claim sexual self-knowledge in Lawrence in contrast to Anderson's failure to know himself. Even his most sympathetic readers now acknowledge the deviousness and deviancy of Lawrence's sexual consciousness, the inadequacy that disguises itself as megalomania or religious exaltation. Lawrence may be more interesting in what he did not know about himself—in the confusion and uncertainties that left him open as a subject for reflection by writers like Norman Mailer and Henry Miller. Howe's discussion of the "Lawrencean orbit" in which Anderson wrote was conducted under the influence of a prematurely secure conception of Lawrence as a normative writer, fostered principally by F. R. Leavis.

There has been a considerable amount of theorizing about influence in recent years. Harold Bloom has distinguished the strong poet as one who in effect cannibalizes his strong predecessor, the poet who would deny the latecomer originality. The denial of the predecessor by the latecomer may not be explicitly asserted in the poem, but it is felt there. It is the weak poet, according to Bloom, who submits to the influence and regards it as benign. I think Bloom is probably right to distinguish between two kinds of poets (the deniers and the accepters of tradition), but I am not happy with the strong–weak distinction. Certainly a writer like Lawrence would seem to represent Bloom's "strong poet." Lawrence remarks: "I don't want to write like them [Goethe, Kant, Galsworthy, Ibsen, etc.]. We have to hate our immediate predecessors to get free of them."[18] An explicit discursive denial or repudiation of influence, of course, does not guarantee a writer's security against it. Nor does the powerful presence of another writer in one's imagination necessarily make for weakness. In any case, other writers are very much present to Lawrence, however much he might protest the tyranny of influence—and, one should add, benignly present.

Perhaps "influence" is not the word we want. Every writer, no matter how original, experiences the presence of other writers, past and present. The question is, what form or forms does that presence take?

Lawrence's presence to American writers reveals itself in the peculiar resistance to him to be found in those whose sympathies with him are the greatest.[19] Thus Henry Miller's extraordinary celebration of *The World of Lawrence* was conceived in hostility; Miller calls him "a little runt, a nasty devil, a dry, thoroughly English type."[20] According to Anaïs Nin, who provided both moral and practical support for Miller's work on Lawrence, Miller's essential hostility to Lawrence was transformed by his reading of Lawrence's short collection of essays entitled *Reflections on the Death of a Porcupine*, which Nin had sent him. According to Nin, in the essay "The Crown," "he found a man, a profound thinker, and a visionary" in contrast, for example, to the persona in "the sickly letters Lawrence wrote" to Mabel Dodge Luhan.[21]

But the initial hostility to Lawrence no doubt reflects a feeling of rivalry: a resentment about Lawrence's pre-eminence in the field of sexual or passional consciousness that Miller regarded as his own. Miller writes to his agent William Bradley: "It was humiliating to me to sit in your office and be requested to write a little brochure about this man or that man in order to introduce myself. I didn't want any introduction. I wanted simply to stand up and let go—be knocked over for it or lauded for it."[22] Miller's resentful declaration of independence is thoroughly Lawrencean in spirit.

Miller's initial hostility becomes transformed into a fruitful resistance. Instinctively, Miller acknowledges that Lawrence as an influence would contradict the very principle of Lawrencean imagination or of Lawrence's understanding of it. A Lawrence-like writer would be *sui generis*. Of course, as we have already noted, this is perhaps illusion or self-delusion. No writer, however *sui generis* he thinks himself to be, is an island unto himself. Lawrence does not hate his predecessors—Blake, George Eliot, Hardy—and even those writers he hates (or says he hates) are bound to him by the emotion of hatred. Only indifference or ignorance can free a writer from tradition, and what writer worth anything would want to pay that price? Miller learns in writing his book that in going through Lawrence he is realizing himself, that "by writing about him . . . one has caught the flame he tried to pass on."[23] What is tradition, after all, but the passing on of the flame. But to catch the flame is not to be influenced—with the idea of submission that influence implies—it is to struggle, to resist, to acknowledge only what is genuinely flame-like. And indeed, this is Lawrence's own way with writers, especially with those he most admired, who meant most to his own imaginative formation: Dostoyevsky, Hardy, the classic American writers.

Miller's Lawrence is both novelist and prophet. "The whole fundamental interest in Lawrence centers upon his appearance as type and the rather obscure relationship of his type to the epoch."[24] "Like Jesus, Lawrence appears in a time of despair, of hopelessness, when there is a strong suicidal trend, racial and individual. *When the end is clearly in sight!*"[25] For Miller, the prophet struggles with and defeats the poet–artist. Confused as a thinker, inadequate as an artist, failed as a man, Lawrence moves forward "as scourge and avenger . . .—with terrifying consistency."[26] Miller's comparisons of Lawrence with others are not with novelists but with the greatest spiritual figures in history: Jesus and St. Francis of Assisi. (Norman Mailer and Bernard Malamud, two other novelists who make strong responses to Lawrence, also emphasize the prophetic and the biographical Lawrence at the expense of the poetic and the artistic.)

Miller's Lawrence is not an entirely coherent or perspicuous portrait. Though its genesis dates back to 1932, the book was published in 1980, the last of Miller's major publications. In an interview for the *Paris Review*, Miller confessed his dissatisfaction with the book's incoherence.[27] In pursuing Lawrence's ideas he found himself frequently driven to contradiction. Nevertheless, the book is marked by a surprisingly serious, almost solemn effort to get at the essential Lawrence. Surprising, because one might expect from this self-confessed "cunt painter" a worldly sensibility reducing, if not demystifying, the spiritualizing tendencies of Lawrence's representations of sexuality.[28] One might also expect that Lawrence's imagination of sexuality would be the focus of Miller's concern. The chapter titles suggest, instead, a religious–metaphysical focus: "The Universe of Death," "Resurrection," "Destiny," "The Sacred Body Philosophy." "The important Lawrence," Miller insists, "is the man who grasped death in his momentary visions."²⁹ Miller's response to the tragic fatalism of Lawrencean characters is expressed in paradoxical fashion. "In Lawrence's novels, an essential capacity of his characters is the ability to wield power over their own fates, or perhaps the ability to abandon themselves to their fates."³⁰

Miller's sharp eye for the sexual drama between men and women enables him to see, though not with complete accuracy, the essential conflict between men and women in Lawrence. The point of the conflict is not victory over the woman, but male autonomy:

> Man's wonderful world of moralities and religions, of codes of honor, of law and justice, or art, in a constant, painful effort to keep alive the illusion of his necessity in the scheme of things, which woman without saying a word, silently and by her mere presence, by her love even, negates. Because woman is amoral, woman is uncivilizing, woman is lethargy and night, woman is destruction in the profound sense that all creation is also destruction.³¹

The male struggle with the female is for self-preservation.

How faithful is this reading to Lawrence's work? The Oedipal struggles as imagined in *Sons and Lovers* make it clear that masculine autonomy depends on liberation from the domination of Magna Mater. But the woman in Lawrence is not inchoate energy and moral listlessness. On the contrary, she is the culture bearer, as Lawrence complains in *Fantasia of the Unconscious*.³² The roles have become reversed. And indeed, in *The Rainbow*, it is the Brangwen women who imagine, virtually against the feminized consciousness of the Brangwen men, a world of male purposes, in which men move dominant and creative. The Brangwen women at least want autonomy for their men.

What is involved in Miller's misreading of Lawrence? Miller is of course right to see Lawrence's desire for male autonomy as an essential self-preserving desire, but in the American way he radicalizes the struggle between male and female. One fable at the heart of American fiction (as Leslie Fiedler has shown in *Love and Death in the American Novel*) is the male fear of and flight from woman. Lawrence's men are "capable" of flight—

particularly in the work of "the middle period": *Aaron's Rod* and *Kangaroo*. And, in *Women in Love*, Birkin's impulses toward flight at times seem stronger than his desire for connection with Ursula. But Birkin does seek the connection and forms it—and Aaron's desire for separateness is merely provisional. Lawrence's last work is all about a new connection with women and with men, indeed with the cosmos based on a sublimated eroticism which he named "tenderness." Miller then exaggerates the drama of male autonomy in Lawrence out of his own deep American mistrust of the female. "Influence" here works in reverse: the imperatives of Miller's own imagination revise Lawrence's work.

The need for male autonomy also determines Miller's reading of Lawrence's putative homosexuality—or of Lawrence's imagination of it. For Miller, it is "not at all a question of homosexuality, but a polarity between men which could embrace the ambivalent value of war, war that spells hatred, cruelty, death.... In this love and hate, this war, it is all a question of man's survival, man's world, man's soul."[33] There is a kind of mystification in this writing that seems to have been absorbed from Lawrence himself. But what Miller is trying to say (Miller notes how often Lawrence's struggle expresses itself in that phrase: what I am trying to say, what I have been trying to say for the past twenty years) is that the essential Lawrence is not about life and connectedness, but about isolation and death—an isolation and death, to be sure, that is aflame with apocalyptic energy. Projecting himself in the figure of Christ, Lawrence annunciates the betrayals he will suffer at the hands of his disciples. In *The Man Who Died* he even sees himself as the creator of the Judases in his own life, because he "tried to lay the compulsion of love on others." But Miller goes further: "Yes, Lawrence was treacherous at the core because he knew no loyalty except to his inner flame."[34] The autonomy of the prophetic artist is the ultimate truth of Lawrence.

It may surprise those readers of Miller who see him as a connoisseur of promiscuous sexuality in *la vie bohème* to find him capturing and valuing Lawrence's puritan seriousness. In fact with his particular knowledge of the French, Miller sees the special importance of Lawrence for the Latin world, for whom the woman is a "toy" (an object, we would now say).[35] (Potential importance perhaps, for Lawrence does not speak to the French precisely because of his puritan seriousness. If he speaks to America, it is in part because of the shared puritan heritage.)

The familiar Henry Miller surfaces when he contests Lawrence's aversion to obscenity. In effect, he defends *Lady Chatterley's Lover* against the charge of obscenity by conceding it and affirming it: "there is no justification for it. Because it requires none."[36] There is some deviousness in Miller's attitude here. Miller is defending a word that signified degradation of what Lawrence and Miller both valued. "Obscenity is pure and springs from effervescence, excess vitality etc. . . . Obscenity is a divine prerogative of man." Of course, this is precisely what obscenity is not for Lawrence. What makes this defense of obscenity devious is that it is also what it is not for Miller in his fiction. It is almost as if Miller were trying to redeem his own calculating, manipulative sexual imagination by alchemizing its obscenities in the alembic of Lawrence's imagination. What Miller's book on Lawrence makes clear is both the necessity of Lawrence for Miller and his distance from him. Miller in his fiction was hardly Lawrence's disciple, but Miller saw Lawrence as a figure of transcendental isolation who represented the deepest aspiration of the soul in the modern period. Miller concludes his book in religious language:

> But this earthly life, though he himself was not to experience it, was a transfigured life which is open to all of us to know and to enjoy. It is as impressive to me now, when I contemplate Lawrence, as it was to the disciples when they contemplated Christ. It is the desire at the bottom of every man's heart when he is truly alone with his soul.[37]

How different both Lawrence and Miller look in the feminist perspective. Kate Millett's notorious all-out attack on male fantasies of sexual domination in *Sexual Politics* (1970) encompasses Lawrence, Miller and Mailer. All three are guilty, but the judgments vary in severity. If Lawrence and his male characters express misogynist views, deny the female the orgasm (Lawrence repudiated "clitoroidal" women) and sometimes allowed fascist attitudes to infiltrate male–female relationships, he at least conceived relationships under the sign of *tenderness* (the working title for *Lady Chatterley*). There is nothing to redeem Miller in his habit of converting and reducing women to sex objects, cunts. Though Lawrence and Miller have in common a bullying attitude toward women, Millett's portraits of them and their work reveal a contrast between tenderness and callousness. Lawrence, for whom Millett has no affection, is used as a stick to beat Miller. Lawrence is bad, but Miller is worse.

The attack on Lawrence and Miller contains the predictable feminist challenges to the canonization of both writers as the modern champions of sexual liberation. This feminist critique had been anticipated in earlier *un*organized ideologies. For a critique to have an effect, it needs something of an ideological consensus behind it, a sense of collective grievance. For all the crudity and didacticism of Millett's attack, it has precisely that force. And it provoked an extraordinary response from the third target of the attack, Norman Mailer, in *The Prisoner of Sex* (1971).

In writing about Miller and Lawrence (in particular about Lawrence), Mailer is without illusions. He acknowledges a fascist tendency in *Aaron's Rod* and *Kangaroo*. He stresses the bully: "[Lawrence] was a momma's boy, spoiled rotten, and could not have commanded two infantrymen to follow him . . . [he was] a Hitler in a teapot."[38] Yet he was also "a great writer, for he contained a cauldron of boiling opposites." Lawrence provokes Mailer to some of his finest, most sympathetic writing:

> he was the blessed breast of tender love, he knew what it was to love a woman from her hair to her toes, he lived with all the sensibility of a female burning with tender love—and those incompatibles, enough to break a less extraordinary man, were squared in their difficulty by the fact that he had the intellectual ambition sufficient to desire the overthrow of European civilization, his themes were nothing if not immense.[39]

Mailer throughout displays a sensitivity to complexity, tone, atmosphere, dialectics in Lawrence that redeems him from Millett's ideological reductiveness. "Millett's critical misdemeanor is to conceal the pilgrimage, hide the life, cover over the emotional odyssey which took him from adoration of the woman to outright lust for her murder, then took him back to worship her beauty, even her procreative beauty."[40] Mailer appreciates as only he can, inward as he is with the experience, the dramatic character of Lawrence's artistic persona. Lawrence is no impersonal artist, paring his fingernails or disappearing from his narratives. His work is his life blood. Wonderful as the work may be, it is personal expression, the artist in a sense transcending the art.

There are so many passages of extraordinary beauty and eloquence in Mailer's account of Lawrence—so much genuine "reverence for life" (that nineteenth-century attitude to which Lawrence is the last great heir), that one must remind oneself how different Mailer's own sensibility is—in its profound wordliness, its attraction to the glamour of high tech, even in its sexuality and its fascination with violence.

Lawrence and Mailer differ radically in the character of their imagination of sexuality. For Lawrence sex should occur only when the gods are present: it is a rite, a sacrament which enables two embodied "souls" to achieve an ecstatic community in a dark beyond. Lawrence is one of the great mystifiers of the sexual act. He tries to imagine a deep sexuality without friction(!) and as a consequence to deny the orgasm to women (in *The Plumed Serpent*). (One wonders how the male manages.) The satisfaction he imagines is sacramental, a satisfaction that his readers have found very difficult to understand—despite feeling both the desire and the obligation to understand it, because of the passion of the language. There is no American novelist I can think of whose sex scenes truly resemble Lawrence's: one must go to *Wuthering Heights* to find anything like Lawrence's imagination of sexuality. Mailer's erotic imagination is charismatic. In a short story like "The Time of Her Time" (in *Advertisements for Myself*) or a novel like *An American Dream*, the world of political power, of urban aggressiveness, of sado-masochistic fantasy is openly available to the lovers. Sexuality is vitality for Mailer, but it is unmystified by the language of religion. The language of "love" in Mailer is secular, pornographic, comic.

There are confusions of sex and power in Lawrence, but it is of a different order from what we find in Mailer. Lawrence with a messianic fervor wanted to save and convert the world, but drew back from what appeared to be a contradiction to his doctrine of spontaneity; Mailer's desire to "revolutionize consciousness" is ultimately a theatrical gesture, a megalomaniacal desire to display himself, redeemed only by a capacity for self-irony, which Lawrence essentially lacked. (Millet says of Miller: his "naive, sexual heroics" would be far better if, as one critic suggests, they had been carried all the way to "self-parody."[41] This occurs in Mailer, for Mailer realizes that all sexual heroism—which has its verbal counterpart in bravado—must be self-parodic. Like any extremism, sexuality becomes available to the comic view.)

It would seem that contact with Lawrence makes for a kind of self-transcendence in both Miller and Mailer. It is as if in thinking about him, writing about him discursively, they discover their best selves. In *The World of Lawrence* and *The Prisoner of Sex* (more than in their fiction), Miller and Mailer passed on the flame.

Miller and Mailer are writers of obvious susceptibility to the Lawrence presence. Bernard Malamud is a writer one would not immediately think of in the Lawrencean mold. There is a vein of nature-celebration running through Malamud's work (see, for instance, *A New Life*) that is Tolstoyan rather than Lawrencean. Yet Lawrence is an inescapable presence in Malamud, in particular in *Dubin's Lives*, a novel about a biographer whose current project is a life of Lawrence. For Malamud, as for Miller and Mailer, it is the figure of Lawrence more than the work itself, or the figure as it manifests itself in both the life and the work, that is of greatest consequence.

Dubin's daughter and Evan Ondyk, a psychotherapist who has an affair with Dubin's wife, on different occasions wonder about Dubin's attachment to Lawrence. The daughter wonders whether Dubin really likes his subject. "You're not much like him."[42] And Ondyk expresses a professional doubt about whether it is good for Dubin, a "radically different" type, to be "living every day with the anger, spleen and hostility of the enraged man."[43] Why should Dubin (or Malamud for that matter) be interested in Lawrence?

What emerges from *Dubin's Lives* is a discriminating portrait of Lawrence. Dubin is not an academic biographer (he is a freelance writer), but his discriminations have about them an academic judiciousness. Dubin knows that Lawrence's sexual doctrine is frequently misunderstood. He stood for marriage, and in particular his own "rough and tumble" marriage with

Frieda, "a vital and enduring relationship." In fact, what Dubin feels most strongly in Lawrence's life and what wears on him most "was the eternal domesticity of Lawrence and his wife."[44] Dubin understands Lawrencean sex or sexuality (a word Lawrence loathed) as a metaphor "for a flowering life." In a single sentence, Dubin is able to distinguish Lawrence's misanthropy from nihilism, a distinction that Lawrence himself, for all his loquacity, did not make clearly. "I doubt he loved mankind but he relished life though he explained it insufficiently."[45]

Why did Dubin, who had written prize-winning lives of Lincoln, Twain and Thoreau, among others, choose Lawrence? "He picked me. There's something he wants me to know." Dubin's Lawrence is not Miller's Christ-figure, nor is he the fecund mother that Mailer finds him to be. Dubin's Lawrence speaks to the troubled domestic lives of Americans in the middle of the century. His own troubled, even violent domestic situation is hardly a model, but the very seriousness with which Lawrence addressed "the passional lives of men"[46] makes him an indispensable figure for Dubin.

Dubin's own troubles with his wife culminate in his impotence with her at the age of fifty-six. Lawrence, we are reminded, became impotent with Frieda at forty-one. Whereas Lawrence's problem may have been organic (his illness finally took its toll), Dubin's "impotence" represents a diversion of libido to a girl young enough to be his daughter. Though there is no convincing evidence that Lawrence had affairs while married, his putative affairs are part of his legend and probably influenced the characterization of Dubin. Both Lawrence and Dubin, for all their supposed and actual infidelities, remained faithful husbands. But there is another feature to the resemblance between Lawrence and Dubin that inadvertently, perhaps, illuminates the treacherous themes of sexuality and impotence in Lawrence and his work. Dubin is not only impotent with his wife; he has a writer's block. Lawrence, as far as we can tell, never suffered from writer's block. His spontaneity was in his writing, not in his sexuality. Perhaps the writing was a compensation for a troubled sexuality—an anxious rush of explanation and defensiveness. I speak of inadvertent illumination, because the novel is not explicit on the subject. Nor for that matter do I recall anybody else remarking the paradox of verbal spontaneity and sexual impotence, the displacement of libido to writing in Lawrence. Could it be that one of the legacies of Lawrence depends upon a misunderstanding of where Lawrencean spontaneity is actually to be found?

There is something oddly belated about Malamud's Lawrence. He is a throwback to the forties and the fifties, when Lawrence was read as a guide to conduct. During the past twenty years, there has been something of a recoil from the moralist claims that Lawrence made, claims that were given the fullest critical endorsement by F. R. Leavis. We now see his problematic sexuality and his politics with much greater scepticism. He is a more interesting figure than the affirmative portraits of him make him out to be. Malamud's Lawrence is not without complexity or without the provocation that makes him something other than affirmative, but the Malamud–Dubin sensibility tends to make him benign rather than *farouche*: he has ceased to be the revolutionary of consciousness. Dubin's Lawrence is not simply domestic, he is domesticated, a figure that does not demand a revolution in our lives. He is someone *l'homme moyen sensuel* can live with.

When we think of Lawrence's presence in our literary consciousness, it is as a figure, a passion, an emotion; when we think of Joyce, the other great "English" novelist of the century, it is as a technique, a style or series of styles. Lawrence has nothing to teach about narrative or about verbal style, at least on the testimony of American novelists most susceptible to him. Mailer, for example, is downright contemptuous of Lawrence's style. Mailer's Lawrence is "abominably pedestrian in his language when the ducts of experience burned dry, he was unendurably didactic then, he was a pill, and at worst, a humorless nag."[47] His conception of character in *The Rainbow* is one of the great imaginative inventions of the century, but it is not at all clear that it has been seminal. One needs the visionary eye to reduce character to its "carbon" essence. And any writer who could do that would need that eye; he would not be able to derive it from Lawrence or from anybody else. The fact is that Lawrence presents himself first as prophet, then as artist. Which is not to say that he has not made extraordinary works of art. But his work is not there for formal imitation. He is rather a challenge, a provocation in his life and in his work as it expresses itself dramatically, poetically and discursively.

If he is a prophetic artist, he is a prophet of a particular puritan kind. Puritanism is of course a species of Protestantism, and it is the protestant consciousness that reenacted biblical prophecy in the modern world. If Christianity concerns renewal and rebirth, the sloughing of old consciousness and forming a new consciousness underneath, Protestantism concerns the renewal of Christianity itself. Lawrence tries to renew the protestant tradition by overcoming the split that it had caused between spirit and flesh. He knew that Catholicism had achieved a more *grac*ious accommodation to the pagan feeling for the body and, at the very end of his life, he even suggested that Catholicism might represent the new way. But this attraction to the Catholic Church should not divert us from the essential fact of Lawrence's protestant–puritan consciousness, nor from the secularized aspect of that consciousness. His gods remain very much his own invention.

Lawrence's puritanism expresses itself most impressively in his preternatural sensibility to what he hates the most—in his connoisseurship of split consciousness. Doubleness or deception is the special gift of the puritan imagination, as Lawrence remarks in his essay on *The Scarlet Letter* with a fascination that is at once sympathetic and hostile.

> Serpents they were. Look at the inner meaning of their art and see what demons they were. You *must* look through the surface of American art, and see the inner diabolism of the symbolic meaning. Otherwise it is all mere childishness. . . .
> Always the same. The deliberate consciousness of Americans so fair and smooth-spoken, and the under-consciousness so devilish. *Destroy! destroy! destroy!* hums the under-conscious. *Love and produce!* cackles the upper consciousness.
> The American has got to destroy. . . . It is his destiny to destroy the whole corpus of the white psyche, the white consciousness.[48]

Lawrence may want a wholeness born of the fusion of spirit and flesh, but the moralizing strenuousness of his effort, the need to provide a religious condition for sex, betrays the irremediable split in his own consciousness.

Never "use" venery at all. Follow your passional impulse, if it be answered in the other being; but never have any motive in mind, neither offspring nor health, nor even pleasure, nor even service. Only know that "venery" is of the great gods. An offering-up of yourself to the very great gods, the dark ones, and nothing else.[49]

He remains a puritan who failed to overcome himself.

The significance of Lawrence's puritanism cannot be overestimated in trying to understand what he has bequeathed to American literature and in particular to the American novel. The blessing and the curse of the American imagination is its puritan heritage. So in a sense Lawrence does not bring to the American imagination the benefits of the alien. His strenuousness, his preachiness, his didacticism have an all too familiar ring. Sexuality carries too many burdens for Lawrence for his imagination of sex to have a liberating effect for Americans. Indeed, he threatens to increase the burdens.[50] (The sexual imagination of American fiction is polymorphously perverse, pleasure- and pain-oriented, fetishistic, experimental, business-like, obscene, hilarious—in the spirit of Miller rather than of Lawrence.) But, if Lawrence does not bring the benefits of an alien, he does bring benefits as a kindred spirit, one is almost tempted to say as a compatriot. Lawrence is Whitman *redivivus*, the poet of protean consciousness, of cosmic affinities. He has plumbed the depths of consciousness as only the greatest American writers have done.

But Lawrence is a latecomer in the imagination of vitality. In Whitman, even the Industrial Revolution is an incarnation of cosmic energy, the imagination does not discriminate between city and country. Lawrence feels nothing but horror for the industrial world, and he lacks sufficient imagination of modern city life. All references to city or town tend to be abstract, homogenizations of its varied life so that it can become the object of condemnation.

"The stupid lights," Ursula said to herself, in her dark sensual arrogance. "The stupid, artificial, exaggerated town, fuming its lights. It does not exist really. It rests upon the unlimited darkness, like a gleam of coloured oil on dark water, but what is it?—nothing, just nothing."[51]

No American novelist—even one who finds life in the modern city uncongenial—can be indifferent to the claim of the city. If he were, he would forfeit the greatest and most significant territory of the novelistic imagination. Whatever else America is, it is the triumphant incarnation of the modern city and of the machine.[52] If America represented the future for Lawrence, it was certainly not in its commercial spirit, its technological genius, its urban and suburban character, or its obsession with money. As we have already remarked, he envisaged rather the possibility of regeneration through a return to pre-Columbian origins. "Americans must take up life where the Red Indian, the Aztec, the Maya, the Incas left off.... There lies the real continuity: not between Europe and the new States, but between the murdered Red America and the seething White America."[53] For Lawrence, America is Taos, not New York or Boston. The villain of the American drama is the Puritan, who diabolizes the energy that Lawrence values. It is the Puritan within Lawrence that perceives this and expresses it with a puritan energy.

What then is the Lawrencean residue in American fiction? Again, it is not so much a question of influence as it is of affinity. It is to be found, for example, in the "impression" of the narrator of Walker Percy's extraordinary first novel, *The Moviegoer* (1961): "For some time now the impression has been growing upon me that everyone is dead."[54] And shortly afterward he speaks of being "enlivened by the hatred which one bears the other. In fact, this hatred strikes me as one of the few signs of life remaining in the world." In *I Rise in Flame, Cried the Phoenix* (1941) (a one act play about Lawrence), Tennessee Williams sees Lawrence as the writer whose passion for life is so intense that it expresses itself as hatred. The Lawrence character, sick and dying, answers his own question: "What is an artist?—A man who loves life too intensely, a man who loves life till he hates her and has to strike out with his fist like I struck at Frieda——."[55]

If there is a moral tendency in modern American fiction, it is the celebration of cosmic life (not in its minimal survivalist form), a celebration threatened by the various claustro- and agora-phobic forms of contemporary urban and suburban life. Some moral philosophers object that vitality is in itself not moral, and vitalism is not a morality. Perhaps not, but it is certainly a condition of the moral life. Without a sufficient measure of the life force, acts of courage and deeds of virtue are impossible.

For Lawrence, the true American destiny is a reversion to archaic modes of life of the Indians. *Studies in Classic American Literature* is a work of demystification. Yet Lawrence himself was something of a mystifier. He could not escape, hard as he tried, an idealizing conception of the Indians. Anyone who visits the Indian Pueblos of New Mexico is struck by the deterioration of the physical culture of the Indians. The flabbiness of the Indian physique ("nourished" on fast foods) is a sad parody of his white American counterpart, who tries to redeem his fallen body by diet and exercise. Lawrence, we know, was overwhelmed by the beauty of New Mexico, overwhelmed because its majestic aridity seemed to him hostile to the human enterprise. He believed (with his Anglo friends like Mabel Dodge Luhan) that the Indians possessed the secret of the landscape. But perhaps the "secret" was no more than the indifference and resistance of the landscape, an indifference and resistance that the European has mastered with the machine. America, the America the world knows, is the most advanced expression of the mechanical (we now call it technological) civilization that Europe invented: Lawrence's anti-European America is a critique of the American apotheosis of Europe. Lawrence is present whenever one hears in modern American fiction the voice of Life (a voice at once moving and futile) against the prevailing forms of American existence.

CHAPTER SEVEN

Lawrence's Cultural Impact

KINGSLEY WIDMER

Lawrence has what many conventional commentators view as "extra-literary" roles. For several generations he has represented various modes of eroticism, marginal styles of living, anti-industrial and other utopian attitudes, and even antithetical cultish apotheosizings.[1] Most of the published discussions of Lawrence as a cynosure of such dissidence are ill-informed and dismissive.[2] Lawrence's biography, along with the romance of *Lady Chatterley's Lover* and other attempted sacralizations of man–woman coupling, has made him for some an archetype of the heroic outsider as lover.[3] His fictions and pronouncements have also been at the center of several contentious cultural–social issues. Three of those will be briefly examined here: the feminist–misogynist disputes; the obscenity–censorship conflicts; and the problematic role as a prophet of enlarged eroticism. But these should be recognized as just the more marked reefs in a considerable body of influence. For the larger part of a century, Lawrence has called forth ranging and intense responses, even magical though contradictory identifications, which go beyond usual literary legacies.

I

Lawrence has served as a focus of contention, especially in the 1970s and 1980s, as both an ideologist of male domination and as an empathetic proponent of female sensibility. It must now seem odd that Lawrence's vehement misogyny was not made more of by earlier readers and commentators. Patently, he exalted male power, not only the phallic, and female subservience, not only as an anti-feminist but also by advocating slavish submission.⁴ Yet his treatments of the issues are often paradoxical. For example, he believed a woman must totally submit to the appropriate man in order to liberate herself into fuller sentience and selfhood.

Lawrence rages obsessively against "wilful women" and dramatizes a veritable legion of "witches" whom he tendentiously drives to renounce independence for patriarchal submission, or to accept emotional or actual suicide for not submitting.⁵ Certainly he held that there should be a creative conflict in male–female "polarity," but not an equal relationship. "Teach a woman to act from an idea and you destroy her womanhood forever. Make a woman self-conscious, and her soul is barren as a sandbag."⁶ A woman's nature is not to think but to submit: "When a woman is thoroughly herself, she is being what her type of man wants her to be."⁷ Lawrence's romance and marriage paradigms in many of his fictions desperately insist on "male purpose" (though there is little purposeful social order) and on female passivity, but they are often intriguingly perplexed—and must appear even more so now. Yet the crux is less the pyrrhic resolution than the erotic-conversion experience of religious dimensions, which leads to a fuller intensity of responsiveness and a new sense of being.

No doubt Lawrence's problems with women damaged his writings. Even he seems to have later recognized that he twisted *Sons and Lovers'* portrayal of working-class life into a misfocus on provincial-protestant petty-bourgeois life, centered on women. He obsessively, and sometimes brilliantly, savaged women, especially in his shorter fictions. He outrageously rejected female orgasm, as in the "Aphrodite of the foam" passage and the denial of clitoral "beak-like friction" in *The Plumed Serpent*. And he made gratuitous attacks on lesbianism in *Lady Chatterley's Lover*. Why, then, for more than a generation, did few commentators on Lawrence consider his misogyny? His readers, always reported as heavily female, and however poignantly masochistic, may have felt that Lawrence's empathetic projection into women made the misogyny more acceptable. Diana Trilling suggests that, for the early decades, his "harshness to women, instead of alienating his female readers, would seem to have fed their well-stimulated appetite for blame" for not being properly happy in submission to males.⁸ Lawrence's generally perceived role as a liberating sexual prophet also obscured discriminations as to what kind of relations he announced. And *heroic* submissions may be persuasive.

However, early on there were some comments in memoirs on Lawrence's harsh ideology towards women.[9] A full case against Lawrence on women was made shortly after his death by his one-time close friend (and wife's sometime lover), John Middleton Murry, in *Son of Woman*.[10] With some vindictive reductiveness, Murry held that the masculine inadequacy of the Oedipal-victim Lawrence led him to grossly compensatory demands for female submission.[11] In contrast, during the same period, Anaïs Nin published a dithyrambic little book which praised Lawrence's empathetic responsiveness to feminine sensuality and sensibility.[12] Her narcissistic obtuseness extended to involving one of her Parisian lovers, Henry Miller, in her worshipful responses. Miller, too, wrote fervently on Lawrence, though his melange of mystical feminine worship and gross sexual usage hardly encouraged appropriate understanding of the paradoxical Lawrence. These two were also to be brigaded in the public mind for a generation because of censorship.

Probably the first intellectually sophisticated counter-statement to Lawrence's misogyny was Simone de Beauvoir's short chapter in *The Second Sex* (1949).[13] Earlier in the book she had commented on what was to become a nexus of feminist reaction, the attack on female orgasm in *The Plumed Serpent*, which she condemned as "dreadful nonsense." Within the confines she gave her chapter—considering only a few novelistic and expository statements of Lawrence on the subordination of women—she makes a reasonable case. She does not consider his misogynistic portrayals or erotic dialectics, and rather dubiously submerges him in a romantic-nature polarity of femininity and masculinity. With Sartrean ontology, she summarizes Lawrence's insistence on women's submissions to purposive phallic males as the exaltation of "the woman who unreservedly accepts being defined as the Other." Her larger context, of course, did not only concern the reduction to the "feminine," but also the radical social issues of women's consequent lack of economic autonomy and full personhood in society.

Beauvoir's feminist argument was largely ignored in the swell of academic criticism of Lawrence during his literary revival. Few commentators discussed his misogyny (as I did in the 1950s).[14]

But at the end of the 1960s, the strong public renewal of militant feminism—the "Women's Liberation" that developed out of the minority protest, anti-war and counter-culture movements as well as changed sexual and economic conditions—prepared the way to see Lawrence as an important symbolic sexual reactionary. The most influential writing seems to have been that of the feminist-publicist Kate Millett. Her *Sexual Politics* included historical chapters around feminist ideology and on exemplary anti-feminists in twentieth-century literature.[15] The long essay on Lawrence, leading into chapters on avowed Lawrenceans, Henry Miller and Norman Mailer, is an angry denunciation of his mistreatment of women characters and his "doctrinaire male-supremacist ethic." It concludes with explication of the novella "The Woman Who Rode Away," which is presented as a "sadistic" exaltation of "the penis as deity," a "pornographic dream" and "demented fantasy" perverting sex into "slaughter" in the form of a ritual "death fuck."

Though she is unoriginal on that novella, except for some vehement language, the pressured argument is representative. Millett also distorts class and sexual issues, and especially the tone of the last part, of *Sons and Lovers* to hold that Paul victoriously exploits women, instead of having been partly defeated by Miriam's puritanic frigidities and by his mother's petty-bourgeois aspirations. To admit that would put women in the wrong. *The Rainbow* becomes an assault on the feminism of the time, instead of its ambiguous affirmation. *Women in Love* is an exercise in the further punishment of independent women, on the way to Lawrence's homosexual misogyny and lust for male power in *Aaron's Rod* and *Kangaroo*. In exposing Lawrence's male "narcissistic" and social "fascistic" tendencies, Millett in revisionist fervor, only lightly touches on the obvious case of *The Plumed Serpent*. The shorter fictions, though often savage about women, are largely ignored, as are the changes in Lawrence and any qualities other than misogyny. In sum, her polemic against Lawrence is relatively uninformed and unanalytic, and seems aimed mostly to serve, as feminists in that period liked to announce, "women's consciousness raising."

The most noted of the anti-feminist counter-attacks was undoubtedly Norman Mailer's *The Prisoner of Sex*.[16] He deployed his considerable talents not just in egomaniacal self-defense against Millett (and more urbane feminists such as Mary Ellmann and Germaine Greer), but also in jousting for his literary heroes Lawrence and Miller. As a grossly macho writer—describing his "sexual instrument" as "The Avenger," dramatizing obsessive wife-murdering fantasies, and repeatedly putting down women as "witches"—Mailer was the proper melodramatic antagonist of public feminism. Yet parts of his counter-polemic are perceptive. He sees Lawrence as "a great writer" who often wrote "abominably," as a man burning "with tender love" though often sunk in humorless tyrannical fantasies. While an extreme ideologue, Lawrence frequently qualified that with a "profound British skepticism." Mailer's Lawrence is a complex figure. Still, Mailer hardly meets the issues—though he apparently thinks he does—in insisting that "never had a male novelist written more intimately about women," and that women love his work because they recognize he is a "sacramental poet" of male–female relations.

Mailer does grant Millett a partial case in treating Lawrence as a "counter-revolutionary sexual politician" since he shows "unmistakeable tendencies towards the absolute domination of women by men." But he scores her too-simple view of Lawrence's sexual "pilgrimage," her "poisoned" selection of fictions, her twisted use of quotes (which he acutely demonstrates) and her tendentious conclusion with the "savage" "The Woman Who Rode Away." Mailer then rides off on his counter-interpretation of Lawrence as preliminary to his own sexual theology. The heroics of erotic "mystery" apply to both. Lawrence is "saying again and again, people can win at love only when they lose everything they bring to it of ego, position, or identity." Quoting Lawrence–Birkin, "they have to deliver themselves 'over to the unknown.'" We do not understand Lawrence unless we recognize him as a religious prophet who showed that in addition to satisfying sexual need, true "sex could heal."[17]

Mailer also presents Lawrence's religious eroticism as underlaid by personal desperation, a "tortured" struggle for manhood of an Oedipal case whose "psyche was originally shaped to be homosexual." His heightened eroticism was a desperately uncertain, and dying, male's quest for self-transcendence. With heterosexual heroics, and against the limitations of the novel form in *Lady Chatterley's Lover*, he achieved a final affirmation of man–woman love. The argument's astute twist comes in insisting that the Lawrencean consciousness was really that of a "beautiful, imperious, and passionate woman."[18] Thus Mailer uses a superior feminine Lawrence against the mere feminists. (They, especially as represented by Millett, are treated as rather imitation men; Mailer apparently follows Lawrence's extreme hostility towards lesbianism.) The would-be he-man Mailer has found an ally in she-man Lawrence.

Mailer's provocative interpretation seems especially important in positively presenting Lawrence as a peculiar sensibility. Unlike most literary discussions, it does not strap Lawrence into the merely normative. But Mailer's Lawrence is also used for rather diabolic dogmatics, including not only an assault on feminists rightly dubious about him but also, like Lawrence, denunciations of masturbation and contraception, to which he nastily adds anti-abortion. Mailerean eroticism must be fearfully dangerous, especially for women. In a rather sick existential leap, it includes a mystical embryology in which fearfully heightened sex results in superior conception. Thus, in a further parallel with Lawrence's exaltation of erotic desire as one of the few ultimate values in otherwise nihilistic modern life, Mailer uses sexual exacerbation in a desperate effort to find "meaning."[19] Though he perceptively won some of the fights, including a more persuasive reading of Lawrence, Mailer has clearly lost the war against the feminists, if one is concerned with fairness or equality, or even decency.

Lawrence, then, had become a sexual totem for both feminists and misogynists to conjure with. His use seems to have been even more widespread than the polemical literature indicates. For example, a best-selling novel and feminist comic confession of the 1970s, Erica Jong's *Fear of Flying*, takes its two final epigraphs from Lawrence.[20] He had become a brooding presence for erotic conflicts.

The feminist use and abuse of Lawrence also brought forth earnestly sympathetic American male defenses of him as one reaching after new erotic awareness, or, whatever his prejudices, achieving an over-arching affirmation of man–woman relationships.[21] Yet a British feminist critic ignored all that and insisted on the old biographical case for Lawrence's sexual ambivalence, homosexual–narcissistic demands and egotistical mistreatment of women.[22] Another, grimly continuing the by now doctrinal line of feminist interpretation of *Sons and Lovers*, saw him as a "ruthless user of women."[23] Mark Spilka, forever re-doing his American positive thinking of the Lawrencean "love ethic," attempted to counter Millett with an emphasis on Lawrence's nicer women characters.[24] The devout Lawrence biographer Harry Moore concluded, yet again, that Lawrence did not really hate women because he finally regarded them "in a way that can only be called religious."[25] With unintentional irony (and like Mailer's argument) this rather confirmed the essential feminist critique that Lawrence did not treat women as fully human.

The pro-and-con feminist–misogynist literary cudgeling often appeared as contradictory as it was widespread. A British journalist wrote a quite imperceptive book in which she confesses to having identified, as a Midlands schoolgirl, with the Ursula of *The Rainbow* in "a quest for the coming out of feminine consciousness." When she read Millett on Lawrence she reacted negatively—to Millett. Amidst potted summaries of Millett and Mailer, and some of Lawrence's fictions, her main argument, if it can be called that, is that Lawrence shows "better than any female novelist ever had, the strength and power of a woman's feelings," and the fact that "she enjoys fucking."[26] Lawrence thus continued his role, more than half a century later, as prophet of sexual liberation.

A more competent and historical account from a feminist point of view draws together some of Lawrence's uses of "suffragist" ideas and women in his early writings. These, however, showed little sympathy with suffragism in his "rejection of reform in favor of individual [sexual] liberation and development."[27] That rings true. With increasing irritation, Lawrence's wartime fictions show an "insistent emphasis on submission and passivity for women" and a "growing anti-feminism." In the post-war anti-woman fictions, Lawrence heavily asserted masculine power. But towards the end he presented a more qualified view, holding up "phallic consciousness" in a somewhat uncertain glorification of male predominance. While this discussion often lacks critical acuteness, and does not respond to the prophetic–erotic role, it suggests some useful historical correction to the simplified denunciations and defenses of gender prejudices.

And certainly Lawrence has been "useful" beyond literary considerations in the misogynist–feminist disputes of the past generation. Yet much of it seems based on the simple-minded proposition that one cannot be both sensitively sympathetic to women and an extreme male chauvinist. Lawrence was obviously both. In spite of the deepened sense of erotic perplexity in the Lawrencean mode, re-statements continue of the stock pious view of Lawrence as one who sought "creative balance between men and women."[28] But, more generally now, there may be a sense of Lawrence as a most peculiar sensibility, and as one who provocatively—unto perversity—contributed to a different, a more conflicted, awareness of man–woman relations. Yet given the insistently extreme masculine–feminine divisions in Lawrence—and in many of the later contenders about Lawrenceanism—there probably can be no adequate resolution of the arguments or the larger issues without far more radical changes in man–woman relations.

II

Germaine Greer, the noted feminist writer and contentious public personality, vehemently told me a few years ago that *any* use of the word "cunt" for a woman or her parts was male degradation and insult. Even, I countered, when used with poetical tenderness by a gamekeeper? Germaine snapped back, "Precisely," and added some well-chosen male degrading obscenities to place properly Lawrence and his apologist.[29] Lawrence's Mellors uses "cunt" (fourteen times), and similar language, in some of the scenes of *Lady Chatterley's Lover*. The apparent authorial intentions, perhaps a bit contradictory, were to challenge hypocritical prudery in language and to turn obscenity, as usually defined, to the poetic service of erotic ritualism. When I recently restated these points to a rather literal-minded Lawrence scholar, he, too, reacted negatively: "Those were and still are foul terms!" This view, important to some feminist and other genteelizing ideologies, seems now widely current.

Curiously, then, part of the Lawrence obscenity issue still appears to be in dispute after more than half a century. Yet Lawrence's obscene language, even in comparative literary terms, is limited in range and confined for the most part to a private and dialect context. Its usage is even, probably unconsciously, somewhat prudish. For Constance Chatterley (no Germaine Greer) does not use it; that may be a weakness in the novel's motif of turning a lady into a woman, and perhaps should be the feminist objection. Mellors' usage tends to the poetically anatomical, not the more reductive synecdoche. Lawrence's other earnest concerns, such as the attacks on social class, redemptive erotic awakening and an apocalyptic anti-industrial social vision, may also raise problems of tone in the minds of readers who do not find obscenity obscene except when it is yoked with the serious.

While the objections to Lawrence's language have continued for more than a half-century, the grounds seem to have shifted. The Anglo-Saxon terminology, whether as anatomical nomenclature, synecdoche or erotic poeticism, now condemned for sexist denigration, was previously denounced for "lewd and lascivious intent," or for "appealing to prurient interest," or for showing a "tendency to deprave and corrupt." These key phrases in the historic obscenity laws are not the same as the current feminist, and other genteelizing, charges.[30] Yet there may be some subterranean links in covert anti-sexuality as well as in moral righteousness connecting the shifting taboos about verbal obscenity.

But the issue in Anglo-American societies is no longer direct censorship of the novel. For, by an odd historical twist, recognized serious novels—and Lawrence's last acquired such a status—have earned a "literary exemption." The redefinition of censorable material developed partly out of the censoring history of sexually errant heroines—not just Constance Chatterley but Emma Bovary, Sister Carrie, Fanny Hill, *et al.* Lawrence served as a crucial figure in that history. Part of the change, of course, was that verbal and sexual mores were only slowly reflected in case and constitutional law. But the change may also reflect a different role for the novel in the middle-class audience's expectations for proper edification and titilation. (Current censorship disputes most often concern pedagogical materials, magazines, broadcast television and stereo records.) A less central cultural form may be less of a focus of contention.

Lawrence's earlier censorship problems notably included the legal suppression of his fourth novel, *The Rainbow*, in London in

1915. Apparently that was for the "obscenity" of the Ursula–Winifred lesbian relationship, though it is not described with any vulgar language or even much direct detail.[31] The continuing effects can also be seen in efforts at self-censoring, in his own withdrawal of the "Prologue to *Women in Love*," which fervently discussed Birkin–Lawrence's homosexual feelings, the euphemizing of sodomy, and other verbal skittishness.[32] Lawrence seems to have been outraged by the treatment of his earnest fiction, which, later on, may have contributed to his more overt defiance of obscenity taboos. In his final novella, *The Man Who Died*, his intentions obviously included obscene blasphemy. He used elaborate sexual puns (an escaped cock as metaphor for virility, erection as resurrection) and a Black Mass coitus between his Christ and a priestess, but he avoided direct vulgar language. After *Lady Chatterley*, he was widely notorious for obscenity and a focus for those he ragingly denounced as "censor-morons." His artistically crude but only mildly sexual paintings were officially prohibited in Britain, and otherwise treated as "obscene." He also discussed obscenity and related issues in polemical essays, of which the most important was the long, defensive "A Propos of *Lady Chatterley's Lover*." Lawrence, never fully libertarian in temper, attacks the snickering and demeaning "dirt for dirt's sake" in a rather puritanic aesthetic of the obscene.[33]

Obscenity issues, then, are not just incidental to Lawrence's writing, as the more decorous commentators have often held, or to his public role. That *Lady Chatterley* could not be legally published (except in bowdlerized form) in Anglo-American countries for more than thirty years clearly defined his image and effect. He was the author of that forbidden "dirty book" which was, however, widely available. Disappointingly to many, the "dirt" consisted of less than a hundred total uses of a few common "obscene" words and a middling degree of description of not unusual heterosexual actions in about a dozen scenes. The censoring furor now seems hugely disproportionate.

However, trial transcripts and public discussions insist that the obscene words were importantly yoked with several other issues.[34] More general sexual candor was usually part of the disputes. So was adultery, which Lawrence presented not as guilty or titillating furtive eroticism but as exalted redemptive mating. And the adultery was compounded by class violation:

the upper-class lady is having serious sex with her husband's *servant*—this was especially offensive to the British. But, as should be evident to the readers of the two earlier drafts of the novel (published as *The First Lady Chatterley* and *John Thomas and Lady Jane*), Lawrence had strongly redeveloped his protagonist so that he was less the working-class man than the sophisticated and self-conscious anti-hero of modern culture, the socially defiant outsider.[35] The anti-class emphasis has been offensive to conservatives and Marxists but positive to the bohemian and the libertarian. That upper-class ladies need liberation, sexually, socially and ideologically, may be viewed as a recurrent conceit of Lawrence's, though it also seems to be a significant appeal to certain kinds of readers, especially would-be dominant males and repressed females.

Such issues enter the necessarily crass censoring cases mostly as moral bias. Charles Rembar, the main *Chatterley* defense attorney in the U.S. censorship cases, claimed to obviate many of the old moral issues and pursue new legal ground in obtaining the sanction of Lawrence's obscenity by "literary merit."[36] It was not the obscenity itself which was held to have such "value"—that would be an intriguing argument!—but that the "lustful" was conjoined with "literary quality" which, "considering the work as a whole," gave it "redeeming social significance." The ostensible "contemporary community standards" of sexual candor, not moral and literary value, had come to be the dominant qualifications of First Amendment freedoms of speech and publication. The issues presented in 1959 came out as a rather teetering balance between what seemed to be generally accepted and the special literary recognition to be accorded the book. For the first time in U.S. censorship case and appellate law, emphasis was put on "expert witnesses" to literary value. The result might be viewed as a social success story for literary critics. Enlarged freedom of expression depended on the judgments of recognized intellectuals, which was quite a change.[37] Another intellectual, Lawrence, now qualified in law as he had for some time in literary culture.

Lawrence's novel partly engendered a series of American literary censorship cases whose combined history produced the policy, in the words of Supreme Court Justice William Brennan, that "a book cannot be proscribed unless it is found to be utterly without redeeming social value,"[38] and literary value is a social value. Curiously, the focus on "book" here was, and remains, partly restrictive on other formats and media as well as on materials not given prestigious cultural sanctions. Libertarians against all censorship should recognize some ironies in the process. Lawrenceans should also recognize some inflation of the author beyond literary and ideological pertinence. In the months following the trials six million copies of *Lady Chatterley's Lover* were sold in the United States.

Rembar, as the key attorney for the chain of cases starting with *Lady Chatterley*, suggests several conclusions for America. "So far as writers are concerned, there is no longer a law of obscenity."[39] That applies to books and to general distribution (school administrators, as well as certain other custodial bureaucrats, maintain other standards in hundreds of places). Technocratic market processing also provides its own order of controls and restrictions. Rembar also, and perhaps typically, concludes (in 1968) with the hopeful prediction that the society is on the way, and not only in the legal sense, to conditions in which "obscenity will soon be gone."[40] That seems to mean that, once the censoring furors and enticements are over, there will be such a healthy attitude towards sexuality that the very impetus to obscenity will disappear. Even Lawrence, a major figure in encouraging such changes, did not take so optimistic a view of the social–sexual warfare which obscenity issues are partly about. Nor has recent literary and social history, despite the admirable decrease in censorship, tended to confirm it. Much of the conflict continues in different guises.

In the year after the Lawrence cases in the United States, Lady Chatterley, as it were, went on trial in Great Britain. As had previously been evident, the London responses more insistently emphasized adultery and class misbehavior. Is this the kind of book, asked the crown prosecutor, "that you would want your wife or servants to read?"[41]

To the American attorney Rembar, the London case was a "low parody" of free-speech issues, since the British defense proceeded to lengthy and legally loose public determination of "what the law ought to be" in moral senses.[42] They were out to prove the lady's virtue, and Lawrence's. A more disinterested reader of the trial transcripts from both countries might note, besides parochial procedural differences (the British were more loose and capricious), that Lawrence's literary and ideological virtue were at issue in both. The British defense pursued both the "obscenity" issues and their exemption from restriction on such various grounds as literary seriousness, situational ethics, spiritualized sexuality, the libidinous countering of mechanization and other moral concerns. Probably the Lawrence side won because earnest virtues were given notable public recognition, in spite of the obscenity.

Even the British prosecutor generally conceded that Lawrence was a "great writer," though not in this immoral book. Hence the British lawyers and literary notables practiced rough applied criticism of the text. The defense presented thirty-five expert witnesses (the prosecution called none, depending mostly on cross-examination, implicitly granting the literary community to the anti-censors), with quite an array of famous writers (including E. M. Forster, C. Day Lewis, Rebecca West), literary critics (including Helen Gardner, Walter Allen, Richard Hoggart, Raymond Williams, Noel Annan), as well as theologians and Anglican priests, a Member of Parliament, a legal scholar and a sweet young lady. The case was heavily made that Lawrence was a morally worthy and great writer. Thus the general cultural evaluation of Lawrence was confirmed in a legal forum, which led to British sales of additional millions of copies of *Lady Chatterley's Lover*.

But many of the issues remained murky. In both the British and American trials, "literary value" was supposedly at issue but not seriously examined. Even at best, the logic was narrowly circular: this was a good book because it was by Lawrence who was a good writer. The trials again confirmed (as I had discovered by working for the defense in a variety of censorship cases) that legal proceedings and broader intellectual concerns are often fundamentally incompatible. Among other conditions, the simplifications of adversarial stances, the frequent reduction of issues to yes/no or narrowly "factual" answers, the pseudo-qualification of "expert" witnesses by public positions, the legalistic game-playing of attorneys and judges, the synthetically ritualistic ambience, and the punitive threats hanging over all, increase the disparities between legal modes and good sense. The crass realities of courtrooms in intellectual matters may be the most pragmatic argument against any kind of official censorship, which must usually end up arbitrary and falsifying.

The problematic aspects of the later-Lawrence eroticism,

such as the attacks on lesbianism or the sexual–social subordination of the woman, hardly appear in the trials.[43] Nor, apparently, do many of the truer responses of the participants. For example, after winning with the jury at the Old Bailey, the chief *Chatterley* defense barrister was quoted as having come out against "the words," which he now felt were in danger of being used by any "scribbler," not just a national literary icon like Lawrence. The learned liberal editor of the published trial record also censoriously concluded: "It was the words that caused all the trouble, putting her Ladyship as an adultress where a more conventionally spoken gamekeeper might have lent her the immunity of Emma Bovary and Anna Karenina."[44] The supposed scholarly defender of literary freedom was not only terribly reductive on the issues, but also did not seem aware that even without "the words" Flaubert's novel was prosecuted in Paris in 1857 (and proscribed numerous times in later and lesser places), and that Tolstoy's self-censored one had avoided proscription because it was vehemently anti-sexual (as Lawrence had pointed out in an essay). Anti-sexuality, and snobbery, are the usual motives in the disapproval of obscenity.

Real freedoms must apply to sometimes obscene "scribblers," and to ex-ladies and their out-class lovers, if they are to be socially meaningful. The legal licensing of *Lady Chatterley* appears to have applied in this way in the past generation, probably enlarging freedom of expression and erotic awareness. Lawrence, the social moralist, may have been partly right, then, in engaging some of the issues of obscenity with which for two generations his role and influence have been yoked. One might also want to employ a few obscenities (in a non-sexist way, of course) for the restrictive quality of mind and feeling often exposed in even the "oh so nice" people in the obscenity disputes. Those tight ones need to be penetrated by some hard ideas in the struggle against the repressions and gentilities which repeatedly come to prevail. That was part of what Lawrence meant, and it remains in temper and purpose an important legacy.

III

Probably Lawrence's most enduring effects, other than the

specifically literary, go beyond obscenity censorings, feminist–misogynist conflicts, and other dissident morals and manners. Lawrence most importantly represents an enlarged and heightened eroticism. His prophetic demand for that, of course, can not be held autonomous from the controversies, or the counterfeiting, of the Lawrencean. For they are but particular applications of a larger insistence on passional consciousness and a call for a radically different sensibility.

This prophecy can also never be fully separated from Lawrence's fictions, poems and other literary works because those depend, in their very vividness and intensity, on the same passional perceptions. The discriminating critic might feel more comfortable if, say, "The Rocking-Horse Winner" and "The Man Who Loved Islands"—or the best poems, the vivid descriptive writing, the sometimes brilliantly provocative essays (as in the extremely influential *Studies in Classic American Literature*)—were the only Lawrence that the culture utilized and some in the society attempted to live.[45] But it has not worked that way. Our cultural ambience has been so affected that varied erotic histories, dissident ideologies and even marriages, reveal Lawrencean influence.

Lawrence's life-long claim was that he stood for the exaltation of "desire," especially in its "deeper" *ne plus ultra*, as against mere intellection. In more notorious metaphors, he demanded "blood consciousness" or "dark knowledge." The focus was most often, though not exclusively, a sexual nexus. Many Lawrence fictions center on the discovery of the deepest desire, an often anguished process that presupposes a culture of repression. Frequently, it is the one heroism in otherwise ordinary life. The realization of authentic desire separates one from rather than reconciles one to the dominant social order. Lawrence radically subverts the traditional moral casuistries of "good" and "bad," and the orderings of restraint, into qualities of passion. As rebellion and conversion experiences, these culminate in new states of being and a radically different responsiveness.[46]

Some strange things have been done with the Lawrencean, but the passional imperative has also often been recognized and utilized. For example, an influential post-World War II dissident social theorist, Paul Goodman, held for years as a fundamental principle: "Follow your deepest impulse!"[47] Some of the impetus may have come from the Lawrence he admired, though, of course, his matrix of an American-Jewish heritage, left-Freudianism and militant homosexuality gave a different cast to the passional imperative than Lawrence's erotically transposed English protestant individualism. In partly related terms, a Reichean cultural theorist has recently argued that Lawrence is one of the true proponents of the "sexual body" as center of all responsiveness, an awareness developing against millennia of false Western dualism.[48] Lawrence is thus repeatedly taken as a positive prophet of a new consciousness.

Such sexual–social libertarians tend to ignore Lawrence's authoritarian fantasies and other complexities. So perhaps more intriguing in posing the issues are some anti-Lawrencean theorists of social culture. For example, several decades ago a noted conservative moralist in the guise of a social scientist, Philip Rieff, presented Lawrence as a leading "revolutionary imagination" and sexual "seer." In *The Triumph of the Therapeutic*, drawing mostly on Lawrence's "psychological" polemics of the early 1920s (he only touches on a few of the lesser fictions), Rieff takes seriously Lawrence's counter-rationalist "religion of Sex."[49] It was a "post-Christian" effort towards the "integration of the inner and outer man," though too heavily remissive to work in an incoherent culture. This is the obverse of the libertarian's Lawrence. The new pagan prophet "staked his cased on a revival of the erotic mode, as a therapeutic release from inwardness," that is, from guilt and other traditional religious repression. Lawrence aimed at "a new therapy of commitment," but it is dangerous because in its "deliberate avoidance of restraining intellectualism, Lawrence's erotic doctrine permits a violence of expression in which anger and hatred represent more powerfully encouraged motives than that of love."[50] A libertarian could respond, as Lawrence did in passages in *Aaron's Rod* and *Kangaroo*, that the "love-disease" has historically brought on more destruction than any mere anger and hatred ever could.[51] Rieff concludes that Lawrence's passional therapy for the manipulative-rationalist denuding of life aimed to be programmatic, but really had no politics, little sense of socioeconomic ordering and, most crucially, no community. So we get "a spurious therapy of commitment to nothing in particular," which thus results in an impassioned cultural "nihilism."[52]

As far as it goes, this seems significantly accurate for much of Lawrence (as I have previously argued in detail) and for some of his influence. But stoic-Freudian sociologists are not prepared to acknowledge partly autonomous individuals or their subversive sub-culture. Not incidentally, Lawrence's last fiction was about a messiah who deconverted from social salvation to erotically intense individual being and a role of permanent defiance. Such dissidence may not be a full social science, or cultural conservation, but its justifications include more responsive and vivid life.

Another dialectical consideration beyond Rieff would be to recognize the ironic reversal of the Lawrencean when it has become a significant part of the culture—neutralization by co-option. An argument of his sort has been suggested by the cultural historian Michel Foucault, who twice uses Lawrence in the key final section of *History of Sexuality*. "'It is sex,' said Kate in *The Plumed Serpent*. 'How wonderful sex can be, when men keep it powerful and sacred, and it fills the world.'" Foucault comments: "We must not think that by saying yes to sex, one says no to power; on the contrary, one tracks along the course laid out by the general deployment of sexuality."[53] This seems an odd comment for *The Plumed Serpent*, Lawrence's exacerbated effort to fuse sex and power (yet also a demonstration that new religions are mostly reprises of old illnesses). But the history of the modernist affirmation of sexuality is more at issue. Foucault earlier argued that the "deployment of sexuality" from nineteenth-century "generalized repression" toward claims "to free oneself both of repression and of domination and exploitation" have not substantially transformed social and political dominations. Instead, we have had the "deployment of sexuality by power" as a more subtle form of the modern "management of life."[54] Like other modernists defining culture by rebellion against earlier modes of repression, Lawrence thought a new vision of sexuality would change the world. It has not been sufficient.

Lawrence renounced his larger sexual–religious views for the more individualistic eroticism of his last writings. Therefore, Foucault's second quotation is taken from the justification for *Lady Chatterley's Lover*: "'There has been so much action in the past,' said D. H. Lawrence, 'especially sexual action, a wearying repetition over and over, without a corresponding thought, a corresponding realization. Now our business is to realize sex. Today the full conscious realization of sex is even more important than the act itself.'" Lawrence (with some irony, given his earlier attacks on self-conscious sex, on intuitive feeling manipulatively corrupted) seems to be arguing for a revolutionary consciousness. But, Foucault suggests, this ostensible move towards fuller liberation turns out to submit sex to "the power mechanisms of sexuality."[55] For Foucault has made distinctions between "sexuality," which is a mode of discourse, and "sex" as the thing itself. When "sexuality," such as Lawrence's writings, becomes "normative"—I think the argument goes—sex defeats the reality by subordinating it to the prevailing modes. Lawrence, like much of the rest of modern sexual consciousness, created erotic responses which served new tactics of domination. The old repressions at least had the virtues of giving meaning to sexual defiance. In effect, Lawrence spread a sexual politics (for that is what normative discourse finally is) which just ended up as more politics. The "sexual revolution" of recent times took place all right, under the aegis of prophets like Lawrence, but as with so many modern revolutions it ended up changing little and has been subordinated to the cultural tyrannies of technocracy.

The counter-arguments might be that liberating sexual consciousness, and all it implies in voluntaristic society and new modes of post-repressive existence, is still continuing. But after AIDS and other reversals, that may seem a bit counter-factual. Or that the liberation was subverted. But that smacks of even more structural-historical paranoia than Foucault's view. Or that it was a false revolution and we await the true one. But that leans to the pathetic and fanatic. After all, the broad diffusion (not just the literary acceptance) of Lawrence's ideas has often resulted in more parody and anomaly than new reality. His obscenity was less realized than given patronizing exemption. His extremity of masculine–feminine was polemically exploited, not (androgynously?) resolved. His passionate rhetoric became gaming discourse for conventional intellectuals; his literature became canonical antiques. And his demands for passional being mostly produce rococo therapies in the pseudo-indulgent culture of a relentless technocratic ordering.

Lawrence raises some of the most perplexed questions of the relation of rebellious culture to dominant society. He may still sound sometimes as a dissident voice, but one which, given his two generations of rather remarkable effects, has been partly victimized by that very process he so aptly noted: "Anything that *triumphs*, perishes."[56] If his prophecy has not completely perished, then, it is because his vivid consciousness of life has not triumphed. His proper heritage would be to go beyond his ambiguous employment to a social–cultural countering which is more than just recognition—to a new mode of intense being. That passional imperative, beyond as well as in his art, may remain his most significant legacy.

Notes

Introduction *Jeffrey Meyers*

1. "A Genius Pain-obsessed," *Manchester Guardian*, March 4, 1930, p. 12.
2. Alastair Niven, "D. H. Lawrence: Literary Criticism and Recent Publications," *British Book News*, September 1985, p. 516.
3. Aldous Huxley, Introduction to D. H. Lawrence, *Letters* (London, 1932), p. xxx.
4. K. L. Godwin, *The Influence of Ezra Pound* (London, 1966), p. 219.
5. Anthony Burgess, *Flame into Being: The Life and Work of D. H. Lawrence* (New York, 1985), p. 5.
6. W. H. Auden, *The Orators* (New York, 1967), pp. vii, 17, 63; W. H. Auden, "D. H. Lawrence as a Critic," *The Griffin*, 5 (September 1956), 4.
7. Interview with Stephen Spender, Boulder, Colorado, April 4, 1985.
8. Interview with Christopher Isherwood, March 11, 1985.
9. D. H. Lawrence, *Letters: Volume II, 1913–1916*, ed. George Zytaruk and James Boulton (Cambridge, England, 1981), p. 218.
10. Karl Shapiro, "Dylan Thomas," *In Defense of Ignorance* (New York, 1955), p. 184. Dylan Thomas, *Selected Letters*, ed. Constantine FitzGibbon (London, 1966), p. 195, acknowledges his debt to the poems about animals and poems in *The Plumed Serpent*.
11. Keith Sagar, "Beyond D. H. Lawrence," *D. H. Lawrence: The Man Who Lived*, ed. Robert Partlow, Jr. and Harry Moore (Carbondale, Illinois, 1980), pp. 264–265.
12. Letter from Seamus Heaney to Jeffrey Meyers, November 12, 1985. Lawrence's "Poetry of the Present" (1919) appears in *Complete Poems*, ed. Vivian de Sola Pinto and Warren Roberts (New York, 1964), pp. 181–186.

13. D. H. Lawrence, *Letters: Volume I, 1901–1913*, ed. James Boulton (Cambridge, England, 1979), p. 544.
14. George Orwell, *Collected Essays, Journalism and Letters*, ed. Sonia Orwell and Ian Angus (New York, 1968), 1:507, 2:202.
15. *Ibid.*, 4:33.
16. See George Orwell, *The Road to Wigan Pier* (London, 1937), pp. 195, 198–200.
17. Alan Sillitoe, "D. H. Lawrence and His District," *D. H. Lawrence: Novelist, Poet, Prophet*, ed. Stephen Spender (London, 1973), p. 46. See also Alan Sillitoe, "Lawrence's Republic," *Time and Tide*, 42 (October 19, 1961), 1756, on *Fantasia of the Unconscious*.
18. D. H. Lawrence, *Collected Letters*, ed. Harry Moore (New York, 1962), p. 952.
19. Letter from Alan Sillitoe to Jeffrey Meyers, January 20, 1985.
20. Letter from David Storey to Jeffrey Meyers, March 3, 1985. See also David Storey, "Slabs of Slate," *New Statesman*, 68 (October 30, 1964), 654–655, on Lawrence's paintings.
21. Letter from Melvyn Bragg to Jeffrey Meyers, March 15, 1985.
22. *The Letters of D. H. Lawrence and Amy Lowell, 1914–1925*, ed. Claire Healey and Keith Cushman (Santa Barbara, 1985), p. 104.
23. Lawrence, "Poetry of the Present," I.183. See William Carlos Williams, "An Elegy for D. H. Lawrence," *Selected Poems* (New York, 1969), pp. 64–67; and Karl Shapiro, "D. H. L.," *V-Letter* (New York, 1944), p. 47.
24. Letter from Karl Shapiro to Jeffrey Meyers, April 21, 1985.
25. Louis Martz, "A Greenhouse Eden," *Theodore Roethke: Essays on the Poetry*, ed. Arnold Stein (Seattle, 1965), p. 25.
26. Neal Bowers, "Theodore Roethke Speaks," *New Letters*, 49 (1982), 11–12.
27. Theodore Roethke, *Selected Letters*, ed. Ralph Mills, Jr. (Seattle, 1968), pp. 116, 104.
28. Theodore Roethke, "Some Remarks on Rhythm," *On the Poet and His Craft*, ed. Ralph Mills, Jr. (Seattle, 1965), p. 83.
29. Letter from Robert Bly to Jeffrey Meyers, October 24, 1985.

30. Galway Kinnell, *Walking Down the Stairs* (Ann Arbor, 1978), p. 54.
31. Interview with Allen Ginsberg, Boulder, Colorado, April 13, 1985.
32. Quoted in Allen Ginsberg, *Allen Verbatim*, ed. Gordon Ball (New York, 1974), p. 150.
33. Quoted in Wyndham Lewis, *Rude Assignment* (London, 1950), p. 203. See Irving Howe, "In the Lawrencian Orbit," *Sherwood Anderson* (New York, 1951), pp. 179–196.
34. Lawrence, *Letters: Volume II*, ed. Zytaruk and Boulton, p. 90; Ernest Hemingway, "Fathers and Sons," *Short Stories* (New York, 1953), p. 491.
35. Donald Spoto, *The Kindness of Strangers* (Boston, 1985), p. 74.
36. *Ibid.*, p. 271. See also Norman Fedder, *The Influence of D. H. Lawrence on Tennessee Williams* (The Hague, 1966).
37. Letter from Norman Mailer to Jeffrey Meyers, February 6, 1985.

    Bernard Malamud has described his fictional use of Lawrence in *Dubin's Lives* (1979): "Lawrence has had little influence on my work, except as Dubin relates to him at his time of life. Dubin ultimately wrote the biography, not I. Lawrence's purpose in the book was to entice Dubin to participate in a fiction that related him sexually to Fanny Beck.... I used a handful of his books to help Dubin achieve a relationship with Fanny." Letter from Bernard Malamud to Jeffrey Meyers, November 5, 1985.

    For Lawrence's influence on other American writers, see: C. E. Baron, "Lawrence's Influence on Eliot," *Cambridge Quarterly*, 5 (1971), 235–248; Robinson Jeffers, *Selected Letters, 1897–1962*, ed. Ann Ridgeway (Baltimore, 1968), pp. 208, 218, 230, 246; Reloy Garcia, *Steinbeck and D. H. Lawrence: Fictive Voices and the Ethical Imperative* (Muncie, Indiana, 1962); Ekbert Faas, "Charles Olson and D. H. Lawrence: Aesthetics of the 'Primitive Abstract,'" *Boundary*, 2 (1973–74), 113–126; and Virginia Carr, *The Lonely Hunter: A Biography of Carson McCullers* (Garden City, N. Y., 1975), pp. 33, 39.

    Lawrence's influence on foreign writers has never been fully explored. But he clearly influenced the passionate, visceral, homoerotic, authoritarian and extremist elements in the novels of Yukio Mishima. Joseph Sommers, *After the Storm: Landmarks of the Modern Mexican Novel* (Albuquerque, 1968), pp. 128–132, discusses the influence of *The Plumed Serpent* on Carlos Fuentes' *Where the Air Is Clear* (1958). And Bengt Altenberg, "A Checklist of D. H. Lawrence Scholarship in Scandinavia, 1934–1968," *D. H. Lawrence Review*, 2 (1969), 275–277, states that Lawrence influenced the primitivist movement which "became a strong force in Swedish literature" in the 1930s.

38. Lawrence, *Letters: Volume I*, ed. Boulton, p. 478.
39. See John Berryman, "Of Suicide," *Love & Fame*, 2nd ed. (New York, 1972), p. 62:

> I still plan to go to Mexico this summer.
> The Olmec images! Chichén Itzá!
> D. H. Lawrence has a wild dream of it.

Richard Eberhart's "Throwing the Apple," *Collected Poems, 1930–1976* (New York, 1976), p. 202, is based on a painting by Lawrence.

40. The first trade editions of *Tropic of Cancer* (1961), *Memoirs of a Woman of Pleasure (Fanny Hill)* (1963) and the *Kama Sutra* (1963), a sort of Lady Chatterjee's Lover, indirectly owed their appearance to Lawrence. His novel also inspired a number of parodies, including *Lady Loverley's Chatter* and *Sadie Catterley's Cover*.

According to *The Times* (London), August 6, 1985, p. 10, the censorship issue is still alive: "Father Patrick O'Grady, the Catholic priest, has banned *Lady Chatterley's Lover* from being performed in his church hall during the Edinburgh Festival. . . . The organizers of *Lady Chatterley's Lover* offered to withdraw all the nude scenes from the play, but Fr. O'Grady refused to compromise."

41. Lawrence, *Letters: Volume I*, ed. Boulton, p. 99. Lawrence also reached a mass audience through the eight films that were based on his work and his life: *The Rocking-Horse Winner* (1949), *L'Amant de Lady Chatterley* (1959), *Sons and Lovers* (1960), *The Fox* (1968), *Women in Love* (1969), *The Virgin and the Gypsy* (1970), *Lady Chatterley's Lover* (1981) and *The Priest of Love* (1981). An interesting book could be written on Lawrence and film.

42. Philip Larkin, "Annus Mirabilis," *High Windows* (New York, 1974), p. 34.
43. William Boyd, *A Good Man in Africa* (New York, 1982), p. 142. Lawrence also appears in a number of other novels. Kay Boyle's "Rest Cure," *The Best Short Stories of 1931*, ed. Edmund O'Brien (New York, 1931), pp. 47–54, describes the dying Lawrence. Helen Corke's *Neutral Ground* (London, 1933) portrays her friendship with Lawrence and the events that inspired *The Trespasser*. Osbert Sitwell's *Miracle on Sinai* (London, 1933) caricatures Lawrence as a bearded, working-class novelist who praises the dark gods but is always accompanied by a maiden aunt. Keith Winter's *Impassioned Pygmies* (New York, 1936) satirizes Lawrence and his circle. Compton Mackenzie's *The South Wind of Love* (London, 1937) and *The West Wind of Love* (New York, 1940) portray his friendship with Lawrence as well as Lawrence's reaction to the war and attack on religion. In Amanda Cross's *In the Last Analysis* (New York, 1964), the murderer is exposed when he cannot identify a passage in *The Rainbow*. In David Lodge's *The British Museum Is Falling Down* (London, 1965), the frustrated comic hero never manages to read the huge pile of Lawrenciana that awaits him in the Reading Room. And Neal Metcalf's *The Pure Gamble* (Menlo Park, California, 1974) concerns a disciple of Lawrence who founds a commune like Rananim.
44. Quoted in Oriana Fallaci, "Hugh Hefner," *The Egotists* (Chicago, 1968), p. 114.
45. Huxley, Introduction to Lawrence, *Letters*, p. xiii.

Chapter Three. Lawrence and English Poetry William M. Chace

1. D. H. Lawrence, *Mornings in Mexico* and *Etruscan Places* (London, 1974), pp. 146–147.
2. D. H. Lawrence, *Letters: Volume I, 1901–1913*, ed. James Boulton (Cambridge, England, 1979), p. 503.
3. D. H. Lawrence, "Poetry of the Present" [Introduction to the American edition of *New Poems* (1919)], in *Complete Poems*, ed. Vivian de Sola Pinto and Warren Roberts (New York, 1964), pp. 182–183.

...ch von Schiller, *Naive and Sentimental Poetry* and *On the ...*, trans. with introduction and notes by Julius Elias ...York, 1966), p. 110. It should be noted that the ...tion of the key terms of this work, *Über naive und sentimentalische Dichtung*, is problematic, for "naive" and "sentimental" carry connotations in English that are foreign to Schiller's argument. "Simple," "unreflective," and "direct" hint at Schiller's intended meaning for the first term; "complicated," "self-reflecting" and "sophisticated" point to the second.

5. *Ibid.*, p. 116.
6. *Ibid.*, p. 105.
7. *Ibid.*
8. James Joyce, *Ulysses* (New York, 1961), p. 212.
9. D. H. Lawrence, *Studies in Classic American Literature* (New York, 1924), pp. 165–166, 164.
10. Schiller, *Naive and Sentimental Poetry*, p. 89.
11. Sandra Gilbert, "D. H. Lawrence's Uncommon Prayers," *D. H. Lawrence: The Man Who Lived*, ed. Robert Partlow, Jr. and Harry Moore (Carbondale, Illinois, 1980), p. 76.
12. Marjorie Perloff, "Lawrence's Lyric Theater: *Birds, Beasts and Flowers*," *D. H. Lawrence: A Centenary Consideration*, ed. Peter Balbert and Phillip Marcus (Ithaca, N. Y., 1985), p. 128.
13. For arguments asserting that influences on Lawrence also included Thomas Carlyle, George Eliot, John Ruskin and Friedrich Nietzsche, see the respective chapters in *D. H. Lawrence and Tradition*, ed. Jeffrey Meyers (London, 1985).
14. W. H. Auden, "D. H. Lawrence," *The Dyer's Hand* (New York, 1968), pp. 287–288.
15. Humphrey Carpenter, *W. H. Auden: A Biography* (Boston, 1981), p. 87.
16. Auden, *The Dyer's Hand*, p. 278.
17. W. H. Auden, "Some Notes on D. H. Lawrence," *Nation*, 164 (April 26, 1947), 484.
18. Auden, *The Dyer's Hand*, p. 288.
19. *Ibid.*, p. 285.
20. Clive James, "Farewelling Auden," *At the Pillars of Hercules* (London, 1979), p. 18.
21. R. G. Cox, "The Poetry of W. H. Auden," *The Modern Age*:

Volume 7 of the Pelican Guide to English Literature, ed. Boris Ford (Baltimore, 1964), p. 383.
22. John Bayley, *The Romantic Survival* (New York, 1957), p. 196.
23. See, for instance, the 1952 review by Robin Mayhead of Thomas' *Collected Poems, 1934–1952* as reprinted in *A Selection from Scrutiny, Vol. I*, compiled by F. R. Leavis (Cambridge, England, 1968). Of those poems, Mayhead writes, p. 127: "Failing to cohere, to build up together into any kind of overall, unified pattern, they consequently fail to make any forceful or even challenging impact."
24. D. H. Lawrence, "Introduction to His Paintings," *Selected Essays* (London, 1950), p. 317.
25. See his letter (May 9, 1934) to Pamela Hansford Johnson, in Dylan Thomas, *Selected Letters*, ed. Constantine FitzGibbon (New York, 1966), p. 122.
26. Bayley, *The Romantic Survival*, p. 191.
27. Dylan Thomas, *Quite Early One Morning* (London, 1954), p. 14.
28. Blake Morrison, *Seamus Heaney* (London, 1982), p. 23.
29. Edward Lucie-Smith, "The Poetry of D. H. Lawrence—With a Glance at Shelley," *D. H. Lawrence: Novelist, Poet, Prophet*, ed. Stephen Spender (New York, 1973), pp. 226–227.
30. Seamus Heaney, "Englands of the Mind," *Preoccupations: Selected Prose, 1968–1978* (London, 1980), p. 152.
31. Interview with Ekbert Faas, "Ted Hughes and *Crow* [1970]," reprinted in Faas, *Ted Hughes: The Unaccommodated Universe* (Santa Barbara, 1980), p. 198.
32. Calvin Bedient, *Eight Contemporary Poets* (Oxford, 1974), p. x.
33. Quoted in Faas, *Ted Hughes*, p. 208.
34. Bedient, *Eight Contemporary Poets*, pp. 112, 114.
35. Hughes himself has made little of the Lawrence connection, saying only that "I read Lawrence and Thomas at an impressionable age.... But this whole business of influences is mysterious. Sometimes it's just a few words that open up a whole prospect. They may occur anywhere. Then again the influences that really count are most likely not literary at all. Maybe it would be best of all to have no influences." Quoted in Faas, *Ted Hughes*, p. 203.

36. Stephen Spender, *World Within World* (London, 1953), pp. 83–84.
37. R. P. Blackmur, "D. H. Lawrence and Expressive Form," *Form and Value in Modern Poetry* (Garden City, N. Y., 1957), pp. 267, 260.
38. A. Alvarez, "Lawrence's Poetry: The Single State of Man," *D. H. Lawrence: Novelist, Poet, Prophet*, ed., Stephen Spender (New York, 1973), pp. 210–211.

Chapter Four. Lawrence and Travel Writers *Jeffrey Meyers*

1. D. H. Lawrence, *Sea and Sardinia* (New York, 1963), p. 55.
2. *Ibid.*, p. 91.
3. D. H. Lawrence, *Studies in Classic American Literature* (New York, 1924), p. 137.
4. D. H. Lawrence, *Aaron's Rod* (New York, 1965), p. 98.
5. D. H. Lawrence, *The Lost Girl* (New York, 1968), p. 318.
6. D. H. Lawrence, *Letters: Volume II, 1913–1916*, ed. George Zytaruk and James Boulton (Cambridge, England, 1981), p. 330.
7. D. H. Lawrence, *Collected Letters*, ed. Harry Moore (New York, 1962), p. 713.
8. D. H. Lawrence, *Twilight in Italy* (London, 1981), p. 160.
9. D. H. Lawrence, *Phoenix*, ed. Edward McDonald (London, 1936), p. 343.
10. Lawrence, *Collected Letters*, ed. Moore, pp. 702–703.
11. For a development of these ideas and a discussion of Lawrence's travel books, see Jeffrey Meyers, *D. H. Lawrence and the Experience of Italy* (Philadelphia, 1982), pp. 12–28.
12. See Jeffrey Meyers, "Memoirs of Lawrence: A Genre of the Thirties," *D. H. Lawrence Review*, 14 (1981), 1–32. I refer to Auden, rather than to both authors, since he clearly dominated the conception and composition of the book, and wrote all the poetic passages on Lawrence.
13. Edward Mendelson, *Early Auden* (New York, 1981), p. 56.
14. W. H. Auden and Louis MacNeice, *Letters from Iceland* (London, 1937), p. 210. John Layard, an English friend Auden met in Berlin, told him about the crankish ideas of the psychologist Homer Lane.

   Auden wrote five appreciative essays on Lawrence: "Psychology and Art To-day," *The Arts To-day*, ed. Geoffrey

Grigson (London, 1935), pp. 1–21; "Heretics," *New Republic*, 100 (November 1, 1939), 373–374; "Some Notes on D. H. Lawrence," *Nation*, 164 (April 26, 1947), 482–484; "D. H. Lawrence," *The Dyer's Hand* (New York, 1962; rpt. 1968), pp. 277–295; "D. H. Lawrence as Critic," *Griffin*, 5 (September 1956), 4–10.

Auden also rented Lawrence's house in New Mexico from Frieda in 1939, adapted "The Rocking-Horse Winner" for radio in 1940 and lectured on Lawrence's poetry at Oxford in 1957.

15. See Rebecca West, *D. H. Lawrence* (London, 1930), p. 22.
16. See Graham Hough, *Two Exiles: Lord Byron and D. H. Lawrence* (Nottingham, 1956).
17. In an apologetic Foreword to the revised edition (1967), pp. 8–9, Auden unconvincingly wrote that when he saw Iceland "for the first time, the reality verified my dream. . . . The three months in Iceland . . . stand out in my memory as among the happiest in my life."
18. Louis MacNeice, *The Strings Are False* (London, 1965), p. 164.
19. Lawrence, *Sea and Sardinia*, pp. 53, 80.
20. [Christopher Isherwood], "*Letters from Iceland*," *Listener*, 18 (August 11, 1937), 311.
21. Auden and MacNeice, *Letters from Iceland*, p. 223.
22. W. H. Auden and Christopher Isherwood, *Journey to a War* (London, 1939), p. 82.
23. Lawrence, *Aaron's Rod*, p. 97.
24. Martha Gellhorn also interviewed Chou En-lai and later described her 1941 trip with Hemingway to the Sino-Japanese war in *Travels with Myself and Another*.
25. Quoted in Brian Finney, *Christopher Isherwood* (London, 1979), p. 201.
26. Lawrence, *Letters, Volume II*, ed. Zytaruk and Boulton, pp. 431–432.
27. Quoted in Finney, *Christopher Isherwood*, p. 202.
28. Christopher Isherwood, *The Condor and the Cows* (London, 1949), p. 51.
29. Lawrence, *Sea and Sardinia*, p. 149.
30. Lawrence, *Letters: Volume III, 1916–1921*, ed. James Boulton and Andrew Robertson (Cambridge, England, 1984), p. 676.

31. Quoted in Finney, *Christopher Isherwood*, p. 201.
32. Two recent good books on South America, which has rarely inspired great travel writing, have followed the Lawrence–Isherwood tradition: Bruce Chatwin's *In Patagonia* (1977) and Paul Theroux's *The Great Patagonian Express* (1979).
33. See Jeffrey Meyers, *Fiction and the Colonial Experience* (Ipswich, England, 1973), pp. 108–111; and Graham Greene, *The Lost Childhood* (New York, 1962), pp. 66–68.
34. See Meyers, *D. H. Lawrence and the Experience of Italy*, pp. 13–17.
35. D. H. Lawrence, *Mornings in Mexico* and *Etruscan Places* (London, 1974), pp. 134, 158.
36. Graham Greene, *Journey Without Maps* (New York, 1961), p. 11.
37. D. H. Lawrence, *Letters*, ed. Aldous Huxley (London, 1932), pp. 628, 631, quoted in Graham Greene, *The Lawless Roads* (London, 1955), p. 108.
38. D. H. Lawrence, *The Plumed Serpent* (New York, 1951), p. 315.
39. See Jeffrey Meyers, "*The Plumed Serpent* and the Mexican Revolution," *Journal of Modern Literature*, 4 (September 1974), 55–72. For an objective view of the religious question, see Lyle Brown, "Mexican Church–State Relations, 1933–1940," *Journal of Church and State*, 6 (May 1964), 202–222.
40. It is significant that Greene did not reply to *Authors Take Sides on the Spanish War* (London, 1937).
41. This was the subject of Evelyn Waugh's *Robbery Under Law* (1939).
42. Henry Miller, *The Wisdom of the Heart* (Norfolk, Connecticut, 1941), p. 172.
43. Henry Miller, *The World of Lawrence: A Passionate Appreciation*, ed. Evelyn Hinz and John Teunissen (Santa Barbara, 1980), p. 38.
44. *Ibid.*, pp. 160, 82, 159.
45. Henry Miller, *The Colossus of Maroussi* (London, 1963), pp. 34, 161.
46. See Roberts W. French, "Whitman and the Poetics of Lawrence," *D. H. Lawrence and Tradition*, ed. Jeffrey Meyers (London, 1985), pp. 91–114.
47. There were also numerous errors in the text that have remained uncorrected in later editions. Miller referred to

Heinrich rather than to *Stefan* George; attributed a quotation from *Lear* to *Macbeth*; did not realize that Thebes was also a city in ancient Egypt. He planned to visit Delos, but could not even think of seeing Mykonos—which was ten minutes away. And he spoke of "all the English poets who had been drowned in the Mediterranean," though only Shelley died that way.

48. Lawrence, *Sea and Sardinia*, p. 10. See also p. 176.
49. See Greene, *The Lawless Roads*, p. 234: "I loathed Mexico—but . . . there were worse places. . . . [America] wasn't evil, it wasn't anything at all, it was just . . . the sinless empty graceless chromium world."
50. See Ernest Hemingway, "L'Envoi" to *In Our Time* (New York, 1970), p. 157, on the King of the Hellenes: "Like all Greeks he wanted to go to America."
51. Miller, *The World of Lawrence*, p. 159.
52. George Orwell, "Inside the Whale," *A Collection of Essays* (New York, 1954), pp. 248–249.
53. Lawrence Durrell, *Bitter Lemons* (New York, 1957), p. 9.
54. Durrell has recently expanded his island books with *Sicilian Carousel* (1977) and *The Greek Islands* (1978).
55. *Lawrence Durrell and Henry Miller: A Private Correspondence*, ed. George Wickes (London, 1963), pp. 294, 300.
56. *Ibid.*, pp. 304, 306. Though Durrell was politically perceptive, he underestimated Archbishop Makarios and wrote in *Bitter Lemons*: "If Enosis came he would be a nobody, like the Archbishop of Crete."
57. Lawrence Durrell, *Spirit of Place*, ed. Alan Thomas (New York, 1971), pp. 156, 161. Durrell also wrote appreciative introductions to *Lady Chatterley's Lover* (New York: Bantam, 1968), pp. vii–xi, and to *Etruscan Places* (London: Folio Society, 1972), pp. 9–11.
58. Orwell, less moderate than Durrell, defended the use of force in the British Empire and stated the English in India "could not have maintained themselves in power for a single week, if the normal Anglo-Indian outlook had been that of, say, E. M. Forster" ("Rudyard Kipling," *A Collection of Essays*, p. 127).
59. *Literary Influences: The Richard Aldington–Lawrence Durrell Correspondence*, ed. Ian McNiven and Harry Moore (New York, 1981), p. 18.

60. Gerald Brenan, *South from Granada* (Cambridge, England, 1980), p. x.
61. Gerald Brenan, *Personal Record, 1920–1972* (London, 1974), p. 18. For my review of this book, see *Modern Fiction Studies*, 21 (1975–76), 605–607. I came to know Brenan well when I lived in a nearby Spanish village during 1971–75. My story, "A World Historical Moment," *Arizona Quarterly* (1986), is based on our last meeting.
62. Lawrence and Brenan would have loathed the current sexual cant expressed, for example, by Carolyn Heilbrun in *Toward a Recognition of Androgyny* (New York, 1973), p. ix: "I believe that our future salvation lies in a movement away from sexual polarization and the prison of gender toward a world in which individual roles and the modes of personal behavior can be freely chosen."
63. Lawrence, "*Mastro-don Gesualdo*, by Giovanni Verga," *Phoenix*, p. 228.
64. Lawrence, *Mornings in Mexico* and *Etruscan Places*, pp. 146–147.

Chapter Five. Lawrence and American Poetry *Roberts W. French*

1. By "the innovative poetry" I refer to that body of verse frequently termed the "new" American poetry, as distinct from the "traditional" American poetry. The new American poetry, which derives ultimately from Whitman and has been the dominant force for the last quarter-century, would include such poets as Williams, Creeley, Rexroth, Ginsberg and Olson; the traditional American poetry, which derives ultimately from English models and was the dominant force until the late 1950s and early 1960s, is represented by such poets as Frost, Ransom, Wilbur, Hecht, most of Roethke and the early Lowell. The divisions, it should be added, are not always clear, and a particular poet may move from one camp to the other.
2. D. H. Lawrence, *Letters: Volume I, 1901–1913*, ed. James Boulton (Cambridge, England, 1979), p. 145.
3. *Literary Essays of Ezra Pound*, ed. T. S. Eliot (New York, 1968), p. 388.

4. Ezra Pound, *Selected Letters 1907–1941*, ed. D. D. Paige (New York, 1971), p. 17. For a thorough discussion of this subject, see Walton Litz, "Lawrence, Pound, and Early Modernism," *D. H. Lawrence: A Centenary Consideration*, ed. Peter Balbert and Phillip Marcus (Ithaca, N. Y., 1985), pp. 15–28.
5. D. H. Lawrence, *Collected Letters*, ed. Harry Moore (New York, 1962), p. 1154.
6. T. S. Eliot, in *D. H. Lawrence: The Critical Heritage*, ed. R. P. Draper (London, 1970), p. 276.
7. T. S. Eliot, *After Strange Gods: A Primer of Modern Heresy* (Charlottesville, Virginia, 1934), p. 41.
8. Eliot, *After Strange Gods*, pp. 65, 35, 64, 67.
9. Karl Shapiro, "The True Contemporary," *Start with the Sun: Studies in the Whitman Tradition* (Lincoln, Nebraska, 1963), p. 224.
10. D. H. Lawrence, *Letters: Volume III, 1916–1921*, ed. James Boulton and Andrew Robertson (Cambridge, England, 1984), p. 141.
11. *Selected Letters of Robert Frost*, ed. Lawrance Thompson (New York, 1964), p. 179.
12. Stanley Kunitz, *A Kind of Order, A Kind of Folly* (Boston, 1975), p. 3.
13. Robert Duncan, in *Towards a New American Poetics*, ed. Ekbert Faas (Santa Barbara, 1979), p. 69.
14. D. H. Lawrence, *Complete Poems*, ed. Vivian de Sola Pinto and Warren Roberts (New York, 1964), p. 184.
15. Louis Simpson, *A Company of Poets* (Ann Arbor, 1981), pp. 351–352.
16. Marvin Bell, *Old Snow Just Melting* (Ann Arbor, 1983), p. 37.
17. Robert Lowell, *Writers at Work: The "Paris Review" Interviews*, Second Series, ed. George Plimpton (New York, 1963), p. 346.
18. A. Alvarez, "D. H. Lawrence: The Single State of Man," *D. H. Lawrence: Novelist, Poet, Prophet*, ed. Stephen Spender (New York, 1973), p. 222.
19. Karl Shapiro, "The Unemployed Magician," *D. H. Lawrence: A Miscellany*, ed. Harry Moore (Carbondale, Illinois, 1959), pp. 378–395.
20. R. P. Blackmur, "D. H. Lawrence and Expressive Form,"

Form and Value in Modern Poetry (Garden City, N. Y., 1957), pp. 255–256.
21. D. H. Lawrence, *Letters: Volume III*, ed. Boulton and Robertson, p. 141.
22. Robert Bly, *Talking All Morning* (Ann Arbor, 1980), p. 177.
23. W. H. Auden, "D. H. Lawrence," *The Dyer's Hand* (New York, 1968), p. 278.
24. T. S. Eliot, "Tradition and the Individual Talent," *Selected Essays* (New York, 1960), pp. 7, 10.
25. Kenneth Rexroth, *With Eye and Ear* (New York, 1970), p. 38; *Bird in the Bush* (New York, 1959), p. vii.
26. Rexroth, *With Eye and Ear*, p. 36.
27. *The Journals of Sylvia Plath*, ed. Ted Hughes and Frances McCullough (New York, 1982), p. 199.
28. *Ibid.*, p. 128.
29. Sylvia Plath, *Letters Home*, ed. Aurelia Schober Plath (New York, 1977), p. 379.
30. Plath, *Journals*, p. 196.
31. *Ibid.*, p. 199.
32. Lawrence, *Complete Poems*, p. 27.
33. *Ibid.*, p. 191.
34. Alfred Kazin, *Contemporaries* (New York, 1982), p. 224.
35. Steven Gould Axelrod, *Robert Lowell: Life and Art* (Princeton, 1978), p. 86; Robert Lowell, "On Freedom in Poetry," in *Naked Poetry*, ed. Stephen Berg and Robert Mezey, (Indianapolis, 1969), p. 124. The three other poets that Lowell mentions are Whitman, Pound and Williams.
36. Bly, *Talking All Morning*, p. 116.
37. *Ibid.*, p. 251.
38. *Ibid.*, pp. 175, 200.
39. *Ibid.*, p. 116.
40. *Ibid.*, p. 280.
41. D. H. Lawrence, *Phoenix*, ed. Edward McDonald (London, 1936), p. 29.
42. *Ibid.*, p. 31.
43. Gary Snyder, in *Towards a New American Poetics*, ed. Ekbert Faas (Santa Barbara, 1979), p. 119.
44. Gary Snyder, *Turtle Island* (New York, 1974), p. 106.
45. Lawrence, *Phoenix*, p. 27.
46. Snyder, *Turtle Island*, p. 107.
47. Allan Seager, *The Glass House: The Life of Theodore Roethke*

(New York, 1968), p. 63; Theodore Roethke, *Selected Letters* (Seattle, 1968), p. 104; Jay Parini, *Theodore Roethke: An American Romantic* (Amherst, Massachusetts, 1979), p. 67.
48. Theodore Roethke, "Some Remarks on Rhythm," *On the Poet and His Craft*, ed. Ralph Mills, Jr. (Seattle, 1965), pp. 82–83. The exact quotation from Lawrence is this: "It all depends on the *pause*—the natural pause, the natural *lingering* of the voice according to the feeling—it is the hidden *emotional* pattern that makes poetry, not the obvious form" (Lawrence, *Letters: Volume II*, ed. Zytaruk and Boulton, p. 104).
49. Roethke, *On the Poet and His Craft*, p. 83.
50. Theodore Roethke, *Straw for the Fire: From the Notebooks of Theodore Roethke, 1943–63*, ed. David Wagoner (Garden City, N. Y., 1974) p. 154.
51. *Ibid.*, p. 194.
52. Letter from Galway Kinnell to Roberts W. French, March 28, 1985; Galway Kinnell, *Walking Down the Stairs* (Ann Arbor, 1978), p. 54.
53. Kinnell, *Walking Down the Stairs*, p. 61.
54. Aldous Huxley, Introduction to D. H. Lawrence, *Letters*, (New York, 1932), pp. xi–xii.
55. *Ibid.*, p. xxx.
56. Kinnell, *Walking Down the Stairs*, p. 52.
57. *Ibid.*, p. 55.
58. *Ibid.*, p. 54.
59. Galway Kinnell, "Poetry, Personality and Death," *A Field Guide to Contemporary Poetry and Poetics*, ed. Stuart Friebert and David Young (New York, 1980), p. 220.
60. *Ibid.*, p. 217.
61. Galway Kinnell, in *The Craft of Poetry*, ed. William Packard (Garden City, N. Y., 1974), p. 107.
62. "Projective Verse," *The New American Poetry: 1945–1960*, ed. Donald Allen (New York, 1960), p. 387.
63 Charles Olson, *Letters for Origin: 1950–1956*, ed. Albert Glover (New York, 1970), p. 63.
64. Charles Olson, *Human Universe and Other Essays*, ed. Donald Allen (New York, 1961), p. 112.
65. Charles Olson and Robert Creeley, *The Complete Correspondence*, ed. George Butterick (Santa Barbara, 1981), III.61.

66. Robert Creeley, in *Towards a New American Poetics*, p. 166.
67. This comment and those following in this paragraph are in a letter from Robert Creeley to Roberts W. French, April 12, 1985.
68. Olson and Creeley, *The Complete Correspondence*, II.126.
69. *Ibid.*, III.99.

Chapter Six. Lawrence and American Fiction   Eugene Goodheart

1. Earlier versions of *Studies in Classic American Literature* were collected under the title *The Symbolic Meaning*, ed. Armin Arnold, with a preface by Harry Moore (London, 1962).
2. D. H. Lawrence, *Studies in Classic American Literature* (New York, 1924), p. 56.
3. *Ibid.*, pp. 57–58.
4. *Ibid.*, pp. 60, 58.
5. *Ibid.*, p. 59.
6. This is not unprecedented. Who has better understood our culture and our politics than de Tocqueville?
7. Tony Tanner, *The City of Words* (New York, 1971).
8. Edward Dahlberg and Herbert Read, *Truth Is More Sacred* (New York, 1961), p. 102.
9. *Ibid*.
10. *The Confessions of Edward Dahlberg* (New York, 1971), pp. 192–193.
11. D. H. Lawrence, "An Introduction to *Bottom Dogs*," *Edward Dahlberg: American Ishmael of Letters*, ed. Harold Billings (Austin, 1968), p. 46.
12. *The Confessions of Edward Dahlberg*, p. 217.
13. William Carlos Williams, *In the American Grain* (New York, 1925), p. 154.
14. Sherwood Anderson, *Winesburg, Ohio* (London, 1983), p. 80.
15. *Ibid.*, pp. 68–69.
16. Irving Howe, *Sherwood Anderson* (New York, 1951), p. 192.
17. Sherwood Anderson, *Dark Laughter* (New York, 1925), p. 145.
18. Joseph Foster, *D. H. Lawrence in Taos* (Albuquerque, 1972), p. 185.
19. By resistance I do not mean a strategy of disarmament

which dismisses his prophetic role and simply affirms the artist. For instance, Saul Bellow discounts *The Plumed Serpent*, politically and morally his most offensive novel, and embraces *The Lost Girl*, an admirable but not very original novel. (*Writers at Work: The "Paris Review" Interviews*, Third Series, ed. George Plimpton, London, 1965, p. 182.) I suspect that the real motive for Bellow's resistance to Lawrence is not Lawrence's spiritual–prophetic character, but the quasi-fascistic doctrine of *The Plumed Serpent*. I can think of no contemporary American writer whose work has a spiritual ambition as powerful as Bellow's.
20. Evelyn Hinz and John Teunissen, Introduction to Henry Miller, *The World of Lawrence* (Santa Barbara, 1980), p. 15.
21. *Ibid.*
22. *Ibid.*, p. 19.
23. *Ibid.*, p. 24.
24. *Ibid.*, p. 77.
25. *Ibid.*, p. 45.
26. *Ibid.*, p. 84.
27. *Writers at Work: The "Paris Review" Interviews*, Second Series, ed. George Plimpton (New York, 1963), p. 182.
28. In a very shrewd essay on Miller, Orwell discerned the practicality of the American businessman in Miller's sexual dealings. In general, Orwell sees Miller as "a completely negative, unconstructive, amoral writer, a mere Jonah, a passive accepter of evil, a sort of Whitman among the corpses." ("Inside the Whale," *A Collection of Essays*, New York, 1954, p. 256.) Does Lawrence represent for Miller an opposing self, an image of contrary realization that he might have wished for himself? Not that Orwell sees much hope in Lawrence's hopefulness. Lawrence's work is "a species of defeatism, because that is not the direction in which the world is moving" (p. 233). But this is not Lawrence's feeling about his own work; nor does it represent contemporary feeling about Lawrence. My point is that Orwell's incisive characterization of Miller illuminates his distance from Lawrence.
29. Miller, *The World of Lawrence*, p. 238.
30. *Ibid.*, pp. 220–221.
31. *Ibid.*, pp. 184–185.
32. The woman as culture bearer is no generalized perception

in Lawrence, but the specific legacy of his experience of his mother—as we see most impressively in *Sons and Lovers*.
33. Miller, *The World of Lawrence*, p. 184.
34. *Ibid.*, p. 141.
35. *Ibid.*, p. 186.
36. *Ibid.*, p. 175. In a *Paris Review* interview, Miller makes a distinction between the obscene and the pornographic. "The obscene would be the forthright, and pornography would be the roundabout.... Obscenity is a cleansing process, whereas pornography only adds to the murk." *Writers at Work: The "Paris Review" Interviews*, Second Series, pp. 182–183.
37. Miller, *The World of Lawrence*, p. 263.
38. Norman Mailer, *The Prisoner of Sex* (Boston, 1971), p. 136.
39. *Ibid.*, pp. 137–138.
40. *Ibid.*, p. 141.
41. Kate Millett, *Sexual Politics* (New York, 1970), p. 295.
42. Bernard Malamud, *Dubin's Lives* (New York, 1980), p. 182.
43. *Ibid.*, p. 322.
44. *Ibid.*, p. 190.
45. *Ibid.*, p. 182.
46. *Ibid.*, p. 321.
47. Mailer, *The Prisoner of Sex*, p. 137.
48. Lawrence, *Studies in Classic American Literature*, pp. 85–86.
49. *Ibid.*, p. 24.
50. In *Life Against Death* (Middletown, Connecticut, 1959), p. 181, Norman O. Brown speaks of Lawrence as "a paradoxically conservative philosopher of sexuality."
51. D. H. Lawrence, *The Rainbow* (London, 1980), p. 448.
52. Bellow discovers vitality in a place that would be death for Lawrence. Ijah, the central character of "Cousins" (in *Him with His Foot in His Mouth and Other Stories*, New York, 1984, p. 259) knows that "there were so many things going on in the *outer* world [of Chicago], the city itself was so rich in opportunities for *real* development, a center of such wealth, power, drama, rich even in crimes and vices, in diseases and intrinsic—not accidental—monstrosities, that it was foolish, querulous, to concentrate on oneself."
53. D. H. Lawrence, "America, Listen to Your Own," *Phoenix*, ed. Edward McDonald (New York, 1936), p. 90.
54. Walker Percy, *The Moviegoer* (New York, 1961), p. 88.

55. Tennessee Williams, *I Rise in Flame, Cried the Phoenix* (New York, 1951), p. 17.

Chapter Seven. Lawrence's Cultural Impact   Kingsley Widmer

1. For a couple of examples of erotic use: see identifying Lawrence as forerunner of American suburban sex games in Gay Talese, *Thy Neighbor's Wife* (New York, 1979); for the use of Lawrence's writings in treating "sexually dysfunctional males," see Patricia Gillan, "Therapeutic Uses of Obscenity," *Censorship and Obscenity*, ed. Rajeev Dhavan (Totowa, N. J., 1978). For a doctrinaire attack on Lawrence for undermining positive industrial attitudes, see Paul Delany, "Lawrence and the Decline of the Industrial Spirit" (Paper at the Centenary D. H. Lawrence Conference, Tufts University, June 14, 1985); for earlier versions, see the immense controversies around C. P. Snow, *The Two Cultures* (New York, 1959); in contrast, Dan Jacobson struggled to place Lawrence on the radical left in "D. H. Lawrence and Modern Society," *D. H. Lawrence: A Collection of Criticism*, ed. Leo Hamalian (New York, 1975), pp. 133–143. For examples of varied cultish apotheosizings, contrast the narrow moralist F. R. Leavis—*D. H. Lawrence* (Cambridge, England, 1930), *D. H. Lawrence, Novelist* (London, 1955), and *Thought, Words and Creativity* (New York, 1976)—and the apocalyptic buffoon Henry Miller—*The World of Lawrence* (Santa Barbara, 1980); and my discussion of his use of Lawrence, *Henry Miller* (New York, 1963), Ch. 5.
2. For condescending discussions, see Diana Trilling, "Lawrence and the Movements of Modern Culture," *D. H. Lawrence: Novelist, Poet, Prophet*, ed. Stephen Spender (New York, 1973), pp. 1–7; and Keith Sagar, "Beyond D. H. Lawrence," *D. H. Lawrence: The Man Who Lived*, ed. Robert Partlow, Jr. and Harry Moore (Carbondale, Illinois, 1980), pp. 258–266.
3. This is evident in many of the unusually large number of memoirs and biographies, and in some of the eight movies made from his works. Even a conservative contemporary

poet, Donald Davie, has confessed that "some of us ... tried to conduct our marriages on Lawrentian principles, with touching and comical consequences" (*TLS*, October 1, 1977, p. 1233). But possibly the romanticizing is being undermined, for example, by the publication of the second half of the autobiographical *Mr. Noon* (1984), in which we see the beloved woman having casual sex with several other men and the Lawrencean lover displaying timorous jealousy and sexual inadequacy.

4. For a few examples in the novels: Alvina in *The Lost Girl* must, even in her own mind, see herself as her Italian peasant's "sacred prostitute" and "slave," and become totally "submissive to his being." Ursula in *Women in Love* must accede to Birkin's sexual and other peculiarities, and abnegate her "will" unto "surrender of her spiritual being." The arguments in *Aaron's Rod* insist that women make "deep unfathomable free submission." Kate in *The Plumed Serpent* must make "submission absolute" to a ranting thug. Constance in *Lady Chatterley's Lover* is praised for being "a passive, consenting thing, like a slave."
5. See my book *The Art of Perversity: D. H. Lawrence's Shorter Fictions* (Seattle, 1962), especially Ch. 3.
6. D. H. Lawrence, *Fantasia of the Unconscious* (New York, 1933), p. 128.
7. D. H. Lawrence, *Assorted Articles* (New York, 1930), p. 38.
8. D. Trilling, "Lawrence and the Movements of Modern Culture," p. 2.
9. See Jeffrey Meyers, "Memoirs of D. H. Lawrence: A Genre of the Thirties," *D. H. Lawrence Review*, 14 (1981), 1–32.
10. John Middleton Murry, *Son of Woman* (London, 1931). He took a somewhat different later view, as in *Love, Freedom and Society* (London, 1957).
11. Lawrence had savaged Murry for unmanliness in "Jimmy and the Desperate Woman" (1924).
12. Anaïs Nin, *D. H. Lawrence: An Unprofessional Study* (Paris, 1932).
13. Simone de Beauvoir, *The Second Sex* (New York, 1971), pp. 39, 214–224.
14. See, for example, my essay "Lawrence and the Fall of Modern Woman," *Modern Fiction Studies*, 5 (1959), 47–56. The philosopher Kathleen Nott commented in periodicals

on Lawrencean "female discipleship," early but eroding "sympathy with the female," and later male dominance and "leadership" obsessions. These articles were later reprinted in *A Soul in the Quad* (London, 1969), pp. 297–319. The sociologist Philip Rieff (1966, cited below) explained that Lawrence's "aggressiveness against women" was part of the paranoia of "religiously burdened men." Part of Lawrence's problem, of course, was ambivalent homoeroticism, on which, see Jeffrey Meyers, "D. H. Lawrence," *Homosexuality and Literature, 1890–1930* (Montreal, 1977), pp. 131–161. Most literary criticism ignores or fudges that issue.
15. Kate Millett, *Sexual Politics* (New York, 1970), pp. 237–293. As with a number of my examples, this is not just academic argument but a larger social effect (Millett was a celebrity and appeared on the cover of *Time*).
16. Norman Mailer, *The Prisoner of Sex* (New York, 1971). The "avenger" is in "The Time of Her Time," *Advertisements for Myself* (1959), wife-murdering fantasies in *An American Dream* (1964), *Tough Guys Don't Dance* (1984) and his biography. For others, see my essay "The Post-Modernist Art of Protest," *Centennial Review*, 19 (1975), 121–135.
17. Mailer, *The Prisoner of Sex*, pp. 98, 99, 101, 107.
18. *Ibid.*, pp. 110, 113. The point had previously been raised by several commentators, such as: "Lawrence was a woman in a man's skin" in H. M. Daleski, *The Forked Flame: A Study of D. H. Lawrence* (London, 1965), p. 13.
19. Mailer, *The Prisoner of Sex*, p. 152.
20. Erica Jong, *Fear of Flying* (New York, 1973), pp. 319, 335.
21. Probably the most elaborated defense is Charles Rossman's monograph, "'You Are the Call and I Am the Answer': D. H. Lawrence and Woman," *D. H. Lawrence Review*, 8 (1973), 255–328. More qualified is Donald Gutierrez, "D. H. Lawrence and Sex," *Liberal and Fine Arts Review*, 3 (1983), 43–56.
22. Anne Smith, "A New Adam and a New Eve," *Lawrence and Women*, ed. Anne Smith (New York, 1978), pp. 9–48.
23. Faith Pullin, "Lawrence's Treatment of Women in *Sons and Lovers*," *Lawrence and Women*, pp. 49–74. I am ignoring many of the fatuous studies, here and elsewhere.
24. Mark Spilka, "On Lawrence's Hostility to Wilful Women:

The Chatterley Solution," *Lawrence and Women*, pp. 189–211. For a larger context of disagreement, see my "The Literary Institutionalization of D. H. Lawrence," *Paunch* (State University of New York, Buffalo), 26 (1966), 4–13, and counter-statements by Spilka, and rebuttals, *Paunch*, 27 (1966), 83–96.

25. Harry Moore, "Bert Lawrence and Lady Jane," *Lawrence and Women*, pp. 178–188, and his many books on Lawrence.
26. Carol Dix, *D. H. Lawrence and Women* (Totowa, N. J., 1980), p. 81.
27. Hilary Simpson, *D. H. Lawrence and Feminism* (DeKalb, Illinois, 1982), p. 42. Later quotes, pp. 78, 122. She erroneously, for example, claims that Clara in *Sons and Lovers* is not allowed sexual satisfaction and that Mrs. Witt in *St. Mawr* is treated positively.
28. Gavriel Ben-Ephraim, "The Achievement of Balance in *Lady Chatterley's Lover*," *D. H. Lawrence's "Lady"*, ed. Michael Squires and Dennis Jackson (Athens, Georgia, 1985), p. 136.
29. Public conversation (Tulsa, December 1980). Greer makes a similar argument in *The Female Eunuch* (New York, 1972), where she also mocks Lawrence, p. 194. She has repeatedly attacked his heightened eroticism: women should now "recognize that we are not so sexy as we thought we were. The Lawrentian myth has been exploded"—in "Dark Age of the Steroid," *Literary Review* (London), 85 (1985), 12.
30. For current discussion of feminist censoring of obscenity, see Marcia Pally, "X-rated Feminism," *Nation*, 240 (July 29, 1985), 784–793.
31. Emile Delavenay, *D. H. Lawrence: The Man and His Work* (London, 1972), pp. 236–242, held the suppression to be punishment for Lawrence's anti-war views. While "obscenity" cases often have a political element, and in the Great War pathological patriotism might apply, the evidence seems quite uncertain. The generally accepted view is summarized by Harry Moore, *The Priest of Love* (New York, 1974), pp. 239–246.
32. The "Prologue" now appears in *Phoenix II*, ed. Warren Roberts and Harry Moore (New York, 1970), pp. 92–108. The story "Sun" was published unexpurgated by the small Black Sun Press (Paris, 1928) after the usual politer edition

(1926). *The Virgin and the Gypsy* got surprisingly vague with the tabooed bedding-down scene of the Rector's daughter and the dark stranger.

33. The materials were collected in *D. H. Lawrence: Sex, Literature and Censorship*, ed. Harry Moore (New York, 1953), which also gives some history, and in *Phoenix II*.
34. Some legal and historical material is provided in *Literary Censorship*, ed. Kingsley and Eleanor Widmer (San Francisco, 1961). See also my essay "Beyond Censorship? The Restrictive Processing of American Culture," *Freedom and Culture*, ed. Eleanor Widmer (Belmont, California, 1970).
35. For this, and other arguments, see my essay "The Pertinence of Modern Pastoral: The Three Versions of *Lady Chatterley's Lover*," *Studies in the Novel*, 5 (1973), 298–313, with elaborate notes.
36. Charles Rembar, *The End of Obscenity* (New York, 1968), mostly pp. 59–160 (documents of the three hearings and trials are in the Appendix).
37. For part of the testimony of Malcolm Cowley and Alfred Kazin, see *Literary Censorship*, ed. Widmer, pp. 94–104. Prefatory material by Archibald MacLeish and Mark Schorer was part of the 1959 Grove Press edition on trial; supporting material came from current book reviews.
38. Rembar, *The End of Obscenity*, p. 120.
39. *Ibid.*, p. 490.
40. *Ibid.*, p. 493.
41. Quoted in *The Trial of Lady Chatterley*, ed. C. H. Rolph (Baltimore, 1961), which includes the larger part of the transcript, plus some summary and commentary, p. 17. The ostensibly more progressive British statute (the Obscene Publications Act of 1959) used a broader definition, "the tendency to deprave and corrupt," than the U. S. law (the prevailing *Roth* decision qualifying the old Comstock Act), but also gave a clearer escape route than the pre-Chatterley American law since it exempted material "in the interests of science, literature, art, or learning." The results were similar.
42. Rembar, *The End of Obscenity*, pp. 152–160.
43. A bit later, there was a peculiar and disproportionately large academic controversy about Lawrence's partly self-censored sodomizing of the lady. For citations, and a

reasonable discussion, see Donald Gutierrez, "'The Impossible Notation': The Sodomy Scene in *Lady Chatterley's Lover*," *The Sphinx* (University of Saskatchewan), 4 (1982), 109–125.
44. Rolph, *The Trial of Lady Chatterley*, p. 250.
45. I have discussed Lawrence's major influence on the poetic and critical views of Melville in "The Modernist Myth of Melville," *Companion to Melville Studies*, ed. John Bryant (Westport, Connecticut, 1985).
46. I have detailed this in several recent studies, including "Desire and Negation in Lawrence's Fiction," *Centenary Essays on D. H. Lawrence*, ed. Gamini Salgado and G. K. Das (London: Macmillan, in press).
47. The issue is noted, though in a somewhat denigrating religious context, by Taylor Stoehr, "Paul Goodman and the New York Jews," *Salmagundi*, 66 (1985), 50–103. Goodman told me in the 1950s of his admiration for Lawrence but I did not emphasize it in my *Paul Goodman* (Boston, 1980).
48. Arthur Efron, "The Mind–Body Problem in Lawrence, Pepper, and Reich," *Journal of Mind and Behavior*, 1 (1980), 247–270. An attempted massive empirical confirmation of the argument appears in his *The Sexual Body: An Interdisciplinary Perspective* (entire Special Double Issue of *Journal of Mind and Behavior*, 1985), which several times cites Lawrence.
49. Philip Rieff, *The Triumph of the Therapeutic* (New York, 1966), pp. 189–231. His earlier discussion serves as an "Introduction" to Lawrence's *Psychoanalysis and the Unconscious* and *Fantasia of the Unconscious* (New York, 1960), pp. vii–xxiii. Some erotic philosophers in this period viewed Lawrence as sexually "conservative," as did Norman O. Brown, *Life Against Death* (New York, 1959).
50. Rieff, *The Triumph of the Therapeutic*, pp. 191, 196, 230, 211.
51. For these, and related passages, see my "Lawrence and the Nietzschean Matrix," *D. H. Lawrence and Tradition*, ed. Jeffrey Meyers (London, 1985), pp. 115–131.
52. Rieff, *Triumph of the Therapeutic*, p. 217.
53. Michel Foucault, *The History of Sexuality*, Vol. *I* (New York, 1978), p. 157.
54. *Ibid.*, pp. 130–131, 155.

55. *Ibid.*, p. 158. This is elliptical unto obscurantism.
56. D. H. Lawrence, *Reflections on the Death of a Porcupine and Other Essays* (London, 1934), p. 17.

Index

Allen, Walter, 168
Alvarez, A., 77, 114–115
Anderson, Sherwood, 137; *Dark Laughter*, 10, 139, 140–141; *Many Marriages*, 139; *Winesburg, Ohio*, 139–140
Annan, Noel, 168
Apollinaire, Guillaume, 118
Auden, W. H., 2, 8, 60, 61–63, 80, 92, 100, 115, 116–117, 182 n14; *The Ascent of F-6*, 90; "In Praise of Limestone," 85; *Journey to a War*, 88–91, 96, 107–108; *Letters from Iceland*, 83–88, 90, 96, 107–108, 183 n17; *The Orators*, 2; "Whither?," 90
Austen, Jane, 26; *Mansfield Park*, 18

Barr, Barbara Weekley, 1
Bayley, John, viii, 14–29, 64, 65
Beauvoir, Simone de, *The Second Sex*, 158
Bedient, Calvin, 74, 75
Bell, Marvin, 114
Bellow, Saul, 191 n19; *Him with His Foot in His Mouth*, 192 n52
Bennett, Arnold, 31, 32, 33, 34, 40
Berryman, John, *The Dream Songs*, 120; "Of Suicide," 178 n39
Blackmur, R. P., 77, 115
Blake, William, 1, 3, 60, 142
Bloom, Harold, 141
Bly, Robert, 9, 59, 116, 122, 123
Borges, Jorge Luis, 93
Bowen, Elizabeth, 20; "Mysterious Kor," 28–29
Boyd, William, *A Good Man in Africa*, 12

Braddon, Mary, *Lady Audley's Secret*, 23
Bragg, Melvyn, 6, 7–8, 53; *The Hired Man*, 34; *Love and Glory*, 36; *A Place in England*, 34–35; *The Silken Net*, 35–36
Brenan, Gerald, 83, 100; *Personal Record*, 105; *South from Granada*, 104–108
Brennan, William, 166
Brett, Dorothy, 1
Brontë, Emily, *Wuthering Heights*, 148
Browning, Robert, 59
Burgess, Anthony, 2
Butler, Samuel, 81
Byron, George Gordon, Lord, 84–85

Campbell, Roy, 80; "To a Pet Cobra," 78–79
Carlyle, Thomas, 1, 3, 180 n13
Carpenter, Humphrey, *W. H. Auden*, 61
Carswell, John, 1
Caskey, William, 92, 94
Chace, William M., viii, 54–80
Chaucer, Geoffrey, *Troilus and Criseyde*, 15
Chekhov, Anton, 20
Coleridge, Samuel Taylor, 132
Compton-Burnett, Ivy, 21
Conrad, Joseph, 94; *Under Western Eyes*, 85
Cooper, James Fenimore, 135–136
Coward, Noël, *Cavalcade*, 35
Cox, R. G., 62
Crane, Hart, 137
Creeley, Robert, 59, 122, 132, 134; *Collected Poems*, 133

Index

Dahlberg, Edward, 136; *Bottom Dogs*, 138; *Can These Bones Live*, 137; *Confessions*, 137
Dana, Richard Henry, 135
Daudet, Lucien, x
Davie, Donald, 194 n3
Day Lewis, Cecil, 168
Dickens, Charles, 29, 81
Dickinson, Emily, 120
Dostoyevsky, Fyodor, 15, 18, 133, 143
Douglas, Norman, 81, 84
Duncan, Robert, 59, 113, 132
Durrell, Lawrence, 20, 83, 107–108; *Bitter Lemons*, 100–104, 185 n56; *Justine*, 101; *Prospero's Cell*, 101; *Reflections on a Marine Venus*, 101; *Spirit of Place*, 101

Eberhart, Richard, "Throwing the Apple," 178 n39
Eliot, George, 1, 40, 142, 180 n13; *Daniel Deronda*, 42
Eliot, T. S., 18, 55, 59, 62, 109, 110, 115, 117; *After Strange Gods*, 111; "Le Roman Anglais Contemporain," 110–111; *The Waste Land*, 134
Ellmann, Mary, 160
Emerson, Ralph Waldo, 121, 132

Faulkner, William, 19
Fiedler, Leslie, *Love and Death in the American Novel*, 144
Flaubert, Gustave, 24; *Madame Bovary*, 164, 169
Fleming, Ian, 26
Fleming, Peter, 89, 91
Ford, Ford Madox, *The Good Soldier*, 16–17
Forster, E. M., 168; *Aspects of the Novel*, 24
Foucault, Michel, *History of Sexuality*, 172–173
Franklin, Benjamin, 135, 139
French, Roberts W., viii, 109–134
Frere, A. S., 1
Frost, Robert, 109, 112–113

Fuentes, Carlos, *When the Air is Clear*, 178

Gardner, Helen, 168
Garnett, David, 1
Garnett, Edward, 18, 113
Gellhorn, Martha, *Travels with Myself and Another*, 183 n24
Gilbert, Sandra, 59
Gindin, James, viii, 30–53
Ginsberg, Allen, 10, 59; "Howl," 118
Gissing, George, 81
Gogol, Nikolai, 15
Gollancz, Victor, 86
Goodheart, Eugene, ix, 135–155
Goodman, Paul, 170–171, 198 n47
Gould, Gerald, 110
Graves, Robert, 59
Green, Henry, 23
Greene, Graham, 25, 83, 100, 107–108; *England Made Me*, 21; *The Heart of the Matter*, 26; *Journey Without Maps*, 94; *The Lawless Roads*, 21, 94–97, 99, 184 n49; *The Power and the Glory*, 21
Greer, Germaine, 160, 163, 196 n29
Groddeck, Georg, 61

Hamilton, Patrick, 21
Hanley, James, 20
Hardy, Thomas, 1, 22, 31, 60, 62, 142, 143; *Jude the Obscure*, 44
Hawthorne, Nathaniel, 135; *The Scarlet Letter*, 152
Heaney, Seamus, 3–4, 73–74, 79–80; "An Advancement of Learning," 67; "Antaeus," 67; "Digging," 68; *Field Work*, 70; "The First Gloss," 70; "The Guttural Muse," 69; "North," 71; "Oysters," 70; *Station Island*, 80
Hefner, Hugh, 13
Hemingway, Ernest, 11, 16, 20, 25; "A Clean, Well-Lighted Place," 15; *Green Hills of Africa*, 10; *In Our Time*, 185 n50; "The Short Happy Life of Francis Macomber," 10; *Torrents of Spring*, 10

Herbst, Josephine, *The Hunter of Doves*, 137
Hilton, Enid, 1
Hoggart, Richard, 168
Homer, 15, 99
Hopkins, Gerard Manley, 4
Horace, *Odes*, 105
Howard, Elizabeth Jane, 49
Howe, Irving, 136, 139, 140–141
Hughes, Ted, 3, 4, 59, 79–80, 181 n35; "Conjuring in Heaven," 75–76; "Crow," 75; *Crow*, 74; "Otter," 72; "Pike," 71–72
Huxley, Aldous, 1, 4, 13, 19–20, 39, 47, 84, 129; "After the Fireworks," 5; *Brave New World*, 5; *Do What You Will*, 5; *Eyeless in Gaza*, 5; *The Genius and the Goddess*, 5; *Point Counter Point*, 5; "Two or Three Graces," 5
Huxley, Juliette, 1

Isherwood, Christopher, 3, 83, 100; *The Ascent of F-6*, 90; *The Condor and the Cows*, 92–94; *Journey to a War*, 88–91, 96, 107–108

James, Clive, 62
James, Henry, 16, 17, 24, 62, 81
Jong, Erica, *Fear of Flying*, 161
Joyce, James, 14, 15, 16, 17, 19, 24, 25, 30, 47, 80, 151; "The Dead," 28; *Ulysses*, 23, 57

Katsimbalis, George, 100
Kavanagh, Patrick, 4, 80
Kazin, Alfred, 121, 136
Keats, John, "Ode to a Nightingale," 129–130
Kinnell, Galway, 9–10, 122, 128, 132; "The Bear," 129–130; *Mortal Acts, Mortal Words*, 130; "These Are the Things I Tell No One," 130–131
Kipling, Rudyard, 20
Koteliansky, S. S., 18
Kunitz, Stanley, 113

Lane, Homer, 61, 182 n14
Larkin, Philip, "Annus Mirabilis," 12
Lawrence, D. H.
  Ideas:
    America, 8, 135–139, 153
    anti-mechanization, 5, 12, 66, 81–82, 106, 123–124, 153, 155
    anti-rationalism, 3, 55–57, 122
    blood-brotherhood, 21
    blood consciousness, 9, 12, 54, 170
    body–soul conflict, 44, 46, 171
    class, 6, 42, 44, 45, 165–166, 167
    commune, 12, 28, 51–52
    consciousness of life, 14, 15–17, 24–27, 50, 98, 134, 148, 174
    influence of predecessors, 1, 58, 60, 109, 141, 142, 143, 180 n13
    marriage, 3, 10
    misogyny, 156–163
    mysticism, 5
    nature, 3, 7, 9, 76–77, 78, 124–125, 126, 129–130, 132
    the novel, 17–18, 50–51
    obscenity, 163–169, 173, 196 n31
    primitivism, 10, 81–82, 94, 98, 105–108, 128, 136, 154, 155
    prophecy, 6, 7, 12, 143, 145, 151–152, 157, 160, 162, 170–171, 174
    puritanism, 137, 152–154, 165
    re-birth, 135–137, 170–171
    self-consciousness, 58–59, 66, 68, 75, 79, 80, 123
    sex, 3, 10, 11, 12, 23, 27, 35, 42, 49–50, 106, 131, 141, 143–153, 160–163, 170, 172–173, 194 n4, 194 n14
    social impact, 12–13, 26, 117, 156–174, 178 n40, 193 n1
    social responsibility, 5
    "spirit of place," 10, 37, 81, 84, 101, 140
    vitalism, 3, 5, 108, 122, 154–155
  Influence of personality, 1, 118, 128, 129, 133–134, 149–150; character in others' novels, 5, 179 n43

Lawrence, D. H. – *continued*
  Influence on genres:
    novel, 4–8, 10–12, 14–29, 30–53, 135–155
    poetry, 3–4, 8–10, 54–80, 109–134; autobiographical, 118, 120; confessional, 120; form, 10, 77–78, 115–117; free verse, 112, 114, 121, 127, 128; "immediate expression," 8–9, 55–59, 64, 113, 117, 119–120, 121, 133; rhythm, 8, 126
    short story, 20
    travel writing, 3, 81–108, 182 n11
  Influence on writers:
    Anderson, Sherwood, 10, 139–141
    Auden, W. H., 2, 61–63, 80, 83–91, 107–108
    Bly, Robert, 9, 59, 116, 122, 123
    Boyd, William, 12
    Bragg, Melvyn, 6, 7, 34–36, 53
    Brenan, Gerald, 83, 104, 108
    Campbell, Roy, 78–79, 80
    Creeley, Robert, 59, 122, 132, 133–134
    Dahlberg, Edward, 136–138
    Duncan, Robert, 59, 113, 132
    Durrell, Lawrence, 20, 83, 100–104, 107–108
    Ginsberg, Allen, 10, 59
    Goodman, Paul, 170–171, 198 n47
    Greene, Graham, 21, 25–26, 83, 94–97, 107–108
    Hanley, James, 20
    Heaney, Seamus, 3–4, 67–71, 79–80
    Hemingway, Ernest, 10–11
    Hughes, Ted, 3, 4, 59, 71–76, 79–80, 181 n35
    Huxley, Aldous, 4–5, 19–20
    Isherwood, Christopher, 3, 88–94, 107–108
    Kinnell, Galway, 9–10, 122, 128–132
    Kunitz, Stanley, 113
    Lessing, Doris, 6, 36, 47–53

  Levertov, Denise, 59, 132
  Lowell, Robert, 120–121
  MacNeice, Louis, 83, 107–108
  Mailer, Norman, 11, 141, 143, 146–150, 159–162
  Malamud, Bernard, 143, 149–151, 177 n37
  Miller, Henry, 83, 98–100, 108, 141, 142–147, 149, 150
  Mishima, Yukio, 177–178 n37
  Muir, Edwin, 78–79, 80
  Oates, Joyce Carol, 59
  Olson, Charles, 59, 132–133
  Orwell, George, 5–6
  Plath, Sylvia, 118–120
  Rexroth, Kenneth, 117–118
  Rich, Adrienne, 59
  Roethke, Theodore, 8–9, 122, 125–128
  Shapiro, Karl, 8, 112, 115
  Sillitoe, Alan, 6–7, 36–42, 46, 47, 53
  Snyder, Gary, 10, 122, 123–125
  Spender, Stephen, 2–3, 76–77
  Storey, David, 6, 7, 42–47, 53
  Thomas, Dylan, 3, 63–66, 80, 175 n10
  Wain, John, 6, 32–34, 39, 53
  Waterhouse, Keith, 6, 31–32, 39, 53
  Waugh, Evelyn, 22, 25–26
  Williams, Tennessee, 11, 154
  Williams, William Carlos, 8, 112, 139
Prose techniques, 20, 21–24; character, 17, 151; hero, 24–26; literary personality, 81–83, 89, 92–93, 101, 104–105; plot pattern, 38, 39, 44, 45; regionalism, 6–7, 31, 37, 140; satire, 87–88; symbolic scenes, 101, 104, 108

Works
Books:
  Aaron's Rod, 38, 39, 51, 89, 145, 147, 159, 171, 194 n4
  Amores, 120
  Apocalypse, 83
  Bay, 120

Lawrence, D. H. – *continued*
  Works – *continued*
    Books – *continued*
      Birds, Beasts and Flowers, 3, 8, 10, 121, 123, 124, 127, 129
      Collected Poems, 120
      Etruscan Places, 54, 87, 91, 94, 99, 108
      Fantasia of the Unconscious, 2, 61, 83, 144
      The First Lady Chatterley, 166
      John Thomas and Lady Jane, 166
      Kangaroo, 2, 21, 145, 147, 159, 171
      Lady Chatterley's Lover, 6, 11, 12, 22–24, 31, 38, 91, 119, 123, 146, 156, 157, 160–161, 163–169, 172–173, 178 n40, 178 n41, 194 n4, 197 n41, 197 n43
      Last Poems, 118, 127, 130
      Letters, 4, 83, 189 n48
      Look! We Have Come Through!, 118, 120, 121
      The Lost Girl, 35, 37, 191 n19, 194 n4
      Love Poems and Others, 110, 120
      The Man Who Died, 5, 119, 165
      Mr. Noon, 25, 194 n3
      More Pansies, 118
      Mornings in Mexico, 21
      Nettles, 118
      New Poems, 120
      Pansies, 118
      Phoenix, 110
      Phoenix II, 110
      The Plumed Serpent, 2, 12, 21, 22, 40, 89, 95, 148, 157, 158, 159, 172, 175 n10, 178 n37, 191 n19, 194 n4
      The Rainbow, 4, 7, 34, 36, 39, 44, 45, 49, 51, 110, 119, 135, 139–140, 144, 151, 153, 159, 162, 164–165
      Reflections on the Death of a Porcupine, 142
      St. Mawr, 22, 89, 137
      Sea and Sardinia, 10, 83, 87–88, 89, 92–93, 99, 101
      Sons and Lovers, 4, 6, 7, 9, 21, 22, 24–25, 38, 40, 119, 144, 157, 159, 162, 178 n41, 192 n32
      Studies in Classic American Literature, 8, 135–139, 152–153, 170
      The Trespasser, 43
      Twilight in Italy, 82, 91, 94, 101
      The Virgin and the Gipsy, 11, 178 n41, 197 n32
      The White Peacock, 9, 22
      Women in Love, 19, 21, 24, 42, 44, 48, 49, 52, 91, 119, 134, 139, 145, 178 n41, 194 n4
    Essays:
      "A Propos of *Lady Chatterley's Lover*," 165
      "The Crown," 142
      "Goats and Compasses," 2
      "Introduction to *Bottom Dogs*," 138
      "Introduction to *New Poems*," 55, 114
      "Prologue to *Women in Love*," 165
      "Review of H. M. Tomlinson's *Gifts of Fortune*," 82
      "Why the Novel Matters," 50
    Poems:
      "Bat," 10
      "Discord in Childhood," 4
      "Fish," 9, 130
      "Hymn to Priapus," 133
      "Kissing and Horrid Strife," 127–128
      "Man and Bat," 125
      "River Roses," 131
      "The Ship of Death," 10, 73
      "Snake," 9, 57–58, 67, 124–125, 126–127
      "The Song of a Man Who Has Come Through," 36
      "Things Men Have Made," 74
    Stories:
      "The Captain's Doll," 20
      "Daughters of the Vicar," 5–6, 35
      "The Fox," 27–28, 178 n41

Lawrence, D. H. – *continued*
  Stories – *continued*
    "Jimmy and the Desperate Woman," 20
    "The Man Who Loved Islands," 170
    "The Princess," 22
    "The Rocking-Horse Winner," 170, 178 n41, 183 n14
    "Sun," 196 n32
    "The Thorn in the Flesh," 6
    "The Woman Who Rode Away," 21–22, 159, 160
    "You Touched Me," 11
Lawrence, Frieda, 27–28, 150
Lawrence, T. E., 90
Leavis, F. R., 14–15, 64, 141, 151
Lehmann, Rosamond, 24
Lessing, Doris, 36; *The Golden Notebook*, 47–52; *The Good Terrorist*, 47, 51, 52; *The Grass is Singing*, 6
Levertov, Denise, 59, 132
Lewis, Wyndham, *Paleface*, 10
Lowell, Amy, 8
Lowell, Robert, 15, 114; *The Dolphin*, 121; *History*, 120; *Life Studies*, 120–121
Lucie-Smith, Edward, 71
Lynd, Robert, 110

MacNeice, Louis, 100; *Letters from Iceland*, 83, 87, 90, 107–108; *The Strings Are False*, 86
Mailer, Norman, 141, 143, 146, 150, 151, 195 n16; *An American Dream*, 148; *The Prisoner of Sex*, 147, 149, 159–162; "The Time of Her Time," 11, 148
Malamud, Bernard, 143; *Dubin's Lives*, 149–151, 177 n37; *A New Life*, 149
Malraux, André, *Man's Fate*, 90
Mansfield, Katherine, 20
Masters, Edgar Lee, 113
Melville, Herman, 81, 133, 135
Mew, Charlotte, 126
Meyers, Jeffrey, ix, 1–13, 81–108; *D. H. Lawrence and Tradition*, 1, 180 n13

Miller, Henry, 19, 83, 108, 141, 153, 158, 159, 160, 191 n28, 192 n36; *The Air-Conditioned Nightmare*, 93; *The Colossus of Maroussi*, 98–100, 184 n47; *Tropic of Cancer*, 178 n40; *The Wisdom of the Heart*, 98; *The World of Lawrence*, 99, 142, 143–147, 149, 150
Millett, Kate, *Sexual Politics*, 146–149, 159–162, 195 n15
Mishima, Yukio, 177–178 n37
Moore, Harry, 162
Morgan, Charles, 18
Morrison, Blake, 69
Muir, Edwin, 79, 80; "Horses," 78
Murry, John Middleton, 110; *Son of Woman*, 158
Murry, Richard, 1

Necker, Jacques, 28
Nietzsche, Friedrich, 1, 180 n13
Nin, Anaïs, 142, 158
Nott, Kathleen, 194–195 n14

Oates, Joyce Carol, 59
Olson, Charles, 59, 133, 134; "Projective Verse," 132
Orwell, George, 5, 33; *A Clergyman's Daughter*, 6; *Coming Up For Air*, 6; *Homage to Catalonia*, 89; "Inside the Whale," 100, 191 n28; *The Road to Wigan Pier*, 6; "Rudyard Kipling," 185 n58
Owen, Wilfred, 62

Percy, Walker, *The Moviegoer*, 154
Perloff, Marjorie, 59
Plath, Sylvia, 118–119; *Journals*, 119–120
Ponge, Francis, "Horse," 9; "Trees Lose Parts of Themselves Inside a Circle of Fog," 9
Pound, Ezra, 2, 59, 62, 109–110, 113, 115, 132, 134; *Personae*, 113
Powell, Anthony, 21, 23
Powys, John Cowper, 39; *Weymouth Sands*, 19; *Wolf Solent*, 19
Pritchett, V. S., 20
Proust, Marcel, 14, 24

Pushkin, Alexander, *Eugene Onegin*, 28
Pym, Barbara, 26

Rembar, Charles, 166, 167
Rexroth, Kenneth, 117–118; "Thou Shalt Not Kill," 118
Rich, Adrienne, 59
Richardson, Samuel, 18
Rieff, Philip, *The Triumph of the Therapeutic*, 171–172, 195 n14
Rilke, Rainer Maria, 62
Rimbaud, Arthur, 133
Roethke, Theodore, 9, 122, 125, 128; "The Bat," 8; "Elegy for Jane," 126; *The Far Field*, 127; "The Long Waters," 127; "The Pike," 8; "The Small," 126; "Snake," 8, 126
Ruskin, John, 1, 3, 18, 81, 180 n13

Sagar, Keith, 3
Sandburg, Carl, 113
Schiller, Friedrich von, *On Naive and Sentimental Poetry*, 56–58, 62–63, 180 n4
Seferis, George, 100
Shakespeare, William, 1, 4, 57; *King Lear*, 74–75
Shapiro, Karl, 3, 8, 112, 115
Sillitoe, Alan, 6–7, 46, 47, 53; *The Death of William Posters*, 6, 38–39; "D. H. Lawrence and His District," 36; *The Flame of Life*, 38–39; *Her Victory*, 41–42; "The Rats," 38; *Raw Material*, 37; *Saturday Night and Sunday Morning*, 37; *Storyteller*, 40–41; *A Tree on Fire*, 38–39; *The Widower's Son*, 41
Simpson, Louis, 114
Snyder, Gary, 10, 122, 123–125; *Axe Handles*, 125
Spender, Stephen, 2–3, 76–77; *D. H. Lawrence: Novelist, Poet, Prophet*, 36; "I Think Continually of Those Who Were Truly Great," 3
Spilka, Mark, 162

Squire, J. C., 110
Stevens, Wallace, 109, 113, 115
Stevenson, Robert Louis, 81, 94
Storey, David, 6, 7, 36, 53; *The Contractor*, 44; *Death of My Mother*, 44; *The Farm*, 44; *Flight into Camden*, 42–43; *In Celebration*, 44; *Life Class*, 44; *A Prodigal Child*, 46–47; *Radcliffe*, 43–44; *Saville*, 45–46; *This Sporting Life*, 43
Szczesny, Berthold, 93

Tanner, Tony, *The City of Words*, 137
Tate, Allen, 137
Taylor, Elizabeth, 24
Thomas, Dylan, 63–64, 80, 175 n10, 181 n23; "Fern Hill," 65; *Quite Early One Morning*, 66; "A Refusal to Mourn," 3; "When All My Five and Country Senses See," 65
Tolstoy, Leo, 3, 15, 17, 18, 22; *Anna Karenina*, 24, 26–27, 169; *War and Peace*, 19
Trilling, Diana, 157
Trilling, Lionel, 136

Untermeyer, Louis, 113

Verga, Giovanni, *Mastro-don Gesualdo*, 106
Vinogradoff, Julian Morrell, 1
Virgil, 15

Wain, John, 6, 39, 53; *The Contenders*, 32–33; *The Pardoner's Tale*, 32, 33–34; *A Travelling Woman*, 33; *A Winter in the Hills*, 32, 33; *Young Shoulders*, 34
Waterhouse, Keith, 6, 39, 53; *Billy Liar*, 31; *Jubb*, 32; *Maggie Muggins*, 31–32; *Thinks*, 32
Waugh, Evelyn, 20, 21, 23, 25; *Brideshead Revisited*, 22; *A Handful of Dust*, 26; *Officers and Gentlemen*, 26
Weekley, Montague, 1
Wells, H. G., 19, 24

Index

West, Rebecca, 1, 168
Whitman, Walt, 1, 8, 10, 58, 59, 60, 98, 109, 112, 113, 115, 116, 120, 121, 126, 135, 153
Widmer, Kingsley, ix, 156–174
Williams, Raymond, 168
Williams, Tennessee, *Battle of Angels*, 11; *I Rise in Flame, Cried the Phoenix*, 11, 154; *Kingdom of the Earth*, 11
Williams, William Carlos, 8, 10, 109, 112, 118, 133; "Elegy for D. H. Lawrence," 112; *In the American Grain*, 111, 137, 139; *Spring and All*, 113
Williamson, Henry, 39
Wilson, Edmund, 136
Wodehouse, P. G., 20–21
Woolf, Virginia, 14, 24, 25, 105, 118
Wordsworth, William, 56, 86, 129

Yeats, W. B., 59, 115; "Under Ben Bulben," x

OHIO UNIVERSITY LIBRARY

Please return this book as soon as you have finished with it. In order to avoid a fine it must be returned by the latest date stamped below.

RETURN BY
JUN 9 1988

RETURN BY
NOV 23 1989

MAY 3 1 1988

ILL to WSU
IL: 5744672
DUE: 3-1-92

RETURN BY
MAR 1 5 1989
MAR 1 4 1989

APR 0 5 1997
APR 1 1 1997

JUN 1 6 2003
JUN 2 5 2003

RETURN BY
MAY 3 1 1989
JUN 2 9 1989

MAY 2 0 1987